Criminology and Social Theory

D0462448

CLARENDON STUDIES IN CRIMINOLOGY
Published under the auspices of the Institute of Criminology,
University of Cambridge, the Mannheim Centre, London School of
Economics, and the Centre for Criminological Research, University
of Oxford

Criminology and Social Theory

**edited by
David Garland
and
Richard Sparks**

OXFORD
UNIVERSITY PRESS

OXFORD

UNIVERSITY PRESS

Great Clarendon Street, Oxford OX2 6DP

Oxford University Press is a department of the University of Oxford.
It furthers the University's objective of excellence in research, scholarship,
and education by publishing worldwide in

Oxford New York

Athens Auckland Bangkok Bogotá Buenos Aires Calcutta
Cape Town Chennai Dar es Salaam Delhi Florence Hong Kong Istanbul
Karachi Kuala Lumpur Madrid Melbourne Mexico City Mumbai
Nairobi Paris São Paulo Singapore Taipei Tokyo Toronto Warsaw

and associated companies in Berlin Ibadan

Oxford is a registered trade mark of Oxford University Press
in the UK and in certain other countries

Published in the United States
by Oxford University Press Inc., New York

First published in *The British Journal of Criminology*,
vol. 40, no.2. Spring 2000

British Library Cataloguing in Publication Data

Data available

Library of Congress Cataloging in Publication Data

Criminology and social theory / edited by David Garland and Richard Sparks.
p. cm.—(Clarendon studies in criminology)
First published in the British journal of criminology, vol. 40, no. 2, Spring 2000.—Verso t.p.
Includes bibliographical references and index.
1. Criminology. I. Garland, David. II. Sparks, Richard, 1961– . III. Series.
HV6025.C746 2000 364—dc21 00–040078

ISBN 0–19–829942–7

3 5 7 9 10 8 6 4 2

Printed in Great Britain
on acid-free paper by
TJ International Ltd, Padstow, Cornwall

General Editors' Introduction

The Clarendon Studies in Criminology series was inaugurated in 1994 under the auspices of centres of criminology at the Universities of Cambridge and Oxford and the London School of Economics, and it now plays a leading role in the field. The series was originally intended to consist almost entirely of research monographs, but there was never an absolute prohibition on collections of papers, and particularly on outstanding collections. *Criminology and Social Theory* is outstanding. It is edited by two scholars who have contributed as much as any to the extraordinary strength of British criminology. Its authors are men and women of distinction. And the criminology it represents has traded ideas with other disciplines for decades, being at the core of social theorizing and intellectually vigorous in proportion. It is certainly noteworthy that four of those authors are not criminologists conventionally conceived but thinkers prominent in their own special domains of social and political theory and social anthropology.

In a sense, *Criminology and Social Theory* could be read as the unplanned fulfilment of an earlier manifesto, *The New Criminology*, which called in 1973 for a 'fully social theory' that would restore criminology to the grand ideas of sociology and political economy. *The New Criminology* did break with much of what had gone before, and those who were touched by it began again to ask some big questions about the social character of crime, the State and the economy. The new criminologists were marxists, and Marxism has become *passé*, wrongly in some respects. But their preoccupation with big ideas and political economy remains in *Criminology and Social Theory* as its chapters stir the embers of Foucault's writings and pursue new, and markedly more sophisticated, conceptions of the State, regulation, governance and the structuring of social representations.

DAVID DOWNES and PAUL ROCK

General Editors' Introduction

Preface

The idea for this collection grew out of a series of conversations we have had over several years about criminology and its role in late modern society. Through the essays that we commissioned for the volume, and through our own contribution, we hope to provoke further reflection and debate about criminology's contemporary situation, its priorities, its political responsibilities, and its relation to other fields of social scientific inquiry.

The materials contained in the present volume were first published in Spring 2000 as a special issue of the *British Journal of Criminology*. We are grateful to the editorial board of that journal for their enthusiastic support, to Juliet Sydenham, Anne Musgrave, and Michael Belson for their help in the production of the book, and to John Louth, our editor at Oxford University Press.

Above all we wish to express our thanks to our contributors for their willingness to accept our invitation and for the seriousness and thoughtfulness with which they responded to our brief.

DG & RS
May 2000

Contents

List of Contributors

ZYGMUNT BAUMAN is Emeritus Professor of Sociology, University of Leeds

JOHN BRAITHWAITE is Professor in the Law Program in the Research School of Social Sciences, Australian National University, Canberra

MAUREEN CAIN is Reader in Sociology of Law and Crime, the Faculty of Law, University of Birmingham

MARY DOUGLAS is Professor of Social Anthropology and Honarary Research Fellow, University College, London

DAVID GARLAND is Professor of Law and Professor of Sociology at New York University

PAUL HIRST is Professor of Social Theory at Birkbeck College, University of London

MICHALIS LIANOS is Director of the Centre for Empirically Informed Social Theory at the School of Social and Historical Studies, University of Portsmouth and co-ordinator of the EURESEARCH project on 'Uncertainty and insecurity in Europe'.

DARIO MELOSSI is Associate Professor of Law, University of Bologna and Visiting Professor of Community Safety, Keele University.

NICHOLAS ROSE is Professor in the Department of Sociology at Goldsmith's College, University of London

RICHARD SPARKS is Professor of Criminology at Keele University

1

Criminology, Social Theory and the Challenge of Our Times

DAVID GARLAND and RICHARD SPARKS

Contemporary criminology inhabits a rapidly changing world. The speed and profundity of these changes are echoed in the rapidly changing character of criminology's subject matter—in crime rates, in crime policy, and in the practices of policing, prevention and punishment. And if we look beyond the immediate data of crime and punishment to the processes that underpin them—to routines of social life and social control, the circulation of goods and persons, the organization of families and households, the spatial ecology of cities, the character of work and labour markets, the power of state authorities—it becomes apparent that criminology's subject matter is centrally implicated in the major transformations of our time.

The questions that animate this collection of essays concern the challenges that are posed for criminology by the economic, cultural, and political transformations that have marked late twentieth-century social life. The restructuring of social and economic relations, the fluidity of social process, the speed of technological change, and the remarkable cultural heterogeneity that constitute 'late modernity' pose intellectual challenges for criminology that are difficult and sometimes discomfiting but which are ultimately too insistent to ignore. To wish them away, to carry on regardless, to pursue the conventional agendas of criminological enquiry in the accustomed way, would be to turn away from some of the most important issues that face contemporary social thought and public policy. It would also be to depart from the canons of clarity, perspicacity and relevance that worthwhile criminological work has always observed. Ever since its emergence in the industrialized, urbanized world of the mid-nineteenth century, criminology has been, or has sought to be, a contemporary, timely, worldly subject. Criminologists——particularly those who draw upon a sociological tradition—have always sought to ground their analyses in a nuanced sense of the world as it is, and as it is becoming, not least because the phenomena of crime and disorder have so regularly been traced to the effects of social upheaval and dislocation. As the essays in this collection demonstrate, the social transformations of late modernity pose new problems of criminological understanding and relevance, and have definite implications for the intellectual dispositions, strategic aims and political commitments that criminology inevitably entails.

How then might criminologists come to terms with the kinds of variation and change that characterize their twenty-first century world? Are criminology's frameworks of explanation adequate to the changing realities of crime and criminal justice and to the expansive hinterland of political, economic and regulatory activity that encircles them? If not, what kinds of adjustment need to be made? What kinds of question must be brought more clearly into focus? How should the scope of our analyses change? And if we are to develop modes of theorizing and forms of empirical enquiry that respond to the social world *in a fully contemporary idiom* then on what kinds of intellectual resources can we draw and in what corners of contemporary thought might these be discovered?

Criminology and 'Crime Talk'

We have already referred to 'criminology' and 'criminologists'. We do so in full recognition of the fact that these are problematic and permeable categories: indeed part of our intent in this volume is to problematize them further and render them more permeable yet. We adopt this approach in a constructive, curious spirit rather than a nihilistic one. At this point in the subject's development there is little to be gained by replacing the term 'criminology' by some more cumbersome or contrived locution. The disinvention of criminology is not by itself a particularly rewarding project and it has been attempted often enough—generally by criminologists themselves—to discourage further efforts in that direction. But is also seem to us that defending the disciplinary identity of criminology against incursions from 'elsewhere' is now as unfeasible as it is undesirable—at a minimum a disdirection of effort, at worst a category mistake. For reasons we outline below, the conception of criminology as an autonomous and self-standing discipline is one that belongs to an earlier stage of its historical development, and the conditions of existence of that particular disciplinary formation are ones from which we are now increasingly and irreversibly cut off. This might mean, as John Braithwaite argues in this issue, that students of crime and crime control will have to learn to think beyond the confines of 'criminology' as it is currently constituted. But whether or not criminology is a subject 'destined for decline' (as Braithwaite puts it), it must be a subject that constantly reconstitutes itself if it is to come to terms with the social and legal worlds that it aspires to comprehend and in which it intends to intervene.

Such claims doubtless ring oddly in view of the scale, embeddedness and, in quantitative terms at least, rude health of contemporary criminology. Measured by the number and size of academic conferences, university departments, enrolled students, research institutes, research grant income, governmental and commercial consultancies, specialist journals and scholarly publications, the subject has never been healthier. But the bullishness and even boastfulness that accompanies the apparent vitality of criminology as an academic discipline (Zahn 1999) is at odds with criminology's more limited success in shaping the public discussion of 'its' issues and its faltering influence on public policy and decision making. The plain historical fact is that the social significance of crime and its control is so pervasive, so complex, and so contentious that no scientific discipline can ever dictate the ways in which these matters will be understood or addressed. Crime and punishment play such integral roles in the politics of contemporary societies, are so densely entangled with our daily routines, so deeply lodged in our emotional lives, so vividly represented in our cultural imagination, that they easily escape any analytical box, however capacious, that criminology may develop for their containment. Given the centrality, the emotiveness and the political salience of crime issues today, academic criminology can no longer aspire to monopolize 'criminological' discourse or hope to claim exclusive rights over the representation and disposition of crime.

It follows that at least some of the intellectual strategies and institutional assumptions that served earlier generations of criminologists well may be becoming less appropriate today. As we will discuss in a moment, the social changes of the last few decades have already prompted a rethinking of the assumptions that were characteristic in the middle years of this century when academic criminology first developed as a specialism. But some of our most contemporary habits of thought also need to be reconsidered. To give an obvious example, changing social arrangements and legal relations have recently effected a change in how criminologists think about questions of regulation and public authority. The continuing erosion of clear-cut distinctions between the public and the private realms of crime control, together with the displacement of the criminal justice state from centre stage in the production of security and crime control, have had a major impact on the ways in which criminology now addresses questions of regulation and control. Criminologists of all stripes—whether engaged in the study of police, or prevention, or criminal justice, or victims—have begun to think 'beyond the state' in ways that reflect this changing terrain. The result is not just a criminology that is better able to address the regulatory and ethical issues thrown up by this redistribution of social authority—though this in itself is a considerable advance. In the process of rethinking these difficult questions, criminologists have also become better able to conceptualize some of the most fundamental issues of social control and social order—a fact to which several of the essays here attest.

Another effect of the changing social world is that the longstanding division of labour in the academic world is beginning to break down and allow new forms of intellectual exchange to occur. One important instance of this is that two forms of criminological work that were usually considered as separate, if not indeed opposed to one another, are increasingly being brought together and 'thought' together. The opposition between (i) a criminology that is interested in social and political theory, in the reflexive sociology of criminological knowledge, and in the testing or transgressing of disciplinary boundaries and (ii) a criminology that has empirical bite and strategic relevance—is an opposition that can no longer be sustained. If, as Zygmunt Bauman (1990: 6) has argued, the aim of the social sciences is to develop 'responsible speech' about their objects of inquiry, then we are obliged to consider how contemporary conditions bear upon that obligation and to be reflexive about the position from which we choose to speak. The reconceptualizations that criminologists are presently undertaking in this regard take place in parallel with sociology's re-readings and reappraisals of the contemporary relevance of its founding or 'classic' texts (See Sparks 1997; Turner 1996). Indeed such is the centrality of many criminological issues to the social organization, governance and everyday life of contemporary societies that these activities of reappraisal cannot really be thought of as separate. (In addition to the essays collected here, see Taylor 1999; Young 1999; Bauman 1998; Wacquant 1999; Garland forthcoming).

Criminology in Its Contexts

We might best approach the criminological present by saying something more substantive about its past. In a recent memoir, one of British criminology's founding fathers, Sir Leon Radzinowicz, looks back over the development of criminology in the twentieth century. For the most part, he expresses quiet satisfaction at the discipline's growth and institutional development, but on the last page of the book he strikes a more discordant, disappointed note: 'What I find profoundly disturbing is the gap between "criminology" and "criminal policy", between the study of crime and punishment and the actual mode of controlling crime . . . The stark fact stands out that, in the field of criminal justice, in spite of the output of criminological knowledge, a populist political approach holds sway.' (Radzinowicz 1999: 469).

Radzinowicz is not the first person to notice this development: there has been a lot of commentary about 'populist punitiveness' ever since Tony Bottoms coined the term a few years ago (see Bottoms 1995). And Sir Leon perhaps overstates the problem a little. Criminological expertise now plays a bigger role in local crime policy than it has ever done before—in crime prevention, crime audits, community policing and in private security—and in Britain at least there is currently more government funding for 'crime reduction' research than ever before. But the divergence between national penal policy and criminological research findings is certainly striking, and it is a divergence that characterizes the USA as much as the UK. Over the last decade, as governments have adopted a more heated form of law and order rhetoric, introduced mandatory minimum sentencing and encouraged a greater use of imprisonment, there has appeared to be a growing gap between expert criminological advice and enacted public policy.

We invoke Radzinowicz's account here not because it is especially original or profound but because it puts the present situation into an interesting historical light, measuring it against what he and his generation had expected. The institutional founders of modern academic criminology, working in the middle decades of this century, quite reasonably supposed that as criminological knowledge became more refined and more robust it would come to play an increasing part in government policy. It is a something of a surprise therefore, to discover that, in some respects at least, the reverse is true. Elsewhere, Radzinowicz (1991) has written about 'Penal Regressions', giving the sense of the reversal of a developmental pattern—a system that has been maturing, becoming more civilized, more modernized, has suddenly regressed. Its development has been arrested, its evolution blocked. This rather unexpected reversal, and the disparity between criminology's success in the academy and its declining role in public life—particularly in national penal policy—provides us with a problem through which we can think about criminology's development over the last 100 years. It provides a point of departure not for a history in the conventional sense but for a history of the present, using the resources of history to reflect upon the problems of our time.

Criminology, in its broadest sense, consists of our organized ways of thinking and talking about crime, criminals and crime control. If we think of it in this way, academic criminology is only the best-elaborated and most scientific sector of a discourse that includes everything from the working categories of penal institutions to the crime images that circulate in common sense and popular culture. Criminology is not just a creature of the academy. It is also located in other social and institutional settings and these other settings have shaped much of its development. To simplify a complex picture we could say that criminology is inscribed in three major social settings or matrices. It is located in (i) the world of the academy—of social science and scholarly discourse, (ii) the world of government—of crime control and criminal justice, and (iii) the world of culture—including mass mediated popular culture and political discourse. These three matrices are loosely linked and mutually conditioning though they are not reducible one to the other. Criminology is nowadays more closely tied into the first than to the others, though 100 years ago, the situation was the reverse. And although academic criminology has attained a degree of autonomy— becoming an activity pursued for the sake of form, as Paul Rock, echoing Georg Simmel, recently put it—it continues to be influenced by government and popular culture.

When we think of the history of criminology we typically think of the development of theory and research within the academy. We cannot begin to describe here the profusion of ideas that has developed in the last century, particularly since the expansion of the academy in the late 1960s. Criminology has been a focal point for most of the intellectual currents of the last 30 years: Marxism, feminism, post-structuralism, postmodernism, all the strands of sociology, social psychology and cultural studies, not to mention occasional incursions from genetics and neurobiology—incursions that will in all likelihood increase in frequency and insistence in the near future. We have seen grand theory and focused empiricism, radical critiques, consultancy work and policy-driven inquiries. If criminology is a *'rendezvous* subject', as David Downes once put it, there has been a great crowd of very diverse people meeting up and passing through, sometimes establishing fruitful exchange, sometimes merely rubbing shoulders in the crowded passages of textbooks and conferences.

But criminology can also be thought of in its other contexts. Its history can be viewed in relation to the world of government and crime control, or in relation to the wider cultural and political universe. We can look at its role in the institutional field, as an element of governing, as a form of knowledge for power, supplying strategic advice for crime control and directing the power to punish. We can also view it as part of popular culture, a constitutive (and constituted) element in the collective experience of crime, a repertoire of frames and narratives through which we make sense of that experience. For present purposes, we will focus on the history of criminology as a functioning element in the field of crime control and, to a lesser extent, in relation to popular culture. We want to ask questions about these two social matrices and about criminology's place within them. Understanding how these matrices have changed in the last 30 years is, we believe, the key to understanding the situation that we currently find ourselves in.

Modern Criminology

When we refer to 'modern criminology' we do not intend to refer to criminological ideas that are up-to-date or contemporary. We are not here concerned, for example, with the 'criminologies of everyday life' or the choice and control theories that have come to prominence recently (Garland 1996, 2000). By 'modern criminology' we mean the framework of problems, concepts and styles of reasoning that emerged at the end of the nineteenth century, produced by the confluence of medical psychology, criminal anthropology, statistical inquiry, social reform and prison discipline—a framework that provided the coordinates for the penal-welfare institutions that developed during the next 70 years (Garland 1985). Modern criminology is no longer quite 'up to the minute', but it was the formative, hegemonic discourse for the first two-thirds of this century. For all their disagreements, the founders of modern British criminology were all proponents of this basic framework. Hermann Mannheim at the LSE, Max Grunhut at Oxford, Leon Radzinowicz at Cambridge, Tom Lodge at the Home Office, Edward Glover and Emmanuel Miller who, along with Mannheim founded the *British Journal of Delinquency*, the forerunner to the *British Journal of Criminology*—all of them shared the same basic commitments. (A reading of American criminology up to and including the President's Crime Commission Report (1967) reveals similar themes.) And although subsequent generations would revise its terms and question its commitments, this version of criminology played a crucial role in establishing the discipline in the academy, in government and in popular culture.

So what was modern criminology all about? With its faith in instrumental reason, its vision of the technocratic state and its commitment to social progress and social engineering, this criminology was emphatically *modernist*. Punishment in general, and retributive punishment in particular, were viewed as irrational and counterproductive, as remnants of pre-modern practices based upon emotion and superstition. Even the traditional liberal principles of proportionality and uniformity were tainted by archaic thinking. The proper management of crime and criminals required individualized, corrective measures adapted to the specific case or the particular problem.

For modern criminology, crime was a social problem that presented in the form of individual, criminal acts. These criminal acts, or at least those which appeared serious, repetitive, or irrational, were viewed as symptoms of 'criminality' and 'delinquency'. They were the surface signs of underlying dispositions, usually to be found in poorly socialized or maladjusted individuals. These underlying dispositions—and the conditions that produce them—formed the proper object of criminological knowledge. They also formed the preferred target for correctional intervention, with penal treatment being focused upon the individual's disposition, and social policy being left to deal with the wider causes. For modern criminology the maladjusted delinquent was the problem and correctional treatment was the solution. As a consequence, the overwhelming mass of minor and occasional offenders were largely neglected by correctionalist practice, which never reached down to the lower levels of the system to deal with routine, petty offending. This perhaps explains the puzzling fact that one of the most frequently used sanctions of the post-war period—the fine—was completely devoid of rehabilitative pretensions, and commanded hardly any criminological attention. It also explains why this criminology was so favourably disposed to decriminalizing minor offending and disorderly behaviour once crime rates began to rise sharply in the 1960s.

This criminological mind-set involved a form of causality that was long-term, dispositional, and operated through the formation of personality traits and attitudes. It focused upon deep-rooted causes, distant childhood experiences and psychological conflicts. Its tendency was to neglect proximate or immediate events (such as temptations or criminal opportunities or victim behaviour) and to assume that surface meanings and conscious motivations are necessarily 'superficial' and of little explanatory value. To this way of thinking, occasional, opportunistic, rationally motivated offending was of little interest—however much it contributed to overall rates of crime—because the conduct involved spoke to no particular pathology and offered no opportunity for expert treatment or correctional reform.

The theories that shaped research changed over the course of the century. At first they were predominantly drawn from medicine and abnormal psychology; later they drew more upon sociology and social psychology. If there was a central explanatory theme, it was the welfarist one of 'social deprivation' and subsequently of 'relative deprivation'. Individuals became delinquent because they were deprived of proper education, or family socialization, or job opportunities, or proper treatment for their social and psychological problems. The solution for crime was a welfare state solution—individualized treatment, support and supervision for families, and the enhancement of the plight of the poor though welfare reform. What is most noticeable, in retrospect, in this criminological scheme, is the relative absence of any substantive interest in crime events, criminogenic situations, victim behaviour, or the social and economic routines that produce criminal opportunities—all of which are becoming central concerns in present-day criminology. Nor was it substantively focused upon primary or secondary crime prevention, since this was assumed to flow from social reforms and community development rather than criminological intervention. These absences, together with its principled opposition to punishment and its focus upon motivation rather than control, meant that this criminology differed considerably from what came later, and, indeed, from what went before.

Although it presented itself as neutral and outside of politics, it was clear that modern criminology combined its faith in scientific expertise and professionalism with a liberal reform tradition. In political terms the discipline was clustered at one end of the spectrum ranging from left to centre left, from revolutionary socialist to middle-of-the-road technocrats. There was never a 'right wing' in British criminology— although radicals tended to treat the more pragmatic reformists of the Cambridge Institute and the Home Office as though they were establishment reactionaries. The real conservative opposition was actually outside of criminology, and consisted of those magistrates, politicians, and sections of public opinion who continued to think of crime in common-sense terms—as straightforward wickedness that ought to be punished or as signals of an incipient moral decline that had to be stopped. The politics of modern criminology were essentially Fabian, technicist and state-centered, typically offering top-down expert solutions for social problems and disorders. The assumption was that the criminal justice state held the solutions to the crime problem and was chiefly responsible for their implementation. Crime policy was best conducted outside of electoral politics, in a bipartisan mode that delegated policy-formation to professionals and practitioners. Policy was to be based upon research findings about the causes of crime and the most effective treatments, not upon political considerations, electoral advantage or irrational public sentiment. Day-to-day decision making was increasingly to be transferred from judges and politicians to criminological experts. This was a criminological framework well suited to a modernist, welfare-oriented social democracy, particularly one in which problems of crime and insecurity were perceived as localized and manageable. If criminal justice was able to become professionalized, self-contained, and somewhat autonomous of the political process, this was precisely because its political assumptions were so closely in tune with the prevailing political culture.

Modern British Criminology and Twentieth-Century Modernism

For the first three-quarters of the twentieth century, modern criminology became progressively more embedded in academic and governmental settings. Beginning from a tiny base in the 1950s, with only a few centres at places like the London School of Economics, Cambridge and Oxford, academic criminology expanded rapidly in the 1960s and 1970s and again in the 1990s until virtually all the universities came to offer criminology courses of some description. In the last 30 years, the

subject has expanded exponentially to become a thriving field of study
and a sizeable, independent discipline. No one can doubt that criminology has 'arrived' as an academic subject. (For a discussion of the
growth of American criminology, see Zahn 1999). Its courses are popular, its research attracts funding, its academic credentials are no
longer in doubt.

For most of the century, a similar pattern occurred in the sphere of
government, as criminological knowledge became an integral part of
policy making and criminal justice practice. The Criminal Justice Act
of 1948 permitted government funding for criminological research. In
1957 the Home Office Research Unit was formed to commission and
to undertake research. The 1959 White Paper *Penal Practice in a
Changing Society* announced that henceforth, crime and penal policy
were to be based upon research findings. The same year, the Institute
of Criminology at Cambridge was established with considerable government support. From 1944 until the arrival of Mrs Thatcher in 1979,
the reports of the Advisory Council on the Treatment of Offenders and
then the Advisory Council on the Penal System formed direct conduits
between the criminological community and government.

Up until recently, the same story could be told with respect to the
penal process. The abolition of the death penalty was a major development that was certainly influenced by the force of criminological opinion. (Nearly every criminologist in Britain joined the abolitionist
campaign, using their scientific credentials in the service of liberal
reform.) So too were the growing use of indeterminate sentences,
parole boards, and social inquiry reports, the welfarist practices of
juvenile justice, children's hearings, social work and probation; the
development of reformatory prison regimes, particularly for young
adults; training prisons; intermediate treatment; and of course the
much-remarked rehabilitative ethos, often honoured in the breach, but
always observed in official discourse—all of which accorded with the
practical programme of modern criminology.

The idea of a science of criminology even began to influence popular
culture. Ever since the BBC ran a popular radio series featuring Cyril
Burt on 'the modern approach' to juvenile delinquency, the criminolo-
gist-as-social-scientist has emerged as a familiar public figure, displac-
ing an earlier image of the criminologist as Sherlock Holmes. Over the
years it has become routine for journalists to contact criminologists for
comments on crime incidents, crime trends and policy questions.
Criminological science, loosely defined, now constitutes one (but only

one) of the voices that make up the standard public conversation about crime.

In obvious and important respects, this brand of criminology appeared to be an integral part of modern society—part of the modernist scheme of things. It fitted with the increasingly rationalized and disciplinary character of the modern social order and its governmental institutions. It enjoyed intimate links with the criminal justice system and the welfare state, and with the more general project of engineering an orderly, peaceable, well-administered society. Until very recently, everyone from Michel Foucault to Sir Leon Radzinowicz imagined that the future was more of the same. Foucault (1977) may have utterly transformed how some of us regard 'criminological reason' and its practical effects, but his work gave no hint that this way of thinking was already in decline, or that the immediate future would be shaped more by anti-modern forces than by modernist ones. It is therefore something of a surprise to discover that in the 1990s, as criminology flourishes in the academy, its influence in national penal policy appears to be diminishing. It is even more surprising to discover that penal policy is increasingly based not upon research findings and expert advice, but instead upon highly politicized articulations of public sentiment that strike many criminologists as ill-informed, explicitly punitive, and downright anti-modernist in character. And it is disconcerting to realize that many of the most talked-about initiatives of crime control—from situational crime prevention to commercial policing and private security—have emerged from outside of modern criminology and its standard repertoire of social solutions.

What has happened to change the fate of modern criminology? What makes a 'modern', 'social', 'scientific' account of crime appear so much less relevant than before. To answer that question we need to alter how we think about modern criminology. We need to see it not as a scientific basis for effective policies, nor even as a species of power/knowledge that is indispensable to a disciplinary society. We need to view it instead as a specific kind of discourse inscribed in a particular set of institutions at a particular historical conjuncture. Modern criminology took shape as an element of the postwar welfare state. It developed as part of a governmental response to a specific problem of order, a certain collective experience and a definite set of class relations. It was a small part of the social solution to the problems of industrial society. Its fortunes have been tied up ever since with the fate of the social, the politics of welfare, and the dynamics of the criminal justice state. When we think about modern criminology's place in government and culture we should bear in mind the conditions of existence on which it relied. Among these we would mention the following: (i) a social democratic form of politics, a cross-class solidarity and a civic narrative of inclusion; (ii) economic conditions that were favourable to welfare provision, public spending, and the development of social services; (iii) the credibility and influence of the new social service professionals and the broad support of political and social elites for the social-welfare style of problem solving; (iv) confidence in the validity of correctionalist ideas and the effectiveness of its practices; (v) the absence of any serious public or political opposition.

These conditions obtained in Britain and elsewhere, to a greater or lesser degree, up until the 1970s. In retrospect, the decade of the 1970s appears as a watershed, in which the intellectual, institutional and political assumptions of modern criminology were challenged, often in the name of a more radical social politics. It was during this decade that there arose a more critical and reflexive style of criminology, and a more explicit questioning of criminology's relation to the state, to criminal justice, and to the disciplinary processes of welfare capitalism. Criminology became, at least for a while, concerned to link its ideas and analyses to the broader themes of social thought and less concerned to be an applied discipline. It became more enamoured of sociological theory and more critical of criminal justice practice. In these years, criminology's centre of gravity shifted a little, becoming more reflexive, more critical, and more theoretical. As it happens, this was a short-lived moment (albeit a crucial one for criminology's subsequent intellectual range and forms of engagement) and one that was more fully developed in Britain than elsewhere, although it had (and still has) important corollaries in continental Europe and North America. And to the extent that criminology began to draw upon social theory, it was the classic sociology of modernism that formed its chief intellectual resource. The work of Durkheim, Marx, Mead and Simmel—and eventually that of Foucault too—provided criminologists with tools to think the modern world and crime's place within in it, though of course the world these theorists described was a 'modern' one that was already undergoing further processes of change. The explanatory tropes developed by the more sociological criminologists were typically those of the sociology of modernity, and the relation of criminology to its social world exhibited all the ambivalence characteristic of modernist knowledge. Thus while one style of criminology immersed itself in the world of criminal justice, constituting itself as a tool of reform and an instrument of social engineering, another more radical approach explicitly distanced itself from these institutions and adopted the mode of utopian critique.

This broadening of criminology's horizons was preceded (and largely prompted) by that convergence of intellectual, cultural and institutional events that is now evoked by the idea of 'the Sixties', as well as by more specifically criminological developments, such as the collapse of confidence in correctionalist criminal justice. The moment did not last long. Before long, new post-correctional forms of crime control emerged and criminology became immersed in applied questions once again—albeit applied questions of a different kind and in a different practical setting. But the critical, theoretical strands that opened up in the 1970s persisted as a continuing (if subordinate) theme in an increasingly diverse and multifaceted field. And, more profoundly, the influence of 'modern criminology' with its institutional affiliations and its epistemological commitments, was greatly diminished. Since that time, the social organization and political culture in which criminology is located have been further transformed by structural changes in ways that have undermined its expert authority and limited its public impact.

From Modernity to 'Late Modernity'

The world that we inhabit today is no longer quite the same as the world out of which modern criminology emerged, nor even the world that the sociology of modernity was developed to explain. The profound social, economic and cultural changes of the last few decades have seemed to undo the certainties of modernist social theory and make their relation to the world much more problematic. Social theorists differ among themselves as to how to characterize these new forms of life. They talk of the emergence of post-modernity, or late modernity, or high modernity; of the coming of the risk society and post-industrialism; of the disorganization of capitalism, of post-Fordism and New Times. All of these terms are problematic of course—perhaps inevitably given the inexactitude of such large-scale generalization and periodization. But what seems clear is that the transformations that they each, in their different ways, attempt to signal will necessitate some intellectual response on the part of criminologists. At the very minimum, this social and intellectual context requires that all of us—

even unreconstructed modernists—develop a new level of reflexivity, and ask ourselves how we are to respond to the challenge of change and upheaval.

Several of the essays contained in this collection suggest that the social matrices within which criminology operates have changed in quite dramatic ways with major consequences for the position of the discipline, the credibility of its instrumental rationality, and the applicability of its social solutions. We might gloss this argument, and simplify these processes rather drastically, by suggesting that in the last 30 years there have been two intertwined transformative dynamics that have changed the way we think and act upon crime (for a more detailed account, see Garland 2001; also Taylor 1999; Young 1999). The first of these dynamics is the cluster of social, economic and cultural changes that we might call, with some imprecision and much question begging, the coming of late modernity. Many of these changes are narrated in the chapters of this collection, so perhaps a telegrammatic summary will suffice here. By 'the coming of late modernity' we mean to refer to the social, economic and cultural configuration brought into being by the confluence of a number of interlinked developments. These include (i) the transformative dynamic of capitalist production and exchange (the emergence of mass consumerism, globalization, the restructuring of the labour market, the new insecurity of employment); (ii) the secular changes in the structure of families and households (the movement of women into the paid labour force, the increased rates of divorce and family breakdown, the decreasing size of the average household; the coming of the teenager as a separate and often unsupervised age grade); (iii) changes in social ecology and demography (the stretching of time and space brought about by cars, suburbs, commuting, information technology); (iv) the social impact of the electronic mass media (the generalization of expectations and fears; the reduced importance of localized, corporatist cultures, changes in the conditions of political speech) and, (v) the democratization of social and cultural life (the 'desubordination' of lower class and minority groups, shifts in power ratios between men and women; the questioning of authority, the rise of moral individualism.)

The second great transformative force was the reorganization of class (and, in the USA, race) relations that occurred in the wake of late modernity's massive disruptions. This was made possible by the shifting economic interests of the skilled working class, the welfare state's self-destructive tendencies, and the economic recessions of the 1970s and 1980s. In the end though, it was the political 'achievement' of leaders like Thatcher and Reagan, with their reactionary mix of free-market economics, anti-welfare social policy, and cultural conservatism. Together these dynamics changed the collective experience of crime and welfare and the political meaning of both. Late modernity brought with it new freedoms, new levels of consumption and new possibilities for individual choice. But it also brought in its wake new disorders and dislocations—above all, new levels of crime and insecurity. The political reaction of the 1980s and 1990s has shaped the public perception of these troubling issues, persuading us to think of them as problems of control rather than welfare; as the outcome of misguided social programmes; as a result of an amoral permissiveness and lax family discipline encouraged by liberal elites who were sheltered from their worst consequences; as the irresponsible behaviour of a dangerous and undeserving underclass—people who abused the new freedoms and made life impossible for the rest of us.

As one of us has argued elsewhere (Garland 1996), the combination of high rates of crime and the failure of the criminal justice state produced a predicament for government that has prompted the volatile and contradictory policies of the last two decades. But more importantly, the experience of high crime rates as a normal social fact has led to the formation of a distinctive culture that has grown up around crime—a culture that changes the conditions in which criminology and criminal policy operate. This cultural formation—which might be called the 'crime complex' of late modernity—is characterized by a distinctive cluster of attitudes, beliefs and practices. High crime rates are regarded as a normal social fact and crime-avoidance becomes an organizing principle of everyday life. Fear of crime is sufficiently widespread to become a political reference point and crime issues are generally politicized and represented in emotive terms. Concerns about victims and public safety dominate government policy and the criminal justice state is viewed as severely limited in its impact. Private, defensive routines are widespread and there is a large market in private security. A high level of 'crime consciousness' comes to be embedded in everyday social life and institutionalized in the media, in popular culture and in the built environment.

The development of a 'crime complex' produces a series of psychological and social effects that exert an influence upon politics and policy. Citizens became crime-conscious, attuned to the crime problem, and many exhibit high levels of fear and anxiety. They are caught up in institutions and daily practices that require them to take on the identity of (actual or potential) crime victims, and to think, feel and act accordingly. This enforced engagement with crime and crime prevention tends to produce an ambivalent reaction. On the one hand, a stoical adaptation that prompts the development of new habits of avoidance and crime prevention routines. On the other, a measure of irritation and frustration that prompts a more hostile response to the danger and nuisance that crime represents in daily life. Sections of the public became less willing to countenance sympathy for the offender, more impatient with criminal justice policies that are experienced as failing, and more viscerally identified with the victim. The posture of 'understanding' the offender was always a demanding and difficult attitude, more readily attained by liberal elites unaffected by crime or else by professional groups who make their living out of it. This posture increasingly gives way to that of *condemning* criminals and demanding that they be punished and controlled. The prospect of reintegrating the offender is more and more viewed as unrealistic and, over time, comes to seem less morally compelling. New criminologies emerge that echo and reinforce these concerns—stressing increased social control and situational prevention, rational choice and disincentives, incapacitation and punitive exclusion.

In these circumstances the rules of political speech change quite dramatically. So does the relationship between politicians, the public and the system's professionals. What was once regarded as a routine bipartisan task that could be delegated to officials now becomes an urgent political priority, freighted with emotional intensity and electoral consequences. From the point of view of politicians, crime and punishment become too important to leave to criminologists. The primary themes of the new penal policies—the expression of punitive sentiment, concern for victims, public protection, exclusion, enhanced control—are grounded in a new collective experience from which they draw their meaning and their strength. They are also rooted in a reactionary thematization of 'late modernity', prompted not just by rising crime but by the whole reactionary current of recent politics. This current, which has been prominent since the late 1970s, characterizes the present in terms of moral breakdown, incivility and the decline of the family, and urges the reversal of the 'Sixties' revolution and the cultural and political liberation that it ushered in. The mobile and insecure world of late modernity has given rise to new practices of control and exclusion that seek to make society less open and less mobile: to fix identities, immobilize individuals, quarantine whole sections of the population, erect boundaries, close off access. (For a discussion of these themes, see Bauman, this issue.)

Criminology and Contemporary Culture

These social changes have produced a situation in which criminology's grip upon the form and content of our thinking about crime is becoming less rather than more monopolistic. In a culture that is now saturated with images of crime and fear of crime, criminology can no longer hope to dominate the ways in which these issues are analysed. Even within the academy, criminology becomes only one of many settings in which crime is discussed. Feminism, cultural studies, economics, town planning, architectural design, film, political science, risk analysis, social theory in its various forms—all of these now take crime as a central theme in their analyses, a central problem in their research. In the new social world, crime has much greater salience than it previously had, and has become much more difficult to contain within the traditional bounds of criminological analysis. In this new political culture, a criminology that disavows emotive and punitive policies, that echoes welfarist rationales and social solutions, that seeks to de-dramatize crime control and delegate it to professional expertise—such a criminology has little affinity with the values and calculations that shape government decisions.

In this new context, criminology has some strategic choices to make. It can see itself as a kind of specialist underlabourer, a technical specialist to wider debates, providing data and information for more lofty and wide-ranging debates. (This is the role that is often assigned, by the culture, to criminological experts. It is also, probably, the one in which many academics are most comfortable.) Or it can embrace the world in which crime so loudly resonates and engage the discussion at this level too. The social and cultural centrality of crime today is an opportunity for criminology to embrace a more critical, more public, more wide-ranging role. Criminological knowledge—the insight and understanding that comes from close and critical study of crime and our institutional responses to it—has never been so relevant, however much governments resist its findings. The circuits for its use and exchange have never been so extensive and so deeply entwined with our social organization and the culture as a whole. One can understand the disappointment of Leon Radzinowicz, and share his frustration at the counter-productive and irrational aspects of present public policy. But there is, in the end, little point in being dismayed when governments behave politically. It is, after all, what they do. Governments do not always listen to reason, and certainly not only to criminological reason. They operate within a context that is defined by instrumental rationality but also by emotions and values, insistent demands and political imperatives. Governments were doing just this in the heyday of modern criminology, but criminologists did not always notice because they shared its politics and took its gestures for real commitments.

The social changes that have marked the last three decades mean that we can no longer 'think' criminology in the institutional contexts and intellectual thought-styles in which it was previous located. For most of its existence, criminology has been located, for all practical purposes, within the institutions of the criminal justice state. As our discussion of modern criminology already suggested, this institutional setting created a specific epistemology that structured how it was that criminology viewed the world and in particular how it theorized the problem of crime and its control. Today the viability of that institutional epistemology has been undercut by a whole series of developments. The revival of private policing and commercialized security; our new awareness that crime is an embedded, generalized, normal feature of the contemporary social world; new sources of knowledge about crime and victimization that do not rely upon the processes of criminal justices; and criminologies that address the crime problem in terms of redesigning systems and situations rather than the prosecuting and punishing individuals—these and similar developments undermine the assumptions from which criminological inquiry has previously been launched. Together they require us to rethink the criminological enterprise and to bring it more into line with the way that crime is experienced, represented and regulated today.

Criminology now has an opportunity—and a responsibility—to engage public discourse in order to address a central issue of our time. If it is to do so, it must understand the terms in which these wider debates and discussions are being discussed and how crime and crime control feature within them. It must also develop a self-consciousness about its intellectual assumptions and its social situation, above all about its links to government and to culture. Criminology's fate is to be redefined by the political culture of which it forms a part. If it is to play a role in shaping its own future then understanding that political culture will be an important first step. It is as a contribution towards that understanding that the present collection aspires to be of value.

The world that we confront in the first months of a new century has changed if not utterly then at least significantly from the one that previous generations of criminologists confronted. For principled modernists like Radzinowicz this can be understood only with dismay and indignation, as the eloquent closing pages of *Adventures in Criminology* make clear. Whilst there continue to be institutional spaces in which criminologists can work, and policy audiences sometimes ready to listen to criminological evidence, the variance between the rationality proposed by modern criminology and the rationales for policing, punishment and control now in ascendancy is striking and perhaps irrevocable. If crime issues have always been a *rendezvous* for various kinds of interests, they are nowadays attracting a much more diverse crowd of people—politicians and interest groups as much as academics and policy makers—whose encounters are frequently abrasive and mutually uncomprehending. Not the least reason for this more emotionally charged and politically divisive conversation is that crime and punishment are now among the most topical, urgent and contentious social questions of our times.

About This Book

It would be claiming too much to suggest that the contributors to this collection share a common set of concerns, topics or diagnoses. The open-textured debate that we wish to see would scarcely be furthered by such uniformity; and in any case the very variety and complexity of the contemporary contexts of crime and justice militates against shared agendas and easy consensus. However, it does seem plausible to argue that there is a new curiosity amongst at least some criminologists about the ways in which their traditional fields of study are currently being reconfigured. Students of state punishment and its surrounding forms of political and moral enterprise have been conscious for some time now that their field is one in which longstanding orthodoxies are being reversed as new techniques, vocabularies and social and economic interests begin to attach themselves to the business of punishing. Similarly, scholars of policing know that the institutions they study are now chronically prey to technological, organizational and political innovations, some of which threaten to render all but obsolete the traditional terms on which questions of effectiveness, accountability and legitimacy have been discussed. And those interested in victims' rights, public safety and the economical management of risk increasingly recognize that these are now pervasive concerns that refuse to fall neatly into the jurisdiction of any particular criminal justice agency or criminological specialism. Meanwhile, the remarkable pace of change that characterizes this field—with its endlessly elaborated regulatory regimes, its fast-developing technologies, its constantly changing managerial vocabularies, and its shifting political salience—combine to create conditions that can easily escape our conceptual languages and make our long-established research agendas seem outmoded and irrelevant. Under such circumstances the special tasks of social theory include those of raising new questions, making new sightings, and seeing connections between apparently unconnected phenomena in ways that allow substantive research to grasp more perspicuously the particularities of its current environment.

None of this is intended to promote or excuse a merely modish questing after novelty, nor the pointless spinning of empty conceptual structures after the manner that Bourdieu scathingly calls 'theoretical theory'. Indeed the renewal and invigoration of contemporary criminological discussion may in certain respects require a work of *recovery* and a reconsideration of 'classical' themes (Bourdieu in Turner 1996). Neither is it our intention to castigate criminology for a lack of interest in theoretical enquiry—a common allegation but one that in our view has often been couched in excessively sweeping and dismissive terms. Instead we hoped to enliven an ongoing discussion by asking a number of scholars—many of whom are not 'criminologists' but whose work seemed to us to bear fairly directly upon issues of criminological concern—to join in the conversation. As this collection shows, many of the most interesting sociological accounts of the present give a prominent place in their analysis to crime, fear of crime, and the calculations of risk and measures of repression to which these give rise. With this in mind, we challenged our contributors to reflect from their various vantage points upon a field that is deeply implicated in the social currents that they had written about in their work, but which also discloses certain unique features and intractable problems of its own. We think that the results contained here suggest the value of this encounter. They lead us to hope that such an engagement can be of mutual benefit in helping us refine and extend our ways of thinking. Perhaps the concrete questions of crime and crime control can provide one measure of the relevance and validity of social theories. Perhaps criminology can replenish its intellectual resources by engaging with the theoretical work of contemporary social theory. To that extent, the aspiration beyond this volume is to continue the supple movement between theoretical reflection and empirical inquiry, between criminology and social theory, between scholarly analysis and the lived social world.

References

BAUMAN, Z. (1990), *Thinking Sociologically*. Oxford: Blackwell.

BOURDIEU, P. with L. J. D. WACQUANT (1996), 'Toward a Reflexive Sociology: A Workshop with Pierre Bourdieu', in S. Turner, ed., *Social Theory and Sociology*. Oxford: Blackwell.

BOTTOMS, A. E. (1995), 'The Philosophy and Politics of Punishment and Sentencing' in C. Clarkson and R. Morgan, eds., *The Politics of Sentencing Reform*. Oxford: Clarendon.

FOUCAULT, M. (1977), *Discipline and Punish: The Birth of the Prison*. London: Allen Lane.

GARLAND, D. (1985), *Punishment and Welfare: A History of Penal Strategies*. Aldershot: Gower.

—— (1996), 'The Limits of the Sovereign State: Strategies of Crime Control in Contemporary Society', *British Journal of Criminology*, 36/4.

—— (2000), 'The Culture of High Crime Societies: Some Preconditions of Recent "Law and Order" Policies', *British Journal of Criminology*, 40/3.

—— (forthcoming). *The Culture of Control: Crime and Social Order in Late Modernity*. Oxford: Oxford University Press.

HOME OFFICE (1959), *Penal Practice in a Changing Society*. London: HMSO.

PRESIDENT'S COMMISSION ON LAW ENFORCEMENT (1967), *The Challenge of Crime in a Free Society*. Washington, DC: US Government Printing Office.

RADZINOWICZ, L. (1991), 'Penal Regressions', *Cambridge Law Journal*, 50: 422–44.

—— (1999), *Adventures in Criminology*. London: Routledge.

SPARKS, R. (1997), 'Recent Social Theory and the Study of Crime and Punishment', in *The Oxford Handbook of Criminology*, 2nd edn, 409–35. Oxford: Oxford University Press.

TAYLOR, I. (1999), *Crime in Context: A Critical Criminology of Market Societies*. Cambridge: Polity Press.

TURNER, S. (1996), *Social Theory and Sociology: The Classics and Beyond*. Oxford: Blackwell.

WACQUANT, L. (1999), *Les Prisons de la Misere*. Paris: Editions Liber-Raisons D'Agir.

YOUNG, J. (1999), *The Exclusive Society*. London: Sage.

ZAHN, MARGARET A. (1999), 'Thoughts on the Future of Criminology—The American Society of Criminology Presidential Address 1998', *Criminology*, 37/1: 1–16.

2

Social Uses of Law and Order

ZYGMUNT BAUMAN

There are many ways of being human, and each society makes its choices. As a matter of fact, if we call a certain assembly of people a 'society', implying that these people 'belong together', make a 'totality', it is due to that choice: a selection, which is at the same time a constraint imposed on the permissible. It is that choice which makes one assembly of people look different from another—that difference which we refer to when we speak of different societies. Whether a given assembly is or is not a 'society', and where its boundaries run, and who does and who does not belong to the society which that assembly constitutes—all that depends on the force with which the choice is made and promoted, and on the compliance with which it is obeyed. The choice boils down to two impositions (or, rather one imposition with twofold effects): of an *order* and a *norm*.

The great novelist/philosopher of our times, Milan Kundera, described 'the longing for order', evident in all known societies (in *La Valse aux Adieux*, here quoted in Peter Kussi's translation (1993: 85)— *The Farewell Party*), as 'a desire to turn the human world into an inorganic one, where everything would function perfectly and work on schedule, subordinated to a suprapersonal system. The longing for order is at the same time a longing for death, because life is an incessant disruption of order. Or to put it the other way around: the desire for order is a virtuous pretext, an excuse for violent misanthropy'.

To be sure, the desire for order does not necessarily stem from misanthropy—and yet it cannot but prompt it, as well as offer an excuse for whatever actions follow that sentiment. Any order is, after all, a desperate attempt to impose uniformity, regularity and predictability on the human world, the kind of world which is endemically diversified, erratic and unpredictable. Since the humans are, as Cornelius

Castoriadis (1989: 103–4) put it, such 'one type of being that creates something else, that is a source of alterity, and thereby itself alters itself', there is no chance that the human world everywhere (except for the graveyards, that is) will ever stop being diversified, erratic and unpredictable. Being human means constant choice. The longing for order is conceivable only thanks to that quality of being: any model of order is itself a choice—although it is a kind of choice which wants to supersede all other choices and put an end to all further choosing. Such an end being not on the cards, misanthropy follows—whether invited or not. The true object of the suspicion, revulsion and hatred which combine into misanthropy is the stubborn, inveterate and incurable eccentricity of human beings, that inexhaustible source of disorder.

The other imposition is that of the norm. Norm is the reflection of the model of order as it is projected on human conduct. The norm tells people what it means to behave in an orderly fashion in a well-ordered society—it translates, so to speak, the concept of order into the language of human choices. Any order is a choice, and so is the norm; but the choice of certain kinds of order limits the range of tolerable behavioural patterns and privileges certain kinds of conduct as normal, while casting all other sorts as abnormal. 'Abnormal' stands for any departure from the favoured pattern; it turns into 'deviation', which is an extreme case of abnormality, a conduct calling for therapeutic or penal intervention—if the conduct in question does not just differ somewhat from the preferred pattern, but transcends the boundary of tolerable choices. The distinction between mere 'abnormality', a matter of attention, treatment and cure, and the much more sinister 'deviation', is never clearly drawn and when drawn tends to be always hotly contested; just like the question of the limits to tolerance, that attitude which makes the difference between them.

Concern with order and norm signals, as a rule, that not everything is as it should be, and that not everything that is can be left in its present state. The very ideas of order and norm are born of that sense of (rectifiable) imperfection, and of the urge to do something about it. Both ideas are therefore constrictive—diversive and selective: the 'should' which they imply cuts into the 'is', leaving out large chunks of human reality. None of the two ideas would make any sense were they all-inclusive, able to accommodate all people and everything people do. The whole point about 'order' and 'norm' is precisely the opposite— the emphatic declaration that not everything that exists at present can find room in the postulated, properly functioning assembly and not every choice can be accommodated there. 'Order' and 'norm' are sharp knives pressed against the society as it is; they are first and foremost about separation, amputation, excision, expurgation, *exclusion*. They promote the 'proper' by sharpening the sights on the improper; they single out, circumscribe and stigmatize parts of reality denied the right to exist—destined for isolation, exile or extinction.

'Order' performs the job of exclusion directly—enforcing special regimes upon those meant to be excluded; excluding them through subordinating to the special regime. 'Norm' acts indirectly—making the exclusion look more like self-marginalization. In the first case, excluded and banished are those who 'breach the order'. In the second, those who 'are not up to the norm'. In both cases, though, it is the excluded themselves who are charged with the guilt of their exclusion; the perspectives of order and norm alike apportion the blame in advance deciding *a priori* the issue of responsibility and blame against the excluded. It is their actions—*wrong* actions—that brought the plight of exclusion upon them.

In the process of exclusion, the excluded themselves are cast as the principal, perhaps the sole, agency. Being excluded is presented as an outcome of social *suicide*, not a social *execution*. It is the fault of the excluded that they did nothing, or not enough, to escape exclusion; perhaps they even invited their fate, making the exclusion the foregone conclusion. Excluding them is an act of good sense and justice; those who do the exclusion might feel sensible and righteous, as becomes the defenders of law and order and guardians of values and standards of decency.

The excluded are unfit to be free agents, *quod erat demonstrandum*. Horrid things would follow were they let loose. They would bring all sorts of disasters upon themselves as much as on all the others. And so the depriving of the excluded of the freedom to act which they are bound to misuse or waste, apart from being necessary for the protection of law and order—is also called for in the best interests of the excluded; policing, control-ling and supervising the conduct of the excluded is also an act of human care and charity, a profoundly moral duty.

What this perspective leaves out of sight and prevents from being considered is the possibility that—far from bearing responsibility for their sorry fate—the excluded might be at the receiving end of forces which they have been given no chance of resisting, let along control-ling. That some among them might 'breach the order' since they have been marked for exclusion because of what they are, for the traits they possess but did not choose to have, not because of what they have done; that they have been excluded because 'people like them' did not fit an order of *someone else's*, not of their own, choice. And, above all—that some among the excluded happened to be 'not up to the norm' not for the lack of trying and not because of malice aforethought, but due to the lack of resources without which 'living up to the norm'—the resources other people have, that they do not; resources which are in short supply and therefore cannot be had by all, not in sufficient measure.

These two aspects—protection of order from those who have 'excluded themselves', and protection of the excluded from the dire consequences of their self-exclusion— intertwine and merge in the urge to 'do something' about the excluded part of the population—the impulse which draws its impetus and strength from the concern with the installation and preservation of order. To preserve order, the powers of disorder must be disempowered. To support the observance of norm, those in breach of the norm must be seen to be punished. Best of all, they must be seen to be excluded.

The Paradigm of Exclusion

Pierre Bourdieu points out that the state of California, celebrated by some European sociologists as the very paradise of liberty, dedicates to the building and running costs of prisons a budget transcending by far the sum total of state funds allocated to all institutions of higher education. Imprisonment is the ultimate and the most radical form of attention of the government by the political elite in the forefront of contemporary 'time/space compression'.

Spatial confinement, incarceration of varying degrees of stringency and harshness was at all times the prime method of dealing with the unassimilable, difficult to control, and otherwise trouble-prone sector of the population. Slaves were confined to the slave quarters. So were the lepers, the madmen, the ethnic or religious aliens and outcasts. If allowed to wander beyond the allotted quarters, they were obliged to wear the signs of their spatial assignment—so that every passer-by be aware that they belonged to another space. Spatial separation leading to enforced confinement was over the centuries almost a visceral, instinctual fashion of responding to all difference and particularly such difference that could not be, or was not wished to be, accommodated within the web of habitual social intercourse. The deepest meaning of spatial separation was the banning or suspension of communication, and so the forcible perpetuation of estrangement.

Estrangement is the core function of spatial separation. Estrangement reduces, thins down and compresses the view of the other: individual qualities and circumstances which tend to be vividly brought within sight thanks to the accumulated experience of daily intercourse, seldom come into view when the intercourse is emaciated or prohibited altogether: typification takes then the place of personal familiarity, and legal categories meant to reduce the variance and to allow to disregard it render the uniqueness of persons and cases irrelevant.

As Nils Christie (n.d.) pointed out, when personal familiarity prevails in daily life, concern with compensation for the harm done prevails over demand of retribution and punishment of the culprit. However angry we may be with the person responsible, we would not apply to the case the categories of penal law (we would not even think about the case in terms of endemically impersonal categories of crime and punishment, to which paragraphs of law may be applied) 'because we know too much . . . In that totality of knowledge a legal category is much too narrow'. Now, however, we live among people we do not know and most of whom we are unlikely ever to know. It was natural to abstain from resorting to the cold letter of the law if the act which prompted our wrath was seen for what it was—not really like other acts 'of the same category'. 'But this is not necessarily true of the strange kid who just moved in across the street.' And so, says Christie, it is not entirely unexpected (even if not inevitable either), that the consistent trend in our modern society is to give 'the meaning of crime' to 'more and more of what is seen as unwanted or at least dubious acts', and that 'more and more of these crimes are met with imprisonment'.

One may say that the tendency to reduce the variance with the help of legally defined categories, and the ensuing spatial segregation of difference, is likely to become a must, and certainly would grow in demand, since with the advent of modern conditions the physical density of the population tends to become considerably greater than its moral density, and so to be in excess of the absorptive capacity of human intimacy and the reaches of the personal relations network. But one can also reverse the connection and conclude that spatial separation which adds vigour to that reduction is itself a major resource used to prolong and perpetuate that mutual estrangement in which the reductionist operations, also the reductionist impact of criminal law, becomes a must. The tendency to resort to the dry and impersonal letter of law instead of relying on person-to-person negotiation of a common *modus vivendi* is a consequence of the gradual yet relentless demise of what Richard Sennett called 'the multiplicity of contact points'—once the foremost characteristic of city life. When cast in a condition of enforced unfamiliarity guarded and cultivated by the closely supervised space boundaries, held at a distance and barred regular or sporadic communicative access—the Other turns into an Alien and is permanently locked and sealed in that condition, having been effectively 'effaced'—stripped of the individual, personal uniqueness which alone could prevent stereotyping and so outweigh or mitigate the reductionist impact of law—also the criminal law.

As a (thus far) distant ideal of communicative separation, a total isolation beckons, one that would reduce the Other to a pure incarnation of the punishing force of law. Close to such an ideal come American 'state of the art' prisons, like the Pelican Bay in California, the richest of American states which also—to quote Nils Christie's pithy portrayal (Christie 1993)—'favours growth and vivacity' and so plans for eight prisoners for every thousand of population by the turn of the century. Pelican Bay prison, according to the enthusiastic report printed in the *Los Angeles Times* of 1 May 1990, is 'entirely automated and designed so that inmates have virtually no face-to-face contact with guards or other inmates'. Most of the time the inmates spend in 'windowless cells, built of solid blocks of concrete and stainless steel . . . They don't work in prison industries; they don't have access to recreation; they don't mingle with other inmates'. Even the guards 'are locked away in glass-enclosed control booths and communicate with prisoners through a speaker system', and so are seldom, if ever, seen by the prisoners. The sole task left to the guards is to make sure that prisoners stay locked in their cells—that is, non-seeing and non-seen, incommunicado. Apart from the fact that the prisoners are still eating and defecating, their cells could be mistaken for coffins.

At a first glance, the Pelican Bay project looks like an updated, state of the art, super high-tech version of Panopticon; the ultimate incarnation of Bentham's dream of total control through total surveillance. The second glance reveals, however, the superficiality of the first impression.

Panoptical control had an important function to perform; panoptical institutions were conceived above all as *houses of correction*. The ostensible purpose of correction was to bring the inmates back from the road to moral perdition on which they embarked of their own will or on which they had been pushed for no direct fault of their own; to prod them to develop habits which will eventually permit the return of the temporarily excluded into the fold of 'normal society'; to 'stop the moral rot', to fight back and conquer sloth, ineptitude and disrespect or indifference to social norms—all those afflictions which made the inmates incapable of 'normal life'. The vision of Panopticon was conceived at the times of work ethic—when work, hard work and constant work, was seen as simultaneously the recipe for godly, meritorious life and the basic rule of social order. Those were as well the times when the numbers of smallholders and craftsmen unable to make ends meet were growing unstoppably—while the machines which deprived them of livelihood waited in vain for the compliant and docile hands ready to serve them. And so in practice the idea of correction stood for the intention of setting the inmates to work—drilling them for the lifetime of useful work, profitable work. In his vision of Panopticon Bentham generalized the experience of widespread contemporary efforts to resolve the genuine, irksome and worrying problems confronted by the pioneers of the routine, monotonous, mechanical rhythm of modern industrial labour.

At the time when the project of Panopticon was sketched, the lack of willing labour was widely seen as the main obstacle to social improvement. The early entrepreneurs bewailed the resistance and unwillingness of potential labourers to surrender to the rhythm of the factory labour; 'correction' meant, under the circumstances, overcoming that resistance and making the surrender more plausible.

To sum it up: whatever their other immediate destinations, all kinds of panoptical-style houses of confinement were first and foremost *factories of discipline—more precisely, factories of disciplined labour.* More often than not, they were also instant solutions to that ultimate task—they set the inmates to work right away, and particularly to the kinds of work least desired by 'free labourers' and least likely to be performed of their own free will, however seductive were the promised rewards for drudgery. Whatever their declared long-term purpose, most panoptical institutions were, right away, *workhouses.*

The designers and promoters of the 'House of Correction', set in Amsterdam in the early seventeenth century, envisaged the production of 'healthy, temperate eaters, used to labour, desirous of holding a good job, capable of standing on their own feet, and God-fearing' and listed a long inventory of manual occupations in which the prospective inmates should engage to develop such qualities—like shoemaking, manufacture of pocketbooks, gloves and bags, edgings for collars and cloaks, weaving of fustians and worsteds, linen cloth and tapestry, knitting, woodcarving, carpentry, glass blowing, basketry etc. In practice, the productive activity in the House was very soon, after a few half-hearted attempts to follow the initial brief, confined to the rasping of Brazilian logwood, originally named as a means of punishment only—a particularly crude and exhausting labour unlikely to find willing performers if not for the coercive regime of the House of Correction (Sellin 1944).

Whether the houses of correction in any of their many forms ever fulfilled their declared aim of 'rehabilitation', 'moral reform', 'bringing the inmates back to social competence', was from the start highly debatable and remains to this day a moot question. The prevailing opinion of researchers is that contrary to the best of intentions the conditions endemic to the closely supervised houses of confinement worked *against* the 'rehabilitation'. The outspoken precepts of the work ethic never squared well with the coercive regime of prisons, under whatever name they appeared.

In the thoroughly considered, closely argued and backed with comprehensive research opinion of Thomas Mathieson—'throughout its history, the prison has actually never rehabilitated people in practice. It has never led to the people's 'return to "competence" ' (Mathiesen 1990). What prison did instead was to *prisonize* their inmates (Donald Clemmer's term)—that is, to encourage them or force them to absorb and adopt habits and customs typical of the penitentiary environment and of such environment only, and so sharply distinct from the behavioural patterns promoted by the cultural norms ruling in the world outside the walls; 'prisonization' was the very opposite of 'rehabilitation'. In fact, it was itself a major obstacle erected on the 'road back to competence' (Clemmer 1940).

The point is however, that unlike the time when the House of Correction was opened in Amsterdam to the applause of learned opinion, the question of 'rehabilitation' is today prominent less by its contentiousness than by its growing irrelevance. Many criminologists will probably go on for some time yet rehearsing the time-honoured yet never resolved *querelles* of penal ideology—but by far the most seminal departure is precisely the abandonment of sincere or duplicitous declarations of 'rehabilitating intent' in the thinking of contemporary practitioners of the penal system.

Efforts to get the inmates back to work may be effective or not, but they make sense only if work is waiting, and they get their animus and credibility from the fact that the work is waiting impatiently. The first condition is today hardly ever met, the second is blatantly absent. Once zealous to absorb ever growing quantities of labour, the capital reacts now nervously to the news of falling unemployment; through its stock-exchange plenipotentiaries it rewards the companies for laying off the staff and cutting the number of jobs. Under these conditions, confinement is neither a school for employment nor the second best, forcible method to augment the ranks of productive labour when the ordinary and preferred, 'voluntary' methods fail—to bring into the industrial orbit the particularly reluctant and obstreperous categories of the 'masterless men' or to fill the particularly odious and repulsive jobs. It is rather, under the present circumstances, an *alternative to employment*; a way to dispose of, to incapacitate or remove out of sight a considerable chunk of the population who are not needed as producers and for whom there is no work 'to be taken back to'.

In a blatant opposition to the work-ethic commandments, the pressure today is to *dismantle* the habits of permanent, round-the-clock, steady and regular work; what else may the fashionable slogan of 'flexible labour' mean? The strategy commended today is to make the labourers *forget*, not to *learn*, whatever work ethic in the days of the modern industry's ascent was meant to teach them.

Labour can conceivably get truly 'flexible' only if the present and prospective employees lose their trained habits of day-in-day-out work, daily shifts, permanent workplace and steady workmates' company; if they do not get used and habituated to any job, and most certainly if they abstain (or are prevented) from developing vocational attitudes to any job currently performed and give up the morbid inclination to fantasize, let alone assume, job-ownership rights and responsibilities.

On their latest annual meeting held in September 1997 in Hong Kong, the managers of the International Monetary Fund and the World Bank severely criticized German and French methods to get more people back to work. They saw such efforts as going against the grain of 'flexibility of the labour market'. What the latter requires, they said, is the revocation of 'too favourable' job-and-wages-protecting laws, dismantling of all 'distortions' which stand in the way of unalloyed competitiveness, and breaking the resistance of the existing labour against the withdrawal of their acquired 'privileges' (cf. Marti 1997), that is of the rules protecting stability of their employment, their jobs and incomes. In other words—what is needed are new conditions which would favour habits and attitudes diametrically opposed to those which the work ethic prophesied and which the panoptical institutions expected to implement that ethic were to promote. According to the managers of planetary finances, labour must de-learn their hard trained dedication to work and give up their hard won emotional attachment to the workplace as well as the personal involvement in its well-being.

In this context the idea of the Pelican Bay prison as the continuation and a high-tech version of the early industrial workhouses whose experience, ambitions and unresolved problems the project of the Panopticon reflected, looks much less convincing. No productive work is done inside the concrete walls of Pelican Bay prison. No training for work is intended either—there is nothing in the prison's design which may set the stage for such activity. Indeed, for its inmates the Pelican Bay is not a school of anything—even of a purely formal discipline. The whole point of the Panopticon, the paramount purpose of the constant surveillance, was to make sure that the inmates go through certain motions, follow certain routines, do certain things. But what the inmates of the Pelican Bay prison *do* inside their solitary cells *does not matter* at all. What *does matter* is that they stay there. Pelican Bay prison has not been designed as a factory of discipline or disciplined labour. It was designed as the *factory of exclusion* and of people habituated to their status of the *excluded*. And since the mark of the excluded in the era of the time/space compression is enforced *immobility—what the Pelican Bay prison brings close to perfection is the technique of immobilization.*

If the concentration camps served as laboratories of a totalitarian society, where the limits of human submission and serfdom were explored, and if the Panopticon-style workhouses served as the laboratories of industrial society, where the limits of routinization of human action were experimented with—the Pelican Bay prison is a laboratory of the 'globalized' (or 'planetary', in Alberto Melucci's term) society, where the techniques of space-confinement of the rejects and waste of globalization are tested and their limits are explored.

Prisons in the Post-Correction Age

Apart from the rehabilitating function, Thomas Mathiesen in the already quoted book scrupulously examines other widely used assertions meant to justify the use of imprisonment as a method of resolving acute and noxious social problems, such as the theories of the preventive role of prisons (in both universal and individual sense), of incapacitation and deterrence, of just retribution—only to find them all, without exception, logically flawed and empirically unsustainable. No evidence of any sort has been thus far found and collected to support, let alone to prove, the assumptions that prisons perform the roles ascribed to them in theory, and that they achieve any degree of success if they try to perform them—while the assumed justice of most specific measures which such theories propose or imply fails the simplest tests of ethical soundness and propriety (for instance: 'what is the moral basis for punishing someone, perhaps hard, in order to prevent entirely different people from committing equivalent acts?'; the question all the more ethically poignant and worrying for the fact that 'those we punish to a large extent are poor and highly stigmatized people in need of assistance rather than punishment' (Mathiesen 1990: 70)).

The number of people in prison or awaiting likely prison sentences is growing, and fast, almost in every country. In America, their total number already exceeds the number of students in all colleges of higher education. The network of prisons enjoys nearly everywhere a building boom. State-budget expenditure on the 'forces of law and order', mainly the active police force and prison service, are on the rise throughout the globe. Most importantly, the proportion of population in direct conflict with the law and subject to imprisonment is growing on apace, which signals more than a purely quantitative increase and suggests a 'greatly increased significance of the institutional solution as a component in criminal policy'; it signals, moreover, that there is a presumption taken by many governments and enjoying wide support of public opinion that 'there is an increased need for disciplining of important population segments and groups' (Mathiesen 1990: 13).

What the sharp acceleration of the punishment-by-incarceration suggests, in other words, is that there are some new and large sections of the population targeted for one reason or another as the threat to social order, and that their forcible eviction from social intercourse through imprisonment is seen as an effective method to neutralize the threat, or at least to calm the public anxiety which that threat evokes.

The proportion of the population serving prison sentences varies from one country to another—but rapid growth seems to be a universal phenomenon throughout the 'most developed' tip of the world. The US, notoriously, is in the lead and far ahead of the rest—between 1979 and 1993 the proportion of people locked in prisons grew from 230 to 532 per 100,000 of population (in some areas the ratio is much higher— in the district of Anacostia where most of the poor population of Washington is condensed, half of male residents of the 16–35 years' bracket are either awaiting trial or already in prison or on probation (Zucchini 1997))—but the acceleration of pace is marked elsewhere as well: through the same 15 years the comparable figures in Canada went up from 100 to 125, in Britain from 85 to 95, in Norway from 44 to 62, in Holland from 23 to 52 (Christie 1994).

Since the growth is not confined to a selected group of countries but well-nigh universal, it would be probably misleading—if not down-right futile—to seek the explanation in the state-bound policies or in the ideologies and practices of this or that political party (even as it would be similarly wrong to deny the modifying impact such policies may exert on accelerating or slowing down the growth). Besides, there is no evidence that the trust in prison as the principal tool to resolve what has been defined as vexing and anxiety-arousing problems has become anywhere a serious, let alone contentious, issue in electoral battles; the competing forces, even if miles apart on other hot issues of the day, tend to manifest a complete agreement on this one; the sole publicly displayed concern of each of them is to convince the electorate that it will be 'tough on crime' and more determined and merciless in pursuing the imprisonment of criminals than its political adversaries have been or are likely to be. One is tempted to conclude, therefore, that the causes of the discussed growth must be of a supra-party and supra-state nature—indeed, of a global rather than local (in either ter-ritorial or cultural sense) character. In all probability, these causes are more than contingently related to the broad spectre of transformations subsumed under the name of globalization.

One evident cause of the discussed growth is the spectacular promo-tion of the issues classified under the 'law and order' rubric in the panoply of public concerns, particularly as such concerns are reflected in the learned and authoritative interpretations of social ills and in political programmes promising to repair them. In my *Postmodernity and Its Discontents* (1997) I argued that whether or not Sigmund Freud was right when suggesting that the trading off of a considerable part of personal liberty for some measure of collectively guaranteed security was the main cause of psychical afflictions and sufferings, unease and anxiety in the 'classic' period of modern civilization—today, in the late or postmodern stage of modernity it is the opposite tendency, the inclination to trade off a lot of security in exchange for removing more and more constraints cramping the exercise of free choice, which generates the widespread sentiments of fear and anxiety. It is these sentiments which seek their outlet (or are being channelled) in the concerns with law and order.

To comprehend fully this remarkable 'transfer of anxiety' one needs to reunite what the language in its sometimes excessive zeal to divide and circumscribe, has separated. The emotional/attitudinal unity which underlies the allegedly distinct, since linguistically set apart, experiences of security, safety and certainty is difficult to notice for the English-speaker, but much better grasped by the speakers of German— thanks to the otherwise uncommonly rare frugality of their language: the German word *Sicherheit* grasps all three experiences (of safety, security and certainty) and refuses to accept their mutual autonomy which English speakers are linguistically trained to take for granted.

Freud wrote of *Freiheit* and *Sicherheit*, not of 'freedom' and 'security'. If *Freiheit* was made vulnerable by the early modern quest for *Sicherheit*—that is, the triune compound of safety, security and certainty of order—the same *Sicherheit* is the prime victim of the late modern career of individual freedom. Since we would be hardly able to tell apart the three kinds (or the three ingredients) of unease were it not for the three different words that suggest three separate semantic fields, there is little wonder that the dearth of risk-free, that is *secure*, choices, and the growing unclarity of the game-rules which renders uncertain most of the moves and above all the outcomes of the moves, tend to rebound as perceptions of threats to *safety*—first the safety of the body, and then of property, that body-space extension. In the ever more insecure and uncertain world the withdrawal into the safe haven of territoriality is an intense temptation; and so the defence of the territory—'safe home' becomes the passkey to all doors which one feels must be locked up and sealed to stave off the triple threat to spiritual and material comfort.

A lot of tension accumulates in the result around the quest for safety—much in excess of the safety's carrying power. And where there is a tension, a political capital will surely be spotted by clever investors and expedient stock-brokers. No wonder that the appeals to the safety-related fears are truly supra-class and cross-party, as are the fears themselves. It is perhaps a happy coincidence for the political operators and hopefuls that the genuine problems of insecurity and uncertainty have condensed into the anxiety about safety; politicians can be supposed to be doing something about the first two just because being seen to be vociferous, tough-tongued and keeping busy about the latter.

Happy coincidence, indeed, given that the first two worries are, in fact, intractable. Governments cannot seriously promise anything but more 'flexibility of labour'—that is, in the ultimate account, more insecurity and ever more painful and incapacitating insecurity. Serious governments cannot promise certainty either; that they must concede freedom to notoriously erratic and unpredictable 'market forces' which, having won their exterritoriality, are far beyond the reach of anything the hopelessly 'local', territory-bound governments can do, is almost universally taken for a foregone conclusion. Fortunately for the increasingly impotent governments, doing something, or be seen to be doing something, about fighting the crime which threatens personal safety is, however, a realistic option—and one containing a lot of electoral potential. *Sicherheit* will gain little in the result, but the ranks of voters would swell.

Safety: the Tangible Means to an Elusive End

Tapering the complex issue of *Sicherheit* to that of personal safety has other political advantages as well. Whatever one may do about safety is a shortcut to the notorious 'feel good factor'—for the reason of being incomparably more spectacular, watchable, 'televisable' than any move aimed at the deeper, but much less tangible and apparently more abstract, layers of the malaise. Fighting crime, like crime itself, and particularly the crime targeted on bodies and private property, makes an excellent, exciting, eminently watchable show. The mass media producers and scriptwriters are well aware of this. Were one to judge the state of society after its dramatized representations (as most of us do, whether or not we are ready to admit it to others and to ourselves)—not just the proportion of criminals to the 'ordinary folk' would appear to exceed by far the proportion of the population already kept in jail, and not only the world as a whole would seem to be divided primarily into the criminals and the guardians of order, but the whole of human life would seem to navigate the narrow sea-passage between the threat of physical assault and fighting back the potential attackers.

The overall effect of all this is the self-propelling of fear. Preoccupation with personal safety, inflated and overloaded with meanings beyond its capacity due to the tributaries of existential insecurity and psychological uncertainty, towers yet higher over all other articulated fears, casting all other reasons of anxiety in a yet deeper shade. Governments may feel relieved: no one or almost no one would press them to do something about things which their hands are much too short and feeble to grasp and hold. No one would accuse them either of remaining idle and doing nothing of real relevance to human anguish and fear—when watching daily documentaries, dramas, docudramas and carefully staged dramas disguised as documentaries, telling the story of new and improved police weapons, high-tech prison locks and burglar and car-theft alarms, short sharp shocks administered to the criminals and valiant security officers and detectives risking their lives so that the rest of us may sleep in peace.

Building new prisons, writing up new statutes which multiply the number of breaches of law punishable with imprisonment and make the lengthening of prison sentences mandatory—all these measures increase the popularity of governments; they show the governments to be tough, resourceful and determined, and above all 'doing something', not just, explicitly, about the personal safety of their subjects, but by implication about their security and certainty as well; and doing it in a highly dramatic, tangible and visible, and so convincing, fashion.

The spectacularity—the versatility, harshness and promptness of punishing operations matters more than their effectiveness, which— given the endemic listlessness of public attention and short life-span of public memory—is seldom tested anyway. It even matters more than the actual volume of detected and reported crimes. It helps, of course, if time and again a new kind of crime is brought to public attention and found to be particularly repulsive and horrifying as well as ubiquitous, and if a new detecting/punishing campaign is launched. Such occasional prodding of anxiety-prone imagination helps to keep the public mind on the dangers rooted in crime and the criminals and prevents the public from reflecting why, despite all that policing promised to bring the coveted *Sicherheit* about, one goes on feeling unsure, lost, and frightened as before.

There is more than a happy coincidence between the tendency to conflate the troubles of the intrinsic insecurity and uncertainty of the late modern/postmodern being in a single, overwhelming concern about personal safety—and the new realities of nation-state politics, particularly of the cut-down version of state sovereignty characteristic of the 'globalization' era.

To focus locally on the 'safe environment' and everything it may genuinely or putatively entail, is exactly what the 'market forces', by now global and so exterritorial, want the nation-state governments to do (effectively barring them from doing anything else). In the world of global finances, state governments are allotted the role of little else than oversized police precincts; the quantity and quality of the policemen on the beat, efficiency displayed in sweeping the streets clean of beggars, pesterers and pilferers, and the tightness of the jail walls loom large among the factors of 'investors' confidence', and so among the items calculated when the decisions to invest or cut the losses and run are made. To excel in the job of the precinct policeman is the best (perhaps the only) thing state government may do to cajole the nomadic capital into investing in its subjects' welfare. The shortest roads to economic prosperity of the land, and so hopefully to the 'feel good' sentiments of the electors, lead through the public display of the policing skill and prowess of the state.

The care of the 'orderly state', once a complex and convoluted task, on a par with the multiple ambitions and wide and multifaceted sovereignty of the state, tends to taper in the result to the task of fighting the crime. In that task, though, an increasingly privileged, indeed a leading role, is allocated to the policy of imprisonment. The centrality of crime-fighting does not by itself explain the prison boom; after all, there are other ways as well to fight back the real or alleged threats to the citizens' personal safety. Besides, putting more people in jail and for a longer time has not thus far been shown to be the most effective among these ways. One would guess therefore that some other factors favour the choice of prison as the most convincing proof that indeed 'something is being done', that the words have flesh and bones: to posit imprisonment as the crucial strategy in the fight for the citizens' safety means addressing the issue in contemporary idiom, using the language readily understood and invoking commonly familiar experience.

Today's existential opportunities and choices are stretched along the hierarchy of the global and the local, with global freedom of movement signalling social promotion, advancement and success, and immobility exuding the repugnant odour of defeat, of failed life, of 'being left behind'. Increasingly, globality and locality acquire the character of contrary values—and paramount values with that, values most hotly coveted or resented and placed in the very centre of life dreams, nightmares and struggles. Life ambitions are more often than not expressed in terms of mobility, free choice of place, travelling, seeing the world; the life fears, on the contrary, are talked about in terms of confinement to a place, lack of change, being barred from places which others traverse easily, explore and enjoy. 'Good life' is the life on the move; more precisely, the comfort of being confident of the facility to move elsewhere in case staying on no more satisfies. Freedom came to mean above all freedom of choice, and choice has acquired, conspicuously, a spatial dimension.

In the era of time/space compression, so many wonderful and untried sensations beckon from afar, that 'home'—though as always attractive as an idea—tends to be enjoyed most in the bitter-sweet emotion of homesickness. In its solid, bricks-and-mortar embodiment, 'home' breeds resentment and rebellion. If locked from outside, if getting out is a distant prospect or not a feasible prospect at all, the home turns into jail. Enforced immobility, the condition of being tied to a place and not allowed to quit, seems a most abominable, cruel and repulsive state; it is the blank prohibition to move, which renders that condition especially offensive. Being prohibited to move is a most potent symbol of impotence and incapacitation—and the most acute of pains.

No wonder, therefore, that the idea of prison sentence as simultaneously the most effective method of disempowering the potentially harmful people and a most painful retribution for ill deeds, is resonant with contemporary experience and so easily 'makes sense' and altogether 'stands to reason'. Immobilization is the fate which people haunted with the fear of their own immobilization would naturally wish and demand to be visited upon those whom they fear and consider deserving a punishment most harsh and cruel. Other forms of deterrence and retribution seem woefully lenient, inadequate and ineffective—painless—by comparison.

Prison, though, means not only immobilization, but eviction as well. This adds further to its popular attraction and approval as the effective means to 'strike at the roots of danger'. Imprisonment means protracted, perhaps permanent exclusion (with the death penalty offering the ideal pattern by which the length of all other sentences is measured). This meaning also strikes a highly sensitive chord. The slogan is to 'make our streets safe again'—and what else promises better to fulfil this slogan than the removal of the carriers of danger into spaces out of sight and out of touch—spaces they cannot escape?

The ambient *Unsicherheit* focuses on the fear for personal safety; that in turn sharpens further—on the ambivalent, unpredictable figure of the Stranger. Stranger in the street, prowler around the home . . . burglar alarms, watched and patrolled neighbourhood, guarded condominium gates—they all serve the same purpose: keeping the strangers away. Prison is but the most radical among many measures—it is different from the rest in the assumed degree of effectiveness only, not in kind. People brought up in the culture of burglar alarms and anti-theft devices would tend to be the natural enthusiasts of prison sentences, and ever longer prison sentences. It all ties up together very nicely—the logic seems to be restored to the chaos of existence.

The Out of Order

'Today we know', writes Thomas Mathiesen, 'that the penal system strikes at the "bottom" rather than at the "top" of society' (Mathiesen 1990: 70–2). Why this should be the case, has been amply explained by the sociologists of law and practices of punishment. Several causes have been repeatedly discussed.

The first among them are the admittedly selective intentions of law-givers, concerned as they must be with the preservation not of 'the order as such', but of a *certain specific* kind of order. The actions most likely to be committed by people which that order has no room for, by the underdog and the rejected, stand the best chance to appear in the criminal code. On the other hand, robbing whole nations of their resources is called 'promotion of free trade'; robbing whole families and communities of livelihood is called 'downsizing' or just 'rationalization'. Neither of the two has ever been listed among criminal and punishable deeds.

Moreover, as every police unit dedicated to 'serious crime' would have found out, the illegal acts committed at the 'top' are exceedingly difficult to disentangle from the dense network of daily and 'ordinary' company dealings. In the activity which openly pursues personal gain at the expense of other people, the borderline between the moves allowed and disallowed is necessarily poorly defined and always contentious—nothing to compare with the comforting unambiguity of the act of safe-breaking or forcing a lock. No wonder that, as Mathiesen finds out, the prisons 'are above all filled by people from the lower strata of the working class who had committed theft and other "traditional" crimes'.

Poorly defined, the crimes 'at the top' are in addition awfully difficult to detect and yet more difficult to prosecute. They are perpetrated inside a close circle of people united by mutual complicity, loyalty to the organization and *esprit de corps*, people who usually take effective measures to spot, silence or eliminate the potential whistleblowers. They require a level of legal and financial sophistication virtually impossible to be penetrated, let alone appropriated, by outsiders—particularly by lay and untrained outsiders. And they have 'no body', no physical substance, they 'exist' in the ethereal, imaginary space of pure abstraction: they are, literally, *invisible*—it takes an imagination on a par with the imagination of the perpetrators to spy out the substance in an elusive form. Guided by intuition and common sense, the public may well suspect that some theft played its part in the history of fortunes—but to point one's finger to it remains a notoriously daunting task.

Furthermore, only in rare and extreme cases do the 'corporate crimes' come to court and into public view. Embezzlers and tax cheaters have an infinitely greater opportunity for an out-of-court settlement than do pickpockets or burglars. Apart from anything else, the agents of local orders are all too aware of the superiority of global powers and so would consider it a success if they got as far as that.

As if to protect the 'crime at the top' even better, vigilance of the public in this area is at best erratic and sporadic, at worst non-existent. It takes a truly spectacular fraud, a fraud with a 'human touch', where the victims—pensioners or small savers—can be personally named (and even then it takes all the imaginative and persuasive gifts of a small or not that small army of the popular press— journalists) to arouse public attention and keep it aroused for longer than a day or two. What is going on during the trials of high-level fraudsters defies the intellectual abilities of the ordinary newspaper readers and TV watchers; besides, it is abominably short of the drama which makes the trials of simple thieves and murderers such a fascinating spectacle.

More importantly, though, the 'crime at the top' (usually an extraterritorial 'top') may be in the last account a principal or contributing cause of existential insecurity, and so directly relevant to the endemic Unsicherheit which haunts the denizens of late modern society and makes them so obsessed with personal safety in the first place—but by no stretch of imagination can it be conceived of as, of itself, a threat to that safety. Any danger which may be sensed or surmised in the 'crime at the top' is of an altogether different order. It would be extremely hard to envisage how bringing the culprits to justice may alleviate the daily fears ascribed to the more tangible dangers lurking in the rough districts and mean streets of one's own city. There is, therefore, not much electoral capital which can be squeezed out of 'being

seen as doing something' about the 'crime at the top'. And there is little political pressure on the legislators and guardians of order to strain
their minds and flex their muscles in order to make the fight against
that kind of crime more effective; no comparison here with the public
hue-and-cry against the car thieves, muggers or rapists, as well as
against all those responsible for law and order who are suspected of
being too lazy or lenient in transporting them to prison, where they
belong.

Last but not least, there is that tremendous advantage the new global
elite enjoys when facing the guardians of order: order is local, while the
elite and the free-market laws it obeys are translocal. If the wardens of
a local order get too obtrusive and obnoxious, there is always a possibility to move away if things get locally too hot for comfort; 'globality'
of the elite means mobility, and mobility means the ability to escape
and evade. There are always places where local orders do not clash
with global market usages, or where the local guardians of order are
glad and willing to look the other way in case a clash does happen.

All these factors taken together converge on a common effect: identification of crime with the (always local) 'underclass'—or, which
amounts to much the same, on criminalization of poverty. The most
common types of criminals in public view come almost without exception from the 'bottom' of society. Urban ghettos and no-go-areas are
seen as the breeding ground of crime and criminals. And conversely—
sources of criminality (of that criminality which truly counts—criminality seen as the threat to personal safety) appear to be unambiguously
local and localized.

Donald Clemmer coined in 1940 the term 'prisonization' to denote
the true effects of confinement, sharply different from the 're-educating'
and 'rehabilitating' impact ascribed to imprisonment by its theorists
and promoters. Clemmer found the inmates being assimilated into a
highly idiosyncratic 'prison culture', which—if anything—made them
even less fit than ever before for life outside the walls, and less capable
of following the rules and usages of 'ordinary' existence. Like all cultures, prison culture had a self-perpetuating capacity. Prison was and
remains, in Clemmer's opinion, a *school of crime*.

Fourteen years later Lloyd W. McCorkle and Richard R. Korn
(1954) published another set of findings, which brought into relief the
mechanism making prisons into such schools of crime. According to
their data, the whole police/judicial process culminating in imprisonment is, in a sense, one long and tightly structured ritual of symbolic

rejection and physical exclusion. Rejection and exclusion are humiliat-
ing and meant to be such; they are meant to result in the
rejected/excluded accepting their social imperfection and inferiority.
No wonder the victims mount a defence. Rather than meekly accepting
their rejection and converting official rejection into self-rejection, they
prefer to reject their rejectors.

To do that, the rejected/excluded resort to the means at their dis-
posal, which all contain some measure of violence; the sole resource
that they may increase their 'nuisance power', the only power they can
oppose to the overwhelming might of their rejectors/excluders. The
strategy of 'rejecting the rejectors' quickly sinks into the stereotype of
the rejected, adding to the image of crime the traits of the criminals'
inherent proclivity to recidivism. At the end of the day, prisons emerge
as the principal tools of a self-fulfilling prophecy.

This does not mean that there are no other causes of crime and no
genuine criminals; it means, though, that the rejection/exclusion practised through the prison system is an integral part of the social production of crime, and that its influence cannot be neatly disentangled from
the overall statistics of the incidence of criminality. It also means that
once prisons have been identified as outlets for mostly the lower class of
'underclass' elements—one would naturally expect the self-confirming
and self-perpetuating effects to be at their most emphatic, and so the
criminality to be 'most evident', at the 'bottom' reaches of society.

Prisons as Testing Grounds of Order Maintenance

Clemmer and McCorkle and Korn conducted their research among the
inmates of prisons and articulated their findings in terms of the effects
of imprisonment. One can suppose, though, that what they sought and
found was not so much the effects of prison as such, as of the much
wider phenomena of *confinement*, *rejection* and *exclusion*. That, in
other words, prisons served there as laboratories in which trends ubiq-
uitously (though in a somewhat more dilute form) present in 'normal'
life could be observed in their condensed and purified shape (Dick
Hebdige's seminal study *Hiding in the Light* corroborates this guess).
Were this supposition correct, then the effect of 'prisonization' and the
widespread choice of 'rejecting the rejectors' strategy with all its self-
propelling capacity would go a long way towards cracking the myste-
rious logic of the present-day law-and-order obsession; also towards
explaining the apparent success of the stratagem of substituting that

obsession for the serious attempt to face up to the challenge of the accruing existential insecurity.

It might also help to understand why the rejection from global freedoms tends to rebound in the present tendency toward self-enclosure and fortification of localities. Rejection prompts the effort to circumscribe localities after the pattern of concentration camps. Rejection of the rejectors prompts the effort to transform locality into a fortress. The two efforts reinforce each other's effects and between them make sure that fragmentation and estrangement 'at the bottom' remain the twin siblings of globalization 'at the top'.

The fortifications built by the better off majority and the self-defence-through-aggression practised by those left outside the walls have a mutually reinforcing effect well predicted in Gregory Bateson's theory of 'schismogenetic chains'. According to that theoretical model, schism is likely to emerge and deepen beyond repair when a position is set up in which

The behaviour x, y, z is the standard reply to x, y, z . . . If, for example, the patterns x, y, z include boasting, we shall see that there is a likelihood, if boasting is the reply to boasting, that each group will drive the other into excessive emphasis of the pattern, a process which if not restrained can only lead to more and more extreme rivalry and ultimately to hostility and the breakdown of the whole system.

The above is the pattern of 'symmetrical differentiation'. What is its alternative? What happens if the group B fails to respond to the x, y, z kind of challenge by the group A with an x, y, z type of behaviour? The schismogenetic chain is not then cut—it only assumes the pattern of the 'complementary', instead of symmetrical, differentiation. If, for instance, assertive behaviour is not responded to in the same currency, but meets with submissiveness, 'it is likely that this submissiveness will promote further assertiveness which in turn will promote further submissiveness.' The 'breakdown of the system' will follow all the same (Bateson 1973).

The overall effect of the choice between the two patterns is minimal, but for the sides tied by the schismogenetic chain the difference between the patterns is one between dignity and humiliation, humanity and its loss. One can safely anticipate that the strategy of symmetrical differentiation would always be preferred to the complementary alternative. The latter is the strategy for the defeated or for those who accepted the inevitability of defeat. Whatever the value of this hypothesis, though, one can safely expect that some things are bound to emerge victorious, whichever strategy is chosen: the new fragmentation of the city space, shrinkage and disappearance of public spaces, falling apart of urban community, separation and segregation—and above all the exterritoriality of the new global elite and the forced territoriality of the rest.

If the new exterritoriality of the elite feels like intoxicating freedom, the territoriality of the rest feels less like a homeground, and ever more like prison. The present-day trends in prison policies reflect the latter experience, as much as they expand its horizons. It may yet transpire that what Silicon Valley did for our wired-computerized-interwebbed existence, the Pelican Bay prison might have done for the future life conditions of the multitudes who failed to jump on the fast moving train of globalization or were pushed out of it.

References

BATESON, GREGORY (1973), *Steps to an Ecology of Mind*, 41–2. Frogmore: Paladin.

BAUMAN, ZYGMUNT (1997), *Postmodernity and its Discontents*. London: Polity Press.

CASTORIADIS, CORNELIUS (1989), 'Anthropology, Philosophy, Politics', lecture given in Lausanne in 1997, in Thesis, 49, translated by David Ames Curtis.

CHRISTIE, NILS (1993/94), *Crime Control as Industry: Towards Gulag, Western Style?*, 86–7. London: Routledge. (In the second edition the question mark has been removed.)

—— (n.d.), *Civility and State*, unpublished manuscript.

CLEMMER, DONALD (1940), *The Prison Community*. New York: Holt, Reinhart and Winston.

KUNDERA, MILAN (1976), *La Valse aux Adieux*. Paris: Gallimard, quoted in Peter Kussi, trans. (1993) *The Farewell Party*. London: Faber and Faber.

McCORKLE, LLOYD W. and KORN, RICHARD R. (1954), 'Resocialization Within Walls', in *Annals of American Academy of Political and Social Science*, 88–98.

MARTI, SERGE (1997), 'Le FMI critique les méthodes anti-chômage de Bonn et Paris', report from the Hong Kong meeting, *Le Monde*, 19 September.

MATHIESEN, THOMAS (1990), *Prison on Trial: A Critical Assessment*, 40. London: Sage.

SELLIN, THORSTEN (1944), *Pioneering in Penology: the Amsterdam Houses of Correction in the Sixteenth and Seventeenth Centuries*, 27–9, 58–9. Pennsylvania, PA: University of Philadelphia Press.

ZUCCHINI, LAURENT (1997), 'Ségrégation ordinaire à Washington', *Le Monde*, 25 September.

3

The New Regulatory State and the Transformation of Criminology

JOHN BRAITHWAITE

Carved in Stone

When I entered the University of Queensland in 1969, there was a large sandstone building with Zoology carved over the entrance. Next to it Botany was carved into the stone. Behind was a newer building called Microbiology. Today, these disciplinary divides don't mean much. The big organizing themes of the biological sciences are molecular biology (transformed by the DNA revolution), evolutionary biology and ecology—all themes that run right across the old biologies based on types of organisms.

Comparable change is descending upon the social sciences. This essay will attempt to explain why. It will contend that some of the scholars who are currently thought of as criminologists might become central influences in the social sciences, even though criminology itself, according to this analysis, is destined for decline. Most of the contributors to this collection, including this one, come from the discipline of sociology, which is already in decline. The risk is that in 20 years our collection will be read as a dialogue between a dead and a dying discipline.

But for the moment sociology is far from dead and criminology is booming. Criminologists have only recently begun to think of themselves as belonging to a discipline, though most continue to have a healthy scepticism of criminology going the way of disciplines they have escaped. In North America, where criminology is most disciplined, there now may well be more university scholars who identify themselves as criminologists than as philosophers or geographers. There are certainly more of the former in government research posts.

The criminology boom is not fed by the intellectual accomplishments of the field, but by the continuous growth in public sector employment in the criminal justice system combined with new expectations that police should be university graduates, and by even stronger growth in private policing. This criminology expansion is so sustained that the criminal justice building will probably still stand on the university campus a century from now. My prediction is that just as there is exciting biology going on in the zoology and botany buildings today, in future we might see criminology abandoned inside the criminal justice building in favour of studies of regulation, child development, restorative and procedural justice and other yet unforseeable organizing ideas. Why? Because of a shift from a Keynesian state to a new regulatory state. Perhaps 'new' should be in inverted commas because all its individual elements are old, and similarly with 'state' since the most important feature of the new regulatory state is that most of the regulation is neither undertaken nor controlled by the state.

The nightwatchman state which preceded the Keynesian state will be conceived as one where most of the steering and rowing (Osborne and Gaebler 1992) was done in civil society. The Keynesian state that succeeds it has the state do a lot of rowing, but was weak on steering civil society. The new regulatory state that is most recent in this chronology holds up state steering and civil society rowing as the ideal.

From the Nightwatchman State to the Keynesian State

The nightwatchman state of classical liberal theory had functions more or less limited to protecting its citizens from violence, theft, fraud and promulgating a law of contract (Nozick 1974). Until the nineteenth century most of the steering and most of the rowing in the regulation of social life was done in civil society rather than by the state. Oliver McDonagh (1977) has documented the pattern of government growth in Victorian England that began the journey from the nightwatchman to the Keynesian state. Part of the same pattern was professionalizing the nightwatchman functions themselves with the Peelian revolution in policing from 1829.

The most decisive shift to the Keynesian state was the New Deal in the United States, when a great variety of national regulatory agencies assumed a degree of expert central state control of formerly unregulated activity. It took something as terrible as the great crash to end the nightwatchman state, with the libertarians fighting a rearguard action to the very end. When Richard Whitney, President of the New York Stock Exchange, appeared before Senate staff investigators who were setting up the Securities and Exchange Commission in 1933, he said: 'You gentlemen are making a great mistake. The Exchange is a perfect institution.' (McCraw 1984: 194).

Compared with what went before and with the more Hayekian policy that followed it, the Keynesian state justified quite a lot of rowing by the state, without paying much attention to steering regulatory activities in civil society. In practice, of course, it was still a liberal capitalist society where a great deal of steering and rowing continued to be undertaken by institutions of civil society such as the stock exchange. But the mentality of the Keynesian state was general belief that the state could do the job, including the job of policing; the debate was no longer with liberal minimalism (Hayek was a marginalized, 'out-of-touch' intellectual) but with socialism. Under the ideology of the Keynesian state, the response to every outbreak of disorder was to increase central state policing resources. Social workers, probation officers and other welfare workers employed by the state also acquired ever more resources and powers under the same Keynesian disposition.

From the Keynesian State to the New Regulatory State

Following the lead of the Thatcher government in Britain, during the 1980s and 90s thousands of privatizations of public organizations occurred around the world. Contrary to the Hayekian philosophy of Thatcherism, deregulation did not always go hand in hand with privatization (Ayres and Braithwaite 1992: 7–12). Rather we saw what a number of scholars have discussed as the rise of a new regulatory state (Majone 1994; Loughlin and Scott 1997; Parker 1999a). Hence, when British telecommunications was deregulated in 1984, Oftel was created to regulate it; Ofgas with the regulation of a privatized gas industry in 1986, OFFER with electricity in 1989, OfWat with water in 1990, and the Office of the Rail Regulator for rail in 1993 (Baldwin et al. 1998). When the Thatcher government radically shifted the provision of nursing home beds from the public to the private sector (Day and Klein 1987), 200 little nursing home inspectorates were set up in district health authorities to upgrade the previously cursory regulatory oversight of the industry. This led Patricia Day and Rudolf Klein as early as the mid-80s to be speaking of the rise of a new regulatory state in the health and welfare sector, replacing the Keynesian welfare state.

Privatization combined with new regulatory institutions is the classic instantiation of Osborne and Gaebler's (1992) prescription for governments to steer but not to row.

The rise of the new regulatory state was partly European catch-up with the New Deal, partly a fresh phenomenon shaped by European Commission imposition of regulatory standards on states (Majone 1994). IMF and World Bank conditionality requiring former communist and developing economies to implement 'good governance' initiatives have also been important in globalizing the new regulatory state (Braithwaite and Drahos 2000). But the new regulatory state is qualitatively different from the New Deal in its reliance on self-regulatory organizations (Clarke 1986), enforced self-regulation (Braithwaite 1982) and other responsive regulatory techniques that substitute for direct command and control. Responsive regulation also flows into strategies for regulating already private institutions through compliance systems, codes of practice and other self-regulatory strategies.

The decentring of the state and 'rule at a distance' are evident in other contemporary intellectual currents, including the 'regulated self-regulation' of neo-corporatist theory (Streeck and Schmitter 1985) and the work of Marsh and Rhodes (1992) on 'policy communities' and 'issue networks' as more important in some ways than states as policy makers (see Crawford 1997). The latter echoes Meidinger's (1987) analysis of 'regulatory communities' of state, business and NGO policy networks with a shared epistemic frame.

While the development of the concept of the new regulatory state by regulatory scholars predates the popularity of late-Foucauldian ideas of liberal governmentality, in the 1990s regulatory scholarship began to be influenced by Foucault's (1991) governmentality lectures. There is no doubt that at the end of his life Foucault was grasping at similar phenomena, albeit in a way that lacked the concrete referents of the scholars of the new regulatory state, or of his own earlier work on disciplinary power with its detailed analyses of practices such as imprisonment (Garland 1997).

For the late Foucault, successful government operates through a capacity of both those who govern and those who are governed to regulate their own behaviour. What Foucault meant by a progressive governmentalization of the state was a move away from direct domination or law enforcement toward indirect rule through inventing technologies for the regulation of conduct, technologies which reshape the institutions within which individuals regulate their own conduct (Hindess

1996). Foucault believed that we 'live in an era of "governmentality" first discovered in the eighteenth century' (Foucault 1991: 91). This account is more or less compatible with the new regulatory state chronology of (1) eighteenth century 'police' in the pluralized, privatized regulatory sense that one sees for example in the writings of Adam Smith (1978), followed by (2) the rise of the Peelian project of a unified state monopoly of 'the police', culminating with (3) the ascendency of Keynesianism that re-pluralizes into (4) the new regulatory state from the 1980s. On both accounts, the Keynesian mentality obscures both the eighteenth and late twentieth century reality of a state that is not a unified set of instrumentalities. What we must study today is strategies of regulation by state and non-state actors, where the state is both a subject and an object of regulation (by the IMF, Moody's, the Security Council, the International Organization for Standardization and the World Trade Organization, among other institutions).

The substantive topics studied by eighteenth-century scholars of police were almost identical in range to those researched by contemporary regulatory scholars, so many of whom moved beyond a base in criminology (like Clifford Shearing and his colleagues). In France and Germany in the eighteenth century, included among the topics covered by 'police regulations' were security, customs, trade, highways, foodstuffs, health, labour standards, fire, forests and hunting, streetlife, migration and immigrant communities (Pasquino 1991: 110). Both eighteenth century scholars of police, of which there were thousands (Pasquino 1991: 112), and the equally numerous researchers of the new regulatory state, share an interest in integrating explanatory and normative theories (eg Loader 1998; Crawford 1997). For most of the police scholars, the normative theory tended to utilitarianism: 'The object of police is everything that has to do with maintaining and augmenting the happiness of its citizens' (Von Hohental 1776). For the new regulatory scholars, the normative frame tends to involve a blend of neo-liberal and Keynesian welfarist objectives, well illustrated by Shearing's attraction to a neo-republican concern with freedom as non-domination (see Brogden and Shearing 1993). More broadly, new regulatory scholars blend police, liberal and Keynesian mentalities of governance. The marriage of police and the market effected in the writing of Adam Smith (1978)[1] is in turn married to a nostalgia for certain Keynesian virtues, as we will see below.

[1] Adam Smith's agenda of fostering competitive markets by eliminating both public and private monopolies and liberalizing trade is shared by most scholars of the new

The new regulatory state has touched even the heartland of the Keynesian state in Australia, with job placement services for the unemployed being privatized and subjected to the regulatory standards of what was initially called the Employment Services Regulatory Authority. The criminal justice system has not been immune to the vectors of the new regulatory state. As in so many nations, in Australia we have seen ten private prisons built during the 1990s, though the new institutions for regulating them have been rather limited (Harding 1997; for Britain see Hood et al. 1998). Again, Hayekian marketization combined with Keynesian regulation of markets.

Much more dramatic has been the privatization of policing, with most developed economies having today more private than public police (Shearing and Stenning 1981, 1983, 1987). As early as the 1950s in the US private security personnel outnumbered public police. But the huge taxpayer investment in public police during the 1960s restored a roughly equal balance of the private and public by 1970, only to see the 1.1 million private police by 1982 standing at almost double the public police (Johnston 1992), increasing to 2 million in 1994, thrice the public police (Bayley 1994). In South Africa the preponderance of private over public police is much more profound than in the United States or Europe. There, not only have private replaced public police at sporting events, in high-rise buildings and in gated housing communities for the wealthy, but on the streets in the nightlife areas of the cities nightclubs and restaurants employ the armed private security personnel who patrol to help us to feel safe as we park along the street. Increasingly, the governmental role is to regulate the standards of these private security providers. In Papua New Guinea, which may have even a worse crime problem than South Africa, the new regulatory state has on some occasions taken the fascinating form of Justice Ministers and Police Commissioners negotiating gang surrenders whereby Rascol gangs hand over their weapons and give various other self-regulatory under-

regulatory state. Where they differ is that new regulatory state researchers are highly attracted to many Keynesian forms of regulation, of banking, stock markets and labour standards, for example, that would not have been in the least congenial to Smith. Moreover, new regulatory state students utterly reject Smith's ironically statist and authoritarian approach to 'security': 'In every civilized nation death has been the punishment of the murther(er), but in barbarous nations a pecuniary compensation was accepted of, because then government was weak and durst not meddle in the quarrels of individuals unless in the way of mediation . . . In the laws of all nations we have the remains of this ancient state of weakness' (Smith 1978: 476). For new regulatory state theorists who find much that is attractive in decentralized restorative justice, this 'weakness' of pre-mercantilist states was an attractive one.

takings in return, among other things, for help by the government to set them up in employment in the private security industry! (Dinnen 1996).

The biggest difference between the new regulatory state of criminal justice versus telecommunications, for example, is that whereas private sector growth has been coupled with public sector decline in telecommunications, this is far from universally true with criminal justice. Public prison building has been as expansive as private prison construction during the 1990s. Between 1970 and 1990 the number of public police increased from a low of 22 per cent in Japan (which was the lowest per capita to start with) to a high of a 97 per cent increase in Australia (Bayley 1994: 37), with Britain and the United States falling in the middle at 35 per cent and 64 per cent growth respectively. Where we do find some public sector retrenchment with criminal justice is in the employment of social workers and with other types of welfare provision for offenders, ironically at a time when the evidence clearly no longer sustains a 'nothing works' conclusion. While the welfare state is wound back, the punitive state is not. Andrew Scull's (1977) prediction that the fiscal crisis of the Keynesian welfare state would lead to decarceration has happened with mental patients but not with criminals. Indeed, we might say that with recent cuts to the defence establishments in most states, the Keynesian punitive state stands alone as the major exception to 'the hollowing out of the state' (Jessop 1993).

Associated with the neo-liberal economic policies of the 1980s and 90s have been much higher levels of unemployment than the levels possible in the Keynesian world of the 1950s, 60s and early 70s. Part of the ideological strategy of Bush-Reagan and Thatcher-Major, copied by many other states, was to blame the victims for a slothful welfare mentality, but most of all through the war on drugs. In the United States by 1994 there were 678,300 black men behind bars, more than were enrolled in higher education (Mortenson 1996: 4). The impression that the United States has a lower unemployment rate than some European nations today disappears if you correct the unemployment rate by adding those in prison. In 1980, there were 31,000 Americans in prison or jail for selling or using drugs; by 1994, there were 400,000 (mostly unemployed when arrested and black) (Reuter 1997: 264).

But the simultaneous expansion of the new regulatory state to monitor privatized security and the punitive state is beginning to take a financial toll. The state that has gone further than any other in winding back Keynesianism, New Zealand, has been the state that has gone furthest with the new social movement for 'restorative justice' (the most important manifestation of the new regulatory state in criminal just-ice). Part of the appeal was the fiscal windfall from reducing the num-ber of juvenile justice institutional beds. A close competitor to New Zealand as the most liberal economy in the world is Singapore, the only state that has nominated 'restorative justice' as the officially sanctioned model of its juvenile (but not its adult) justice system (Singapore Subordinate Courts 1997). The Howard conservative government in Australia was elected in 1995 with a justice policy which committed it to expansion of restorative justice initiatives. In the event, while it has cut federal police numbers substantially and while all Australian juris-dictions do have some kind of restorative justice programmes, the expenditure on the latter has been minimal and the cuts to the former are being reversed. The US Attorney General and the British Home Secretary are giving speeches about picking up restorative justice ini-tiatives without really taking any significant policy turns.

Risk Society and the New Regulatory State

Clifford Shearing (1995), who I will construe as the quintessential scholar of the new regulatory state, believes with Beck (1992), that we have become a risk society in which preventive governance (O'Malley (1992) calls it 'prudentialism', Feeley and Simon (1994) an 'actuarial logic') has become more important. In this, Shearing follows in the footsteps of a variety of regulatory scholars, including Albert Reiss (1989), Carol Heimer (1985), Nancy Reichman (1986), Peter Manning (1989), Charles Perrow (1984), Ellen Baar (1989), Joseph Sanders (1989), Susan Shapiro (1989), Diane Vaughan (1989) and Keith Hawkins (1989) who made the study of risk a central theme of the sociology of regulation during the 1980s. Shearing sees a difference between feudal governmentality as decentralized rule from the centre (sovereignty devolved) and a marketized mentality that devolves authority itself. Here he picks up on Beck's (1992: 104) idea that the 'universalism of the market' engenders a mentality of loss-reduction, a risk-focused strategy. This combines with the imperative to respond to certain risks that are extreme (and extremely difficult to manage) which have come with the late twentieth century. Let me give two illus-trations of what I want to construe as the key connections between risk society and the new regulatory state.

One of the ironies of financial markets is that the engineering of new products to spread risks (derivatives such as futures contracts) has increased systemic risks. The collapse of Barings, England's oldest merchant bank, once referred to as the 'sixth great power in Europe' (Ziegler 1988), by the derivatives trading of a single employee in Singapore, led the development of various risk-reduction strategies coordinated by the International Organization of Securities Commissions and the Basle Commission on Banking Supervision. But the most revealing response to the Barings collapse from the perspective of the new regulatory state was by J. P. Morgan, which had succeeded Barings and the Rothchilds in the late nineteenth century as the most powerful banking house in the world. J. P. Morgan released for general use in October 1994 its own proprietary risk management model, RiskMetrics, accompanied by the data set on the volatilities of different types of financial products used with the model (Dale 1996: 165). As a big player, J. P. Morgan realized that it was in a community of shared fate with smaller players like Barings which used less sophisticated risk management technologies than RiskMetrics. Trading in derivatives actually does not generate new kinds of risks, but risks that can get out of hand with a rapidity obscured by the complexity of secondary markets. The risks of derivatives trading had to be made more transparent to fend off the systemic risk of a major financial collapse.

The second illustration is another of a community of fate (Heimer 1985). Joe Rees (1994) showed how following Three Mile Island, the American nuclear industry shared self-regulatory technologies that they had previously kept secret from one another. They believed another Three Mile Island would see the mentality of the risk society wipe them all out. They set up an industry self-regulatory organization which seems to have been more effective than state regulation alone, though state regulation in the background was an important element of their success. For example, scrams (automatic emergency shutdowns) declined in the US from over seven per unit in 1980 to one in 1993. After the Chernobyl disaster, this self-regulatory programme globalized under the auspices of the World Association of Nuclear Operators (WANO). WANO pairs all nuclear power plants in Russia with sister plants mostly in Germany who help them upgrade to international standards of risk management.

What do these two cases illustrate?

1. The centrality of the mentality of risk management in regulation.
2. The globalizing logic of risk management and how it decentres the regulatory role of the state compared with transnational

corporations, and hybrid private/public international regulators such as WANO, IOSCO and the Basle Commission on Banking Supervision.
3. The possibilities for what Rees (1994) calls 'communitarian regulation' within communities of fate.

Fourthly, these cases illustrate the limited relevance of criminology, with its focus on the old state institutions of police-courts-prisons, to the crimes which pose the greatest risks to all of us. Even at the level of state institutions, one would never grasp from reading criminology journals that the combined numerical strength of public police had not only fallen behind that of private police, but by 1984 in Australia the combined strength of the 100 largest governmental business regulatory agencies had risen to approximately equal the number of public police (Grabosky and Braithwaite 1986). As in Adam Smith's (1978) account, the most consequential domain of 'police' is not the regulation of safety on the streets, but business regulation and self-regulation. 'Future generations will look back on our era as a time when one system of policing ended and another took its place' (Bayley and Shearing 1996: 585). Perhaps the alleged success story of state policing of hot-spots in New York under Mayor Giuliani is a different story of state policing resurgent. Yet the more neglected and more interesting Giuliani story from a new regulatory state perspective is the 1990s liberation of New York from the grip of organized crime told by James Jacobs (1999). This was accomplished by a shift of reliance away from criminal enforcement (usually followed by the replacement of one jailed mafioso with another) and toward a regulatory strategy (e.g. using licensing powers to deny licences to mob-controlled firms).

The Progressive Collapse of the Peelian Vision

Shearing (1995: 82) interprets Peel's vision of policing as unifying the machinery of policing within the state 'in the form of an expert system staffed by professionals':

Peel hoped that this development would shift the focus of policing from remedying the past to colonizing a future. What actually happened was quite different. The police soon found that they could not watch over directly and that they had to rely on citizens to do their watching for them. Policing was re-privatized rather than de-privatized. The result, with very few exceptions, was not an unremitting watch, but a system for identifying breaches of the peace. This result was the opposite of what Peel envisaged. (Shearing 1995: 82)

This was true of the business regulatory agencies as well. They grew to be more significant law enforcers than the police (who once covered their responsibilities) because the corporatization of the world during the twentieth century changed it to one in which most of the things done for good or ill in the world are now the acts of corporations rather than individuals (Braithwaite and Drahos 2000). This same corporatization also meant that the greatest regulatory capabilities lay with corporations rather than states. By the mid-90s for the first time, a majority of the largest 'economies' in the world were transnational corporations rather than states (Anderson and Cavanagh 1996). So in my time as a Commissioner with the Trade Practices Commission in Australia, the most significant things the Commission did were to set up the Society of Consumer Affairs Professionals in Business and the more general Australian Compliance Professionals Association (Parker 1999b). A Peelian professional project of surveillance, but privatized surveillance (Halliday and Carruthers 1996).

Criminologists tend to see community policing writ small as something public police do when they realize that the Peelian project has failed. Something to make state police more effective by getting the community to help them. Shearing sees it writ large as primarily private activity articulating the possibility of loosely coupled 'bubbles of governance' by 'private governments'. Actually, the process is not just a possibility; it is underway:

[These bubbles of private governance] include such spaces as communities of library users, the residential communities that North Americans term 'gated communities', communities of shoppers at malls, and so on. Together, these communities, or arenas of governance, form a complex and expanding archipelago of private governments that together establish what we might term an emerging 'neo-feudalism'. One of the features of this new feudalism is that the contracts that establish these arenas of governance are, in part, contracts that set out such things as the proper expectations (rights) and responsibilities (duties) of community members. An ubiquitous example is the contract that persons enter into as library user. Most libraries today require, as part of this contract, that members agree to submit themselves to electronic scanning as they enter and leave the book collection. Similar contracts are required if one wishes to fly . . . In our contemporary world we move around this feudal-like archipelago of governance by moving from one contractual community to another. Each of these bubbles has its own mode of governance and its own rules . . . (Shearing 1997)

Shearing connects the rise of restorative justice in schools, churches, business organizations, ethnic communities and through ad hoc institutions such as the South African Truth and Reconciliation Commission to the evolving practice and imperatives of local risk management more motivated by the Peelian vision of making the future safer than by post-Peelian resort to punishing the past: 'Restorative justice seeks to extend the logic that has informed mediation beyond the settlement of business disputes to the resolution of individual conflicts that have traditionally been addressed within a retributive paradigm' (Shearing 1997: 12). Moreover, Shearing concludes that unlike the retributive paradigm, the restorative paradigm 'does not call into being consequences that conflict with the aims of an actuarial approach to security' (as practised by business and business regulators) (Shearing 1997: 14). Because a combination of predominantly restorative justice in business regulation with heavy reliance on self-regulation among communities of shared fate seems to be doing better at reducing risks of nuclear scrams than police are doing at reducing the risks of rape, a major reassessment is beginning to occur (Braithwaite 1999). This reassessment will pose a challenge not only to mainstream criminology, but also to feminist criminology, which for its greater part continues to be dominated by the myopia of police-court-corrections.

Injustice and the Hayekian Vision

Friedrich Hayek was Margaret Thatcher's hero and is a sometime hero of Clifford Shearing[2] as well. Thatcher and Shearing converge on the view that something like the configuration of changes I have called the new regulatory state was inevitable for the reasons Hayek articulated. As economies became larger and more complex, the central state could not acquire the local knowledge to intervene effectively. It tried to pick winners but regularly picked losers in circumstances where knowledgeable locals could see the loss coming: 'knowledge of the circumstances of which we must make use never exists in concentrated or integrated form but solely as the dispersed bits of incomplete and frequently contradictory knowledge which all the separate individuals possess' (Hayek 1949: 77). Hayek's (and Thatcher's) prescription for empowering local knowledge was the market—a price that reflects aggregated local preferences and that delivers profits to those in the best position to know and exploit local knowledge.

[2] Personal communication with Clifford Shearing. To reinforce the shame Clifford may experience at my letting his Hayekianism out of the closet, I want to say all the ideas in this section are stimulated by conversations with him!

Shearing's prescription is different. While he sees Hayek's analysis of local knowledge as the key to understanding the direction of change in criminal justice practice,[3] he sees myopic marketization as a path to insecurity.[4] This is because Shearing regards security for the poor as the best hope for security for the rich. Yet a free market in security as we had in the eighteenth and early nineteenth century delivers private policing services only to the rich, leaving the poor unprotected (and let us be frank, unregulated). Policing works best 'where it is least needed and worst where it is most needed' (Bayley and Shearing 1996: 595). For Shearing, the market mentality engenders deep inequalities in security, especially in his beloved South Africa. Yet it is a global mentality that has colonized all our sensibilities. This leads him to conclude that there is no alternative but to work with these sensibilities and seek to harness them in a transformative way. Shearing is no utopian dreamer; he is a Foucauldian schemer.

I am fully aware that in an ideal world it might not be appropriate to work within the terms of neo-liberal discourses, and that a more radical critique might be appropriate. Nevertheless, I am persuaded that this is strategically the most useful thing to do at the moment. This does not mean that it may not be possible at some other moment to launch a direct assault on the market mentality as a source of inequality. This is, however, not that moment. (Shearing 1995: 83)

The implication of the analysis in this paper is that he is right in that judgement. So what is to be done? In the South African context, Shearing's strategy has three related components:

First, engage the state in ways that will provide for a relocation of control over tax revenues in a manner that will provide blacks with purchasing power. Second, establish blacks as powerful customers with the ability to control their security. Third, do this in a manner that will have currency in the present South African political climate. (Shearing 1995: 83)

---

[3] Hayek and Shearing even share a similar position on the limits of quantitative data in explanatory theory: 'the sort of knowledge with which I have been concerned is knowledge of the kind which by its nature cannot enter into statistics and therefore cannot be conveyed to any central authority in statistical form' (Hayek 1949: 83). 'Any approach, such as that of much of mathematical economics with its simultaneous equations, which in effect starts from the assumption that people's *knowledge* corresponds with the objective *facts* of the situation, systematically leaves out what is our main task to explain' (Hayek 1949: 91).

[4] Put another way, Shearing buys Hayek's explanatory theory of the limits of knowledge available to central planners, while rejecting the normative theory of the economy that he erects on this foundation.

The idea at the cusp of the market and community empowerment mentalities is that instead of a police budget, there should be a policing budget; instead of a court budget, a disputing budget that leaves space for
communitized restorative justice (see also Bayley and Shearing 1996).
In South Africa, enabling this meant breaking the legal framework for
centralized state control over policing:

We persuaded the multi-party forum that drafted the constitution to accept a
legal framework that distinguishes between the provision of security and the
provision of police. This has resulted in provisions in the constitution that
enable the new legislature to establish laws that will give at least part of the
budget for security to local levels of government. (Shearing 1995: 84)

Shearing then used Swedish foreign aid to set up the Community Peace
Foundation in South Africa, which employs local people to work with
local NGOs and communities to set up safety committees. These committees are developing their own local theories of why certain kinds of
crime are prevalent in their communities and designing a responsive
prevention plan. Hayekian local knowledge and local ordering.
Peacemaking or restorative justice conferences often become occasions
that supply the motivation to plan locally to prevent a recurrent threat
to citizen safety.

The next step is to lobby for the actual restructuring of security budgets so that these committees can bid for policing and peacemaking
funds. The step after that is to 'find a way of bringing these plans
together as part of a larger municipal plan' (Shearing 1995: 86). The
South African Attorney-General has publicly articulated his support
for the programmatic praxis of the Community Peace Foundation in an
article he wrote in the *Sunday Times* of 28 July 1996, 'Bringing Justice
to All Our People'. The work of the Community Peace Foundation has
the backing of the Cape Town Police, the provincial and national governments. An Argentinean version of the Community Peace
Foundation strategy is already being put in place.

Philip Stenning has prepared a paper for the Toronto City Council,
which has endorsed it, calling for a pluralizing of policing by enabling
safety committees of housing estates and other institutions of civil society to compete with the Toronto police for a policing budget allocated
by a citizen board answerable to the Council. Mulgan (1993) has also
developed a 'democratic version of competitive tendering' which in the
British context has been subjected to a thoughtful critique by Crawford
(1997: 311). At the time of writing policing as opposed to police budgets are also being discussed in Northern Ireland.

Retrieving Keynesian Virtues

A paradox of the security budget idea developed by Stenning and Shearing is that it requires central control of a healthy revenue in order for the problems of security to be solved, a Keynesian rather than a Hayekian budget. Ultimately it does require a strong state. Shearing's (1993) work on regulatory space highlights the dangers of a conception of regulation where the state indirectly controls self-regulation delegated to civil society:

The public interest, it is argued, is likely to be better served by dialogue and contest than by a system of coordination and state oversight. A contested view of the public interest rather than one that is authoritatively settled by the state can warrant, for example, Greenpeace-style actions that totally reject and undercut the state's conception of the public interest. (Grabosky *et al.* 1993: 7)

This much is agreed. The richer democracy is one where different elements of the state, international society, business and NGOs are all regulating one another. However, there is no escape from some privileging of an ultimate oversight that has the special legitimation that a decent electoral process can supply. This privileging is especially important in respect of accountability for the allocation of funds raised by taxes and for the deployment of violence. In the worst cases, rare as they are, there is a need to restrain people forcibly, lock them up against their will, even shoot them. These powers are so dangerous that the only place we should locate them is in those places surrounded by the maximum of checks and balances. The republican tradition has to greater or lesser degree erected these around the institutions of state violence and enforced state taxation.

There is also no doubt that there are quite a few policing functions that will simply be more efficiently and decently provided by public police. The strength of the research agenda that animates a widening circle beyond the Toronto-Cape Town core of Shearing, Stenning, Doob, Bayley, Nina and Ndlovu is that it concedes as much and embarks on a programme of empirical discovery of what is better provided publicly, by markets or by communities.

Restorative justice founders when the welfare state is not there to support it. If a restorative justice conference agrees with a young offender that he should commit to a drug rehabilitation programme and funding is not available at that time and place for the programme, then restorative justice is likely to fail. It often does fail in Australia and

New Zealand for precisely this reason. Ken Polk's (1994) work is an enduring testimony to the importance of what he calls 'developmental institutions' that pave transition paths from school to work. The US War on Poverty of the 1960s was barely beginning to discover how to build such institutions when it fell victim to the demise of the Keynesian state. In the early 90s, the Keating Labor government was barely beginning to relaunch this programme of R&D through the labour market programmes of its Job Compact when the more Hayekian government of John Howard swept them away.

Criminologists lobbied for the Job Compact on the grounds that it had good prospects of reducing crime (Braithwaite and Chappell 1994). Nothing captures disenchantment with the Keynesian state among criminologists more than the widespread belief that the evidence shows that the level of unemployment and inequality makes no difference to the crime rate. In fact, the evidence is not consistent with this belief as many scholars have contended for a long time (Braithwaite 1979). When the economy improves, there are short-term increases in opportunities and diminutions of guardianship of persons and property that pushes crime up at the same time as substitution of legitimate for illegitimate opportunities for work pushes it down (Cantor and Land 1985; Kapuscinski *et al.* 1998). Those short-term effects are minor compared to the long-term effects of long-term unemployment, whole generations of truly disadvantaged people, year after year, being left without hope, giving up on their own future, but much more importantly (Weatherburn and Lind forthcoming) on the future of their children. The element of the Keynesian state we might retrieve here is a state that can eliminate long-term unemployment. As the Keating government concluded, it makes good economic sense, partly for reasons of combating crime and drug abuse, to fund an offer to every long-term unemployed person of a publicly funded (or subsidized) job or training place. After they finish the programme, if they return to long-term unemployment, they should immediately have publicly funded employment offered to them again. Long-term unemployment can be abolished in developed economies; criminologists who have been overly seduced by the Hayekian tradition have been ineffective in explaining why.

So a strong state is needed: (1) to provide welfare services to restorative justice programmes in civil society, (2) to eliminate long-term unemployment, (3) to fund contestable safety and disputing budgets, and (4) to fund the continuation of state police and courts where they can operate more efficiently and in a more rights-respecting way than markets or communities. In short, there is no appeal in returning to the mentality of the nightwatchman state of classical liberal theory with its weak rowing and weak steering capabilities. There is little appeal in returning to a fully Keynesian mentality of a state that is strong on rowing itself but weak on steering civil society. There is limited appeal in a new regulatory state which does all the steering and leaves all the rowing to markets and civil society. What we might aspire to is a state which is strong on rowing in the Keynesian ways specified in this section and strong on steering, combined with strong markets and communities in civil society that are also strong on both rowing and steering.

Sweeping Across the Disciplines to Become an Educated Scholar of the New Regulation

There is a joke about the economist who has successfully predicted six of the last two recessions. Economics is a discipline with limited predictive power for the reasons articulated by George Soros (1994) in *The Alchemy of Finance*. Whenever a theory successfully formalizes truths about how local markets work, those locals with the most contextually rich and timely local knowledge will act to transform a true theory into a false one. If the theory says the market will go up when certain things happen, those in the know may buy when they can see those things are about to happen and sell after they do, so that the effect of the theory precedes its cause (and a fall in price rather than the predicted rise comes after the cause). According to Soros, economic theory must be reflexive because its objects are not like objects in physics; they are thinking actors capable of asserting themselves as subjects who render the theory the object.

What I want to suggest is that the kind of study of regulatory institutions illustrated in the work of Shearing, applied to phenomena like J. P. Morgan's RiskMetrics and the Basle Committee's regulatory deliberations, may be more useful to understanding how to avert recessions than neo-classical economics. I sat for four years between 1983 and 1987 on the Economic Planning Advisory Council as Prime Minister Hawke and Treasurer Keating explained to us why they had to float the dollar, deregulate the finance sector, privatize Qantas, eventually give us 'a recession we had to have' with the highest unemployment of our lifetime. What raged around that table was a contest between Keynes, who was being pushed aside, and Hayekian deregulation. In retrospect, what we should have been discussing was the nuts and bolts of a regulatory design for a new kind of world where Keynesian pump-priming no longer worked.

In those days, I also used to say that in four years of day-long monthly meetings, no one ever raised the effect on crime of a policy as a reason for changing the policy. This seemed at the time a sensible judgement of the limited significance of my discipline. By the early 1990s, however, I was convinced that we could abolish long-term unemployment and that the long-term effects on crime and drug abuse were important parts of the reason why the considerable economic costs of doing so made the Job Compact sound economic policy.

Economics as a discipline cannot comprehend the latter arguments because its models of unemployment and crime are simply about the costs and benefits of crime measured against the costs and benefits of employment. They miss the main game of how the demoralization of unemployment ruins lives of the children of the unemployed, through the medium of abusive and uncaring parenting by adults who have lost hope (Weatherburn and Lind forthcoming). Economics might be reformable if its micro-foundations were sensitive to empirical evidence from the discipline of psychology as to how economic behaviour is motivated. But not only is that sensitivity largely absent, also largely absent are psychologists interested in confronting it.

To be good scholars of the institutions of the new regulatory state, we need to be able to draw on analytic strengths and empirical revelations from disciplines like economics and psychology, as well as from the disciplines of sociology, criminology and political science upon which we have drawn in the foregoing pages. But we also need to integrate normative theory from the discipline of moral philosophy with our explanatory theory (Braithwaite forthcoming). If we do not, we will continue to live in a world where moral philosophers do work relevant to possible worlds that do not or cannot exist. And explanatory theories such as those of deterrence and incapacitation will continue to generate data that are not useful to any morally acceptable policy project. Social science is likely to be sterile without what Parker (1999: 6) calls 'iterated adjustment' between normative and explanatory theory.

We must also learn from the discipline of international relations, given that the risks the new regulation tackles are so frequently global. In doing so, hopefully we can avert the ingrained assumptions of international relations theorists that states are the actors that matter and can be understood as unitary actors. All these disciplines are afflicted with assumptions of this ilk that discipline young minds into myopic methodological dispositions and channels of thought.

A key to progress is to keep constructing new paradigms that sweep across the disciplines in ways that are responsive to new realities of the world, but that fade, like Keynesism, when those realities change. The disciplinary structure of the social sciences is its biggest problem. Criminology as it rises to the heyday of its popularity has now become part of that problem. The work at the Community Peace Foundation in Cape Town and of the University of Toronto criminologists toward fostering a morally grounded comprehension of the new regulatory state seems part of the solution. Like Foucault in the years before his death, they have discovered that liberal governmentality is a seminal topic. Like Hayek, they have discovered that the key public policy nut to crack is the ordering of local knowledge. Their method has an empirical precision that Foucault's lacks and a praxis grounded in an iterated adjustment of explanatory and normative theory that Hayek lacked. This is why my hope is that the new regulatory state scholars will advance the social sciences in more important ways than the Foucauldians, the Hayekians and the positivist economists.

References

ANDERSON, S. and J. CAVANAGH (1996), *The Top 200: The Rise of Global Corporate Power*. Washington: Institute for Policy Studies.

AYRES, I. and BRAITHWAITE, J. (1992), *Responsive Regulation: Transcending the Deregulation Debate*. Oxford: Oxford University Press.

BALDWIN, R., HOOD, C. and SCOTT, C. (1998), 'Regulation Grows Up: Into its Prime or Mid-Life Crisis?', in R. Baldwin, C. Hood and C. Scott, eds., *Socio-Legal Reader on Regulation*. Oxford: Oxford University Press.

BAAR, E. (1989), 'A Balance of Control: Defining the Risk Bearer's Role in the Regulatory Equation', paper presented to the Annual Meeting of the Law and Society Association, Madison, Wisconsin.

BAYLEY, D. H. (1994), *Police the Future*. Oxford: Oxford University Press.

BAYLEY, D. and SHEARING, C. (1996), 'The Future of Policing', *Law and Society Review*, 30/3: 585–606.

BECK, ULRICH (1992), *Risk Society: Towards a New Modernity*. Newbury Park: Sage.

BRAITHWAITE, J. (1979), *Inequality, Crime, and Public Policy*. London and Boston: Routledge and Kegan Paul.

—— (1982), 'Enforced Self-Regulation: A New Strategy for Corporate Crime Control', *Michigan Law Review*, 80: 1466–507.

BRAITHWAITE, J. (1999), 'Restorative Justice: Assessing Optimistic and Pessimistic Accounts', *Crime and Justice: A Review of Research*, 25: 1–127.
—— (forthcoming), 'Republican Theory and Crime Control', in K. Bussman and S. Karstedt, eds., *Social Dynamics of Crime and Control*. Aldershot: Dartmouth.
BRAITHWAITE, J. and CHAPPELL, D. (1994), 'The Job Compact and Crime', *Current Issues in Criminal Justice*, 5: 295–300.
BRAITHWAITE, J. and DRAHOS, P. (2000), *Global Business Regulation*. Melbourne: Cambridge University Press.
BROGDEN, MICHAEL and SHEARING, CLIFFORD (1993), *Policing for a New South Africa*. London: Routledge.
CANTOR, D. and LAND, K. C. (1985), 'Unemployment and Crime Rates in the Post-World War II United States: A Theoretical and Empirical Analysis', *American Sociological Review*, 50: 317–32.
CLARKE, MICHAEL (1986), *Regulating the City: Competition, Scandal and Reform*. Milton Keynes: Open University Press.
CRAWFORD, ADAM (1997), *The Local Governance of Crime: Appeals to Community and Partnerships*. Oxford: Clarendon Press.
DALE, RICHARD (1996), *Risk and Regulation in Global Securities Markets*. New York: Wiley.
DAY, P. and KLEIN, R. (1987), 'Residential Care for the Elderly: A Billion Pound Experiment in Policy-Making', *Public Money*, March, 19–24.
DINNEN, S. (1996), 'Challenges of Order in a Weak State', PhD Dissertation, Australian National University, Canberra.
FEELEY, M. and SIMON, J. (1994), 'Actuarial Justice: The Emerging New Criminal Law', in D. Nelken, ed., *The Futures of Criminology*. London: Sage.
FOUCAULT, M. (1991), 'Governmentality', in G. Burchall, C. Gordon and P. Miller, eds., *The Foucault Effect: Studies in Governmentality*. London: Harvester Wheatsheaf.
GARLAND, DAVID (1997), ' "Governmentality" and the Problem of Crime: Foucault, Criminology, Sociology', *Theoretical Criminology*, 1/2: 173–214.
GRABOSKY, P. and BRAITHWAITE, J. (1986), *Of Manners Gentle: Enforcement Strategies of Australian Business Regulatory Agencies*. Melbourne: Oxford University Press.
GRABOSKY, P., SHEARING, C. and BRAITHWAITE, J. (1993), 'Introduction', in P. Grabosky and J. Braithwaite, eds., *Business Regulation and Australia's Future*. Canberra: Australian Institute of Criminology.
HALLIDAY, T. and CURRUTHERS, B. (1996), 'The Moral Regulation of Markets: Professions, Privatization and the English Insolvency Act 1986', *Accounting, Organizations & Society*, 21/4: 371–413.
HARDING, R. W. (1997), *Private Prisons and Public Accountability*. Buckingham: Open University Press.

HAWKINS, K. (1989), ' "Fatcats" and Prosecution in a Regulatory Agency: a Footnote on the Social Construction of Risk', *Law and Policy*, 11/3.

HAYEK, F. A. (1949), *Individualism and Economic Order*. London: Routledge.

HEIMER, C. A. (1985), *Reactive Risk and Rational Action: Managing Moral Hazard in Insurance Contracts*. Berkeley: University of California Press.

HINDESS, B. (1996), *Discourses of Power: From Hobbes to Foucault*. Oxford: Blackwell.

HOOD, C., JAMES, O., JONES, G., SCOTT, C. and TRAVERS, T. (1998), *Regulation Inside Government: Waste Watchers, Quality Police and Sleazebusters*. Oxford: Oxford University Press.

JACOBS, JAMES B. with FRIEL, COLEEN and RADICK, ROBERT (1999), *Gotham Unbound: How New York City was Liberated from the Grip of Organized Crime*. New York: New York University Press.

JESSOP, B. (1993), 'Towards a Schumpeterian Workfare State? Preliminary Remarks on Post-Fordist Political Economy', *Studies in Political Economy*, 40: 7–39.

JOHNSTON, LES (1992), *The Rebirth of Private Policing*. London: Routledge.

KAPUSCINSKI, C. A., BRAITHWAITE, J. and CHAPMAN, P. (1998), 'Unemployment and Crime: Towards Resolving the Paradox', *Journal of Quantitative Criminology*, 14/3: 215–43.

LOADER, IAN (1998), 'Criminology and the Public Sphere: Arguments for Utopian Realism', in P. Walton and J. Young, eds., *The New Criminology Revisited*. London: Macmillan.

LOUGHLIN, M. and SCOTT, C. (1997), 'The Regulatory State', in P. Dunlevy, I. Holliday and G. Peele, eds., *Developments in British Politics*, 5. London: Macmillan.

MCCRAW, THOMAS K. (1984), *Prophets of Regulation*. Cambridge, MA: Harvard.

MCDONAGH, O. (1977), *Early Victorian Government*. London: Weidenfeld & Nicolson.

MAJONE, G. (1994), 'The Rise of the Regulatory State in Europe', *West European Politics*, 17: 77–101.

MANNING, P. K. (1989), 'Managing Risk: Managing Uncertainty in the British Nuclear Installations Inspectorate', *Law and Policy*, 11/3.

MARSH, D. and RHODES, R. (1992), 'Policy Communities and Issue Networks: Beyond Typologies', in D. Marsh and R. Rhodes, eds., *Policy Networks in British Government*, 249–68. Oxford: Clarendon Press.

MEIDINGER, ERROL (1987), 'Regulatory Culture: A Theoretical Outline', *Law and Policy*, 9: 355.

MORTENSON, T. (1996), 'Black Men in College or Behind Bars', *Overcrowded Times*, 7/2: 4.

MULGAN, G. (1993), *The Power of the Boot: Democratic Dismissal, Competition and Contestability Among the Quangos*, Demos Working Paper. London: Demos.

NOZICK, R. (1974), *Anarchy, State and Utopia*. Oxford: Blackwell.

O'MALLEY, PAT (1992), 'Risk, Power and Crime Prevention', *Economy and Society*, 21/3: 252–75.

OSBORNE, D. and GAEBLER, T. (1992), *Reinventing Government*. New York: Addison-Wesley.

PARKER, C. (1999a), *Just Lawyers*. Oxford: Oxford University Press.

—— (1999b) 'Compliance Professionalism and Regulatory Community: The Australian Trade Practices Regime', *Journal of Law and Society*, 26: 215–39.

PASQUINO, P. (1991), 'Theatrum Politicum: The Genealogy of Capital—Police and the State of Prosperity', in G. Burchall, C. Gordon and P. Miller, eds., *The Foucault Effect: Studies in Governmentality*. London: Harvester Wheatsheaf.

PERROW, C. (1984), *Normal Accidents: Living with High-Risk Technologies*. New York: Basic Books.

POLK, KEN (1994), 'Family Conferencing: Theoretical and Evaluative Questions', in Christine Alder and Joy Wundersitz, eds., *Family Conferencing and Juvenile Justice*. Canberra: Australian Studies in Law, Crime and Justice, Australian Institute of Criminology.

REES, JOSEPH V. (1994), *Hostages of Each Other: The Transformation of Nuclear Safety Since Three Mile Island*. Chicago: University of Chicago Press.

REICHMAN, N. (1986), 'Managing Crime Risks: Toward an Insurance Based Model of Social Control', *Research in Law, Deviance and Social Control*, 8: 151–72.

REISS, ALBERT J. JR (1989), 'The Institutionalization of Risk', *Law and Policy*, 11/3: 392–402.

REUTER, P. (1997), 'Why Can't We Make Prohibition Work Better? Some Consequences of Ignoring the Unattractive', *Proceedings of the American Philosophical Society*, 141: 262–75.

SANDERS, J. (1989), 'Firm Risk Management in the Face of Products Liability Rules', *Law and Policy*, 11/3.

SCULL, A. T. (1977), *Decarceration: Community Treatment and the Deviant— A Radical View*. Englewood Cliffs, NJ: Prentice-Hall.

SHAPIRO, S. (1989), 'Libel Lawyers as Risk Counselors: Pre-Publication and Pre-Broadcast Review and Social Construction of News', *Law and Policy*, 11/3.

SHEARING, C. (1993), 'A Constitutive Conception of Regulation', in P. Grabosky and J. Braithwaite, eds., *Business Regulation and Australia's Future*. Canberra: Australian Institute of Criminology.

—— (1995), 'Reinventing Policing: Policing as Governance', *Privatisierung staatlicher Kontrolle: Befunde, Konzepte, Tendenzen*. Baden Baden: Nomos Verlagsgesellschaft.

—— (1997), 'Violence and the Changing Face of Governance: Privatization and its Implications', *Kolner Zeitschrift fur Soziologie und Sozial-psychologie*.

SHEARING, C. D. and STENNING, P. C. (1981), 'Modern Private Security: its Growth and Implications', in M. Tonry and N. Morris, eds., *Crime and Justice: an Annual Review of Research*,3: 193–245. Chicago: University Chicago Press.

—— (1983), 'Private Security: Implications for Social Control', *Social Problems*, 30/5: 493–506.

——, eds. (1987), *Private Policing*. California: Sage.

SINGAPORE SUBORDINATE COURTS (1997), *Excellence and Beyond*. Singapore: Singapore Subordinate Courts.

SMITH, ADAM (1978), *Lectures on Jurisprudence*, R. L. Meek, D. D. Raphael and P. G. Stein, eds., Oxford: Clarendon Press.

SOROS, GEORGE (1994), *The Alchemy of Finance*. New York: Wiley.

STREECK, W. and SCHMITTER, P. (1985), *Private Interest Government*. London: Sage.

VAUGHAN, D (1989), 'Regulating Risk: Implications of the Challenger Accident', *Law and Policy*, 11/330–49.

VON HOHENTHAL, P. G. G. (1776), *Liber de Politia*. Liptal.

WEATHERBURN, D. and LIND, B. (forthcoming), *The Economic and Social Antecedents of Deliquent-Prone Communities*. Melbourne: Cambridge.

ZIEGLER, P. (1988), *The Sixth Great Power: Barings 1762–1929*. London: Collins.

4

Orientalism, Occidentalism and the Sociology of Crime

MAUREEN CAIN

The difficulties of teaching criminology in a society that self-defines as non-western derive both from lack of materials, and from the lack of a theory to make sense of these materials. The diagnosis for these difficulties can be found in two persistent problems. The most familiar of these, since Said's seminal contribution of 1978, is *orientalism*. This in brief involves the discursive constitution of an often romanticized but also wayward and unknowing 'other' which, because of these besetting albeit (to liberals) endearing characteristics, requires the guidance and advice of the 'us' to find and/or accept its proper place in the world. These days that usually means a relatively subordinate place in an uncontrolled global market, a market which, however, requires as it always has long-term order and predictability, and the security of property in all its sites of production and exchange, in order to function effectively.

In Trinidad and Tobago and the Caribbean an even more problematic tendency of western scholarship and, indeed, of international indirect governance[1] has been *occidentalism*. The opposite of orientalism, occidentalism presumes the 'sameness' of key cultural categories, practices and institutions. There is thus a constant misdiagnosis of problems leading, on occasion, to a misallocation of scarce resources. Moreover occidentalism, like the earlier diagnosed orientalism, may be exported to those whom the occidentalist discourses purport to describe. Both discourses have hegemonic tendencies. What worries me

---

[1] I use this term to cover the full range of international aid-with-strings agreements, from IMF conditionalities to the Good Governance programmes of the ODA/DFID (Clegg and Whetton 1999).

is that both discourses can be found within the broad subject matter of contemporary criminology.

In this chapter, therefore, I first offer a single example of orientalism in criminology; in the following sections I identify examples of occidentalist criminology in the context of Caribbean discourse and practice; next in a brief discussion of the security of Caribbean women I argue that an avoidance of these two discursive aberrations can enhance both practice and understanding; in conclusion, I suggest a more modest agenda than 'comparison' in transnational work, but an agenda which paradoxically may lead to more theoretically (and practically) useful abstractions. Because many examples may be unfamiliar to BJC readers the argumentative ride may seem bumpy; I trust that the landing in women's terrain will make the journey worthwhile.

Orientalism

Since Smith's (1956), classic challenge to the orientalist conception of the Caribbean family form as problematic, since decolonization movements and underdevelopment theorists exposed the ideological basis of the construct of the lazy native (Frank 1967; Said 1978), since Best (1968), and Beckford (1972), challenged both conventional and Marxist analyses of Caribbean political economies, the region has been equipped to resist the hegemonic tendencies of orientalist accounts. Today, it seems to me, it is the West which suffers most from its own orientalist tendencies. Nowhere is this more apparent than in the burgeoning field of informal justice. Let me explain.

Informal justice has been on and off both academic and political agendas at least since Danzig recommended it for the US in 1973 and Christie familiarized the British with the arguments against formal adjudicative procedures and the 'theft' of conflicts by professionals in 1977 (Danzig 1973; Christie 1977). After initial enthusiasm, the schemes proposed were subjected to a welter of criticism from the left (see Cain 1985, 1989), before being reinstated as part of a progressive agenda by Braithwaite's contributions (Braithwaite 1989; Braithwaite and Mugford 1994). Today mediation, the favoured format, is deemed as desirable in cases of divorce and domestic conflict as it is in cases of larceny and criminal damage. It is a favoured process for dealing with neighbour disputes (Dignan et al. 1996). Feminist evidence that weaker parties (women in divorce proceedings and domestic violence cases, children and women in victim-offender mediation sessions) tend to lose out (Fineman 1988; Schneider 1994: 45; Cobb 1997), seems not to have abated practitioner enthusiasm in the UK. In the West Midlands for example some half dozen victim/offender schemes can be identified.[2] What is orientalist about all this? To answer that question it is necessary to consider the early genealogy of the informalist ideal. Nils Christie invited his readers to reconsider the operation of the criminal justice system from a 'sunny hillside of the Arusha province' of Tanzania, where, in an overcrowded house 'a circus, a drama . . . a court case' is underway (p. 2). The characteristics of this event are juxtaposed to those of Scandinavian and, by implication, British courts. The western model is found sadly wanting, and the Tanzanian or 'third world' model proposed in its stead—a model in which victims and offenders sort out *their* conflict face to face to their mutual advantage and that of the community. Acknowledging that in the current system both neighbourhoods and victims are too few, while professional intervention is deemed too great (p. 12), Christie nonetheless argues that the Tanzanian model provides the ideal towards which Western justice should strive.

Merry's critique of this approach was directed more to the American neighbourhood justice movement than to Christie's argument but is none the less pertinent (Merry 1982). *Inter alia* she points out that 'informal' agreements and sanctions are effective in non-industrial societies if and when, and because, they are supported by relevant structures of power. To see such agreements as the amorphous products of consensual minds alone is romantic nonsense (let alone bad sociology). Disputants are in interdependent relationships before and after the conflict, mediators are *familiar* influential people from within the community, and there is pressure to settle from those upon whom the parties are dependent amounting in effect to coercion. None of these conditions is likely to apply in an urban, industrial, western setting.

Moreover 'mediated settlements between unequals are unequal' (Merry 1982: 32). In other words, these strategies work only within particular social contexts, and even in those contexts all is not romantic and power free forgiveness and joy. The model is both flawed and context dependent.

Braithwaite's original model for reintegrative shaming in a process of informal settlement was from a starkly contrasting setting: the

---

[2] This information was given to me by Lystra Hagley who is completing a Ph.D. on t he subject at the University of Birmingham, UK.

ways in which offending companies and individuals are dealt with in the pharmaceutical industry (Braithwaite 1989). However his recent reworking of the idea in relation to juvenile justice (Braithwaite and Mugford 1994), involves a return to romanticism. The practices or 'reintegration ceremonies' described were developed within Maori communities in New Zealand (mainly in Auckland), and their expansion to include Pakeha, their 'importation' by white authorities 'has been riddled with imperfection' (p. 167). In Australia the ceremonies largely involve poor white youth. Like Christie a decade earlier, Braithwaite and Mugford argue that movements towards informal processes of reintegrative shaming are a step in the right direction, even if far from perfect in their new and modified, white, context. One problem is that of rights and protections for underage offenders under pressure from those they love and/or need most. Another, cited by the authors, is that of 'inappropriate net widening' (p. 167).

Let us stick with those two classic and undeniably influential examples. The later model is more theoretically grounded. This reduces its romanticism. However, while the attempt at context substitution—in offenders' choices of relevant others for the support team, in having a child-friendly police officer as the coordinator—acknowledges the structural differences of context (as the models Merry critiqued did not), there is no such recognition of the discursive or cultural ones. As we shall see in the following sections, neither age nor gender is a cultural universal. Each is a discursive construction with a contextual meaning. There is a danger in treating either as a given 'fact' able to underpin a transplanted model.

Thus it would seem that in their romantic reconstructions of the other's dispute settlement processes the classic foundations of the western informal justice movement are orientalist. This limitation may do little harm to those societies from which the models have been generated,[3] but in the host communities to which the models have been imported those who already have rather few enforceable rights may find themselves with even fewer.

Occidentalism 1: the second and third ages of man

I have laboured over the social nature of age so much in recent years (Cain 1996, 1999), that readers of this paper may be referred to these

---

[3] Unless this idealization of the models is used to inhibit further development.

earlier accounts for all but the most cursory of evidential statistical details. Instead I am going to start with a personal anecdote,[4] for I know no other way of making myself understood.

Once upon a time, more than a decade ago now, a woman just turned 50 moved into a hillside house in Trinidad, one of half a dozen middle class homes clustered in the stump of a cul-de-sac: the houses were both reached and isolated by a trace through an older poor to lower middle class village straggling lower down the hill.

One day a few months after the move a 16-year-old youth called to her from across the trace to join him and his sister and friends in a game of table tennis. She expressed thanks but declined. She was pleased by the invitation but did not want to spoil their game. Later her son (early twenties) said 'I'd be really chuffed if they asked me to play table tennis when I was 50. It means they think you're a fun person.'

As the years went by I realized that both my response and that of my son were wrong. There were too many other occasions when people either much younger (one woman was 26), or much older (one was in her eighties) offered companionship or friendship, which by then I had learned the good grace to accept.

The point is that no one saw age as salient in the context described except me. The society is not age-stratified except into one broad group called children who are excluded from adult pursuits, most notably those associated with Carnival such as attending calypso tents or playing (adult) mas. Then there are the rest, who socialize in multi-age and family groups. Even male street corner groups are not age-stratified. Of course people are aware of age and ageing, *viz.* very great respect for and appreciation of the skills and experience of older people, or parties in pubs and clubs for middle class largely 'fair skin' youth. But perhaps the exception proves the rule: these latter events are for 20-somethings and under 35s, not for teenagers.

It seemed to me that this last category, *teenager*, did not offer any real purchase on the ways people behaved.[5] People were children until they were not children any more. So, I am trying to say that age is not one 'thing' cross culturally. Ways of counting age have been developed

---

[4] Anecdotes because I deliberately did not 'make like an ethnographer' in Trinidad. I interpreted my brief as making an effort to be useful from and on the inside—as a teacher primarily, and also as a fundraiser. From such a stance I could not objectify my friends in a text. But some things I remember, more or less—hence, anecdotes.

[5] Every generalization prompts thought of an exception. In Tobago the older children who flock to the island for Great Race Weekend were called teenagers by the hoteliers interviewed by Roanna Gopaul and myself in 1997.

which are quite widely but not universally shared, but even between social groups which count the same way the discourses of age, the benchmarks which matter, the age-appropriate behaviour for each discursively constituted stage, these things will vary, be negotiated and renegotiated as the social and political environment changes. Age after all is not an abstract theoretical category, but very much a feature of local and particular common senses.

For these reasons even at a theoretical level claims that the relationship between age and crime is a cultural universal should be regarded with astonishment. More importantly, such claims should be recognized as expressions of a profoundly occidentalist discourse. Yet Braithwaite (1989: 45–6), makes just such a claim in his list of 'known' relationships which form the foundation of his arguments for reintegrative shaming, and cites others before him who have shared the same presumption.[6] More recently Bayley and Shearing (1996: 598) have made a similarly confident statement as to the criminality of young males.

Knowing that age is lived differently in the Caribbean it should come as no surprise to find that the relationship between age and crime is different too. Indeed, Harriott's work (1996), indicates that the best known, if the most recent, of Caribbean crimes, that of drug trafficking, is dependent organizationally on the continued participation of mature people. And in the Caribbean, as elsewhere, the typical crimes of the mature—family violence, embezzlement, fraud—no doubt flourish to a far greater extent than is registered in the statistics.[7]

All that having been said, the statistics of conventional offences and offenders as explored in three different societies indicate that the age profile of Caribbean offenders is different from that in the 'West'. In

---

[6] John Braithwaite is cited so frequently in this chapter because his work is important, has been influential in practice as well as academically, and because I have read most of it. I therefore challenge with respect, and in the knowledge that it is a far far better thing to be criticized than to be ignored.

[7] In Trinidad and Tobago, in the decade ending in 1997 (the most recent year for which figures are available) there has been a fluctuating rate of serious crimes with peaks in 1988 and 1993. For crimes against the person, however, the trend has been unequivocally up, from 979 reported crimes in 1988 to 1,606 in 1997. Most of this increase is accounted for by the 'other crimes against the person' category which includes unlawful carnal knowledge (possibly affected by a greater willingness to report) and attempted suicide. However, the category including 'embezzlement, false pretences, conversions, larceny under $2,000 and larceny in dwelling houses', collated together in the 'minor crimes' table, has shown a steady decrease over the decade. *Annual Statistical Digest 1997*, Table 46, p. 45 (unverified pre-publication data).

1981 Jones pointed out that whereas in England and Wales the offending peak (ie rate per 10,000), was in the 16 to under-20 age group, with those 10 to under 16 coming second, in Guyana the rate for this youngest group was far below that for those between 16 and 20, and 20 to under 30 (Jones 1981: 39, table 3.9).

In Trinidad and Tobago, Cain (1996) had the opportunity to work from raw data provided by the Probation Department on 1994 cases. In spite of a widespread concern (which turned out to be a moral panic) about growing 'juvenile delinquency and youth crime' (Sampson 1994), it emerged that juvenile matters accounted for only 5 per cent of all prosecutions instituted, and only 1.9 per cent of prosecutions instituted in the serious crime category (ibid., p. 100). One plausible explanation for this is that the age profile of offending is different. Another is that juvenile offenders are not brought to the attention of the authorities. Either explanation would support the central tenet of the argument in this section, that when age is constituted differently age-related social behaviour is different too.

The most convincing data to support this thesis have been provided by F. Braithwaite (1996). His sample was drawn from police files of those sentenced in Barbados in 1993, and as a result his youngest age category is 14–19 years. The young people in this category accounted for only 9.4 per cent of those sentenced. Indeed, those *over* 25, the age at which UK offenders typically 'grow out of crime' (West 1982), constituted 70 per cent of all those sentenced. Even allowing for recidivism and for longer periods on remand than in the UK, the evidence does seem to be accumulating that in the southern Caribbean at least, conventional crime is a grown-up problem, a pattern of adult offending rather than of childish behaviour. Youthful 'offending' either occurs relatively rarely (my preference) or is something that the penal and welfare authorities do not record. This last explanation is less plausible precisely because of the climate of moral panic already alluded to: moral panics typically lead to over rather than under recording.[8]

Rather, then, than straining to prove that the Caribbean is 'really' the same as 'us' would it not be better to acknowledge a difference, not

[8] In Trinidad and Tobago the Sampson Committee which reported on 'juvenile delinquency and youth crime' in 1994 was established because of just such a moral panic, although the Committee's findings did not problematize the young but rather pointed to an increase in interpersonal violence in the wake of structural adjustment programmes and resultant economic polarization.

to romanticize and orientalize it, but not to flatten it out either by means of occidentalizing theory. Perhaps we might acknowledge too that youthful offending is constituted both discursively and structurally by the societies in which it occurs (Brown 1998; Carlen 1996) rather than by a biological moment in human development. In that way some harm to the younger people of the Caribbean may be avoided, some groundless stigmatization; and eventually perhaps, when a wider range of variation has been explored, some improved abstractions about the relationships between age discourses and criminality may be constructed to the benefit of all concerned.

Occidentalism 2: victimization and poverty

Crime survey results from the US and the UK show that people from lower income groups are more at risk of victimization than more prosperous citizens. Since Lea and Young's *What is to be Done* (1984), an entire political programme legitimating crime control measures as part of a purportedly progressive agenda has been constructed around this evidence that the poor suffer most from crime as from every other social ill. No longer, it is argued, can crime be seen as the poor's revenge upon the rich: rather we should regard it as collective self flagellation by the collectively impoverished.

These revelations from western crime victim surveys have given rise to a new case of occidentalism. As Clegg and Whetton (1999: 3), reveal, a White Paper published by the Department of International Development (DFID 1998),

reflect[s] a recognition that the poor and the vulnerable suffer disproportionately from crime and ineffective policing.

While resultant moves to constitute the poor and women and children ('the vulnerable') as 'stakeholders' in relation to good policing, and so to consult them in relation to proposed policing initiatives (ibid., p. 4), can only be welcomed, it appears that the relationship between 'policing, crime, poverty and development' (ibid., p. 5), is not a universal one, and may have been misdiagnosed. Indeed, the data from Trinidad and Tobago and from Brazil (Birju 1998), suggest a very different pattern of victimization. The vulnerability of the poor to criminal predation and violence turns out to be a shaky foundation upon which to model and build new policing regimes across the less developed world.

Direct experience of victimization is commonplace in Trinidad and Tobago[9] so occidentalist theories may be less likely to be given credence than in the unfortunate case of juvenile and youth crime. On the other hand arguments supported by substantial grant aid can come to seem quite plausible unless local organizations are provided with data which enable them to give authoritative voice to an alternative. What is clear is that the alleged greater vulnerability of the impoverished is being used to justify, to legitimate, an increase in the quantum of the policing of the poor. In this context the occidentalist premise needs to be checked.

A victim survey in a multi-ethnic and multi-class area of Trinidad was carried out by Birju between 1992 and 1994 (Birju 1998). His results concerning the relationship between victimization and poverty can be presented very briefly. Birju's calculations as to class are based on what he calls a 'quality of life measure' (p. 236), that is to say, the mean income per member of the household, rather than the income or occupational status of one or more adult member. The key finding (p. 238, Table 7.1), is that 'the lowest average income group is victimized significantly *less* than the middle or upper average income groups— exactly the opposite to [the relationship] found in the "first world". 62 per cent of the lowest average income group had been victimized in one way or another at least once in the previous 12 months, compared with 93.7 per cent in the middle mean income group and 87.1 per cent in the upper group (n=299). The pattern persisted when property crimes (against the household) (p. 239), and all crimes against the person (p. 240), were analysed separately, and even more surprisingly (to a Westerner) the upper mean income group turned out to be more vulnerable to sex crimes than either the middle or lower mean income categories.[10]

Like the author himself, I find it difficult to go beyond this statement of difference to an explanation. But then it is not the 'difference' which needs explaining: that would imply 'our' normalcy and 'their' oddity— orientalism again, the flip side of occidentalist denial. As before what is needed is a range of studies showing different patterns so that

---

[9] Birju's results indicate considerably higher rates of victimization than have been reported in the UK or the US, as well as a radically different distribution of victimization by social class.

[10] The data are presented cursorily here because the author will no doubt wish to publish them in full himself. Suffice it to say, therefore, that the data are presented in tables 7.1, 7.2, 7.3 and 7.5 on pages 238, 239, 240 and 242 of his thesis and that statistical significance at the 0.05 level was achieved in each case.

abstractions identifying (constructing) theoretically valid differences can be formulated, thereby illuminating each and all of the specific concrete situations. What we have, however, is occidentalism, and the export of a model of community policing based on an inappropriate presumption of the generalizability of western victimization patterns. Any expansion of policing must be justified by what it realistically proposes to deliver. An expansion justified by false presumptions and the resultant possibility of a flawed analysis must be viewed with extreme caution, most particularly so when the outcome of this occidentalist approach is most likely to involve a heavier police presence in poorer neighbourhoods.

Occidentalism 3: community safety and neighbourhood watch

As in the cases of the problematization of the young and the need to police the poor for their own good, so too western faith in neighbourhood watch programmes 'has not allowed ideas to violate its profound serenity' (Said 1978: 107). Indeed, even *data* about the limited value of such police sponsored schemes (Bennett 1990), have done little to disturb these serene convictions. In Trinidad and Tobago, however, the local Chamber of Commerce was the prime mover in the establishment of neighbourhood watch schemes, although both the police authorities[11] and the Ministry of Community development became enthusiastic sponsors of the idea. Ground rules for community action were agreed in 1994, rules which importantly prohibited any kind of vigilante patrolling. Elaborate structures of responsibility were put on paper involving both community development officers and the local police, while at neighbourhood level three and four-tier reporting networks were established—designed, it must be admitted, by the local committees albeit with the advice of the authorities. At the apex of these community level reporting networks was someone designated as 'block captain' whose job was to contact the local police. Reportedly, the police were thought to prefer to deal with one person rather than the many individuals involved in the schemes. However at the time that I searched out surviving schemes in late 1997 the formal relationships with both the police and the Ministry of Community Development had ceased to function, although both the Ministry and the Police

[11] Different segments of the police at local level were less receptive to the neighbourhood schemes: see Cain 2000.

Community Relations Branch were able to suggest possible respondents for one chain in my chain referral sample.[12]

An umbrella group of people with standing in the community was also set up at this time, 1994, as a result of local initiatives. Members included retired head teachers, local business people, retired personnel from the security forces, and ministers of religion. Working with the police and the Ministry the umbrella group function was identified as assisting actual neighbourhood groups to become established. Knowhow about the functions of neighbourhood watch, about the appropriate relationship with the police, about structure, and in general terms about how to get going was made available both informally and by providing speakers for local start-up meetings. The support of this group seems to have been effective, for I interviewed members of several active schemes in its catchment area, and heard of others still. Both local groups and the umbrella group in the main research area were originally supported by a designated police constable from the local divisional headquarters. His name appears unfailingly in minutes of those early meetings, and everyone I spoke to had met him. His energy and commitment were praised, as were his assistance in getting meetings going, his advice in the drafting of the groups' constitutions, and his liaison skills.

A grand launch of the neighbourhood watch programme was held at the end of 1994, after a full year of preparation. The Prime Minister and the Commissioner of Police attended, and all seemed set fair. However, the umbrella group never met again after the launch. Some respondents said with embarrassment that they didn't know why or 'perhaps the police lost interest' or 'didn't (suchabody) tell you?'. Others were more definite, with explanations ranging from police hostility to, again, indifference—in that the much praised officer responsible for the schemes on the ground was transferred and no one appointed to pick up his responsibilities. Those are the data. My hunches about the unspoken truth of the matter have no place here.[13]

[12] Other respondents or chains of respondents were identified through personal friends who lived in or adjacent to areas with such schemes, by chance, in the course of interviews with hotel and guest-house owners or reserve police officers or by security officers in the course of patrols. There was not time to follow up all the possible respondents identified, in particular those met while on patrol with security firms. Apart from the obvious advantages of a broader coverage the main consequence of running out of time is that neighbourhoods which had taken the route of employing security firms are underrepresented. Only one representative of such a neighbourhood was formally interviewed.

[13] An adequate explanation would have to explain why the umbrella group did not carry on meeting even without police support, as the local groups did.

The mystery, however, need not concern us, for it inadvertently provided an opportunity to investigate neighbourhood watch schemes which have no official relationship with any state agency. Cut loose from both the police and the Ministry of Community Development a number of the local groups established under the 1994 initiative continue to meet regularly, as do pre-existing residents' groups which added neighbourhood watch to their functions at that time. Both in Trinidad, therefore, and in St Lucia[14] we have the limiting case of an occidental innovation separated from the structures bearing, however indirectly, occidentalist discourse.

What happened in all but one of those cases was that crime and security-related activities ceased to be paramount even in those groups specifically set up for these purposes. The only exception was the single shanty-style district in my sample where I encountered community self protection in the form of a group of young men who allegedly *did* operate in a vigilante style, giving 'no trouble' to residents but watching out for strangers who disturbed the neighbourhood. No information about community social activities was given to me in this neighbourhood, and as it was one of my earliest interviews I did not have the wit to ask.

The residents' associations, according even to the constitutions of the formal ones, are founded to promote 'a sense of community spirit',[15] with the promotion of functions to achieve this end sometimes explicitly mentioned. Preservation and improvement of the communal facilities—open spaces, water and garbage services and so on—is also usually mentioned. Some members of residents' associations told me that promotion of security was added by constitutional amendment in 1994, while in other cases it had always been there, among the other functions but *never* at the head of the list.

For the groups newly established as neighbourhood watch groups in 1994 communal security was ostensibly the reason for their existence. Three years later, however, when I asked them what they did they too described with enthusiasm a much broader range of functions. One of the 1994 groups had expanded the definition of security from crime watch to include fire watch, price watch, and environment watch. More common was an expansion into social events: 'fetes', at Carnival,

---

[14] In St Lucia the 'English Commissioner', A. W. F. Hemmingway, who held the office for three years on secondment (Royal St Lucia Police Force 1993), advocated neighbourhood watch, and the idea caught on among some residents' groups whom I interviewed, even though no organizational steps were taken by the police.
[15] Quotation from a constitution of an organization founded in the 1980s.

Christmas, and possibly Divali; sports days and other events for children. 'Beautification' and the creation of facilities were common: by clearing bush, creating open play or sports areas, assisting with external repairs and decorating, or even, in one more prosperous location, building a pavilion.[16] Security was more directly addressed by fencing the 'drains' (very deep culverts to carry occasional flood waters) to prevent would-be thieves using them for access, providing alarm bells for the elderly, and, importantly, improving communications, oiled by mutual recognition as a result of the social activities and meetings. One area reported that the block captain structure with intermediate reporting stages had broken down because key members were often out, but with informal networks so much enhanced this did not seem to matter.

One or two points that take us a little beyond description can be made here.

(i) *Contact with police.* No one mentioned giving information to the police or receiving information from the police, either when questioned about activities in general or when asked directly about the relationship. While they spoke highly of the initiating constable, and, with some notable exceptions, described the relationship with the police as good (ascribing police deficiencies to lack of resources), they had no formal or routinized contact. In Trinidad they said that officers sometimes passed by, enquiring casually how things were going. When residents defined something as a crime they were willing to send a car to collect an officer. There were complaints, but there was no tension in the ongoing relationship, in spite of reports from two groups of active police hostility in the early days. Crucially, there was no police presence in their planning or deliberations.

(ii) *Participation.* Neighbourhoods varied between 50 and 500 households. Turnout at open meetings was variously described as between one in five and one in 17 households. Most described the usual problem of some committee members being more active than others. All said that the formal social events were very well attended. I was of course talking to the committed in the main (although one respondent indicated that his activities with the residents' group had been slowing down recently). However, even allowing that necessary pinch of salt these

---

[16] For further details see Cain (2000).

three-years-old-plus groups sound as if they are both representative of their neighbourhoods and thriving.

(iii) *Security problems*. One group indicated that it had few problems to start with. Another was concerned about 'snatches' by
strangers passing through the area. Both of these were in St
Lucia. In Trinidad respondents had been worried about house-
breaking, but also and more so about the stealing of fruit, furniture, hoses, equipment and personal items such as toys from
yards and porches. Car theft had also been a problem. In addition there were the experienced incivilities of outsiders making
noise or nuisance or just using public space. My respondents
told me that the petty thefts and car thefts had been dramatically reduced, although the latter still happened on occasion.
The incivilities occurred only rarely now, and were dealt with
by communal, if drastic, preventive action, such as turning an
open space where young outsiders had begun to congregate into
a tennis court!

One constructive lesson and one note of warning may be derived from
this account. The positive lesson is that neighbourhood watch schemes
can be effective for enhancing the quality of life of communities if they
are allowed to develop their own agendas. Those schemes were effective because they located crime problems firmly within their own hierarchy of neighbourhood activities and priorities. They were not
co-opted to a police agenda of information exchange or crime control.
They were more rather than less effective as a result.

On the other hand all the known problems of informal justice or
informal policing apply: (a) community togetherness may involve
keeping others out: the youths driven off by the tennis court probably
had nowhere else to go; (b) communities are most effective when they
are able to generate and mobilize resources. The communities I studied
were not, with one exception, rich, but they were predominantly middle class. They had skills, they had networks, so yes, they could generate resources; (c) community policing is meant to incorporate
community values. Sometimes these values may be at odds with those
which the state or the society as a whole might wish to support.
Sometimes what is *not* said in an open, conversational interview is as
important as what is mentioned. Notably not a single person with
whom I discussed neighbourhood security spoke of security *within* the
households that constituted their community. In all but one area the

community spokesperson was a man. I waited in vain to hear about the networks of friends and safe houses which might have offered greater security to those victimized within the domestic sphere. We may hope that the enhanced sociability helps the women too, but violence within the home is certainly not seen by these neighbourhood groups as having a place on their self-constructed agendas.

In this regard the state police do rather better than the informal watchers, as the next section will reveal. Let me, however, conclude this part of my essay by returning to the theme of occidentalism. As far as neighbourhood watch goes, an occidental idea plainly caught the imagination of many people in Trinidad and St Lucia—people who, as Birju's data (1998) reveal, had a serious problem of repeated minor thefts. Personalized police support in getting neighbourhoods up and running was crucial. Subsequent police withdrawal so that people could construct their own agendas was also crucial. No one made that third crucial input which would have brought the issue of security within the home to the attention of the groups. In the following section I indicate possibilities for change in this regard.

Neighbourhood watch activities in Trinidad and Tobago form the limiting case of occidentalism as I have defined it here. The idea as imported is an English one, and the current Commissioner (the third since 1994), has Bramshill connections. Moreover, the Superintendent in charge of the Community Policing Division told me 'what we are trying to do now is to organize neighbourhood watch groups'.[17] The aims, seen as an integrated package, are 'the enhancement of communities', the identification by the groups of community problems, and the joint mobilization of community and police networks so that resources can be focused on problem solving.

Community enhancement is what the already existing 'police-abandoned' schemes are doing well, so that seems fine. Moreover, the Superintendent welcomed the account I gave him of the wide range of activities undertaken in the name of neighbourhood watch. Problem identification poses more difficulties, because people tend to ask agencies for what they believe they can provide, while agencies themselves with the best will in the world, see or formulate problems that fit their own organizational preconceptions.[18] On how this works in practice I

---

[17] Interview 9 July 1999.

[18] See Brogden (1999), for a further discussion of the functionalist presuppositions of problem-oriented policing which become clear when an attempt is made to transpose this American policing model to different socio-cultural, economic and political contexts.

have no empirical evidence but a later remark of the Superintendent
gave me pause:

You see . . . the whole philosophy of community policing is the police and the
community working together to reduce crime, aimed at reducing crime and disorder, fear, which is something you can't quantify, so that you know we are
working together to reduce that.

These objectives too sound admirable. But the message my data convey
is the paradoxical one that the reduction of crime, disorder and fear is
not necessarily given precedence in any direct sense amongst the activities of a functioning neighbourhood watch scheme. These effects may
occur inadvertently as a result of an improved quality of life, which
includes more frequent and more friendly contacts between people
who live fairly near to each other. But if schemes focus on crime-related
matters, as one respondent told me and as the English experience
proves, people rather quickly lose interest and stop coming to meetings. It is, apparently, by decentralizing crime and becoming more like
multi-purpose residents' associations that the Trinidadian schemes
have achieved success. Because of this I suggest that the role of the
police in neighbourhood watch schemes should not be one of agenda
setting on the occidental model. Initiation, facilitation, and legal and
procedural advice (e.g. no vigilantism) are helpful. Indeed, where they
have expertise the police may suggest areas which need attention, from
traffic pollution to domestic violence. As they are more likely to read
papers such as this than other community members, they might, these
days, suggest that the neighbourhood groups broaden the scope of their
activities beyond crime-watching. But too much pressure for the
instant formulation of actionable problems may well be counterproductive. What must also be avoided—and it is the cusp upon which
success or failure turns—is peddling the occidentalist view that reduc-
tions in crime, fear of crime, and disorder are the sole or main point of
the exercise. The newer schemes in Trinidad wobble on that cusp.

The good news, for the Superintendent and his dedicated team, as
for residents of the neighbourhoods, is that a zero-sum choice between
the home-grown and the imported is not required. Rather, in this area
as in others,[19] what is likely to happen and what is required, is *interactive globalization*. A new idea which resonates with experience, which
seems to make sense, may be derived from anywhere. The trajectory is

[19] See M. Cain (1996), Report to the Leverhulme Foundation on Phase 1 of the Project
Private Policing in the Caribbean, Grant no. RGF/96.

most usually from the more to less powerful, but the recipient groups may, if they choose, if they are strong enough, interact with that idea, re-situate it within their own discourses and practices, modify it, make it their own, and so create an alternative model, which ideally should then find its own place in a global pool of possibilities. The way off the cusp then may be to embrace neighbourhood watch so tightly that it is transformed.

Interactive globalization: the case of violence against women and children

The purpose of this section of the paper is not only to reveal further how both orientalist and occidentalist approaches to understanding are misleading but also to demonstrate the possibility of mutual and reciprocal learning. In order to do this it is necessary in addition to 'clear the underbrush' also of more 'progressive' occidental thinking. I then move on to describe very shortly the practices of some of the women and women's organizations in Trinidad and Tobago and St Lucia that work to prevent violence against women and children. The section as a whole reveals how western criminology, locked in as it is to either orientalist or occidentalist paradigms, is missing the theoretical and political opportunities offered by a familiarity with a wider range of ways of social ordering.

Contacts with first world feminist ideas and practices are easy enough to trace for women working on behalf of women and children in Trinidad and Tobago and St Lucia. Yet the women's movements are nothing if not indigenous in their guiding philosophies and practical approaches. For this reason the struggles against violence against women and children demonstrate clearly the inadequacy of linear notions of direction of influence such as are contained in some conceptions both of globalization and of hegemony and resistance (e.g. Robinson 1996a, 1996b).[20] Not only structural power is in play here— although in play as ever it is—but also a play of philosophies, strategies, tactical opportunities, personal experiences, ethnic awarenesses, organizational capacities, and career trajectories. These form the

---

[20] I make this point in the recognition that oftentimes choices are not open, that economic globalization forecloses some options such as the possibility of nurturing and protecting a small-island economy. I thank Robinson for what I and my students have learned from his resistance to antinomian postmodern orthodoxy. But there is usually more than defensive reaction (resistance) to the ways in which people engage with the powers at play in their environment.

grounds of and result from positive choices.[21] Such choices, if they run counter to a model of anticipated western dominance, have typically been characterized as resistance. Such a conception would leave Trinbagonian and Lucian women in a permanently defensive posture. Such a concept does not fit their experience as they described it to me and as I all too briefly saw it when working with them. Moreover to conceive all non-Western autonomous thought and action as resistance (when it is not custom) denies creativity to these most creative people. The discourse of resistance characterizes the actions of the others from a western perspective. The women I knew, however, and those I talked to, were more interested in seeing about their own business than in what the West was doing. This freed them up to appraise western ideas, colleagues, funds in terms of how all of these potential resources could further their own collectively and locally negotiated agendas. Their engagement with these potential resources was interactive, and could lead to one-sided change, mutual change, or none.

Recent contributions by Trinidadian feminists lend further support to this view. Mohammed (1998), points out that women in Trinidad and Tobago engaged in both cultural and political struggles against colonialism in alliance with men, so that men *qua* men have never been deemed the opposition even while women were fighting for equality. Certainly—to be anecdotal once more—I was informed upon joining that the UWI women's group, like other such groups in the Caribbean, does not exclude men, and the contrast with Anglo-American feminism was explicitly drawn. Indeed, the 'marginalization' of the black male was seen as a serious problem in the society (Miller 1991), needing careful feminist analysis not least because of the misplaced attribution of blame for this problem on the strong black women (p. 25).

The indigenous-yet-globally-aware nature of Caribbean feminist theory and organization is further evidenced by Reddock's (1998), account of the organizational development of the movement in Trinidad. While the earliest and most consistent efforts to organize women were made within the churches, 'new women's movement' of the 1970s was founded on deep roots in the political parties, and, most importantly the labour movement where women held leadership positions until 'responsible' unionism was introduced by the colonial power in response to the pan-Caribbean labour crises of the 1930s (p. 58). At this time too women members of socialist and anti-imperialist

---

[21] Among many such past-marxist formulations the one which best catches the 'flavour' of my argument here is that of Hebdige (1996).

organizations challenged their lack of internal democracy, while at the same time sharing the same struggle.

Pan-Caribbean approaches also have a long history (Reddock 1998). As early as 1936, the First Conference of British West Indies and British Guyanese Women Social Workers was hosted in Trinidad by the Coterie of Social Workers—an organization still in existence. Twenty years later when the British West Indies Federation was founded the Caribbean Women's Association was formed. Then in 1977 a number of nation-specific groups came together to take a position on the UN Decade of Women, and with this development reinforced in 1985 by the formation of an umbrella organization for progressive groups (the Caribbean Association for Feminist Research and Action, CAFRA) (Reddock 1998: 63; see also Nicholas 1990), there has been a consistent attempt to 'define a Caribbean feminism which links women's subor-dination with other systems of subordination—race, class, and nation . . .' (Reddock 1998: 63). In this way Caribbean women have learned from each other as well as and probably more than from the West, whether engaged in local struggles (for example against export processing zones) or struggles in which women globally have been engaged (for example against domestic violence). Thus the influence and support of the 'second wave' movement for gender equality in the West has been important, but it has not defined in any absolute way either the issues to be addressed or the theory shaping the formulation of both issues and strategy.

My own support for this view of globalization, in the context of the women's movement, as an interactive rather than a hegemonic process, is based on 13 interviews with women[22] involved in one way or another in the prevention of violence against women and children. Seven were connected with women's movement NGOs, three held or had held public office but also had NGO connections, and three were involved with violence prevention purely in their official capacity.[23] They range from founder members of single issue violence-prevention groups to organizations concerned with a more general improvement in the

[22] One interview involved two women, another two women and a man. The other eleven were conversations with women alone, usually at their places of work but twice over tea and once in the women's organization's headquarters.

[23] The categories overlap, for example one Minister of State had CAFRA connections; active members of feminist NGOs had jobs as public servants; employees of feminist NGOs might work primarily as professional social workers; only three women gave no hint of connections with a feminist network, and in two of these cases the names were given to me by activists.

condition of women; from ad hoc response groups to government-funded NGOs with employed staff; from women coming out of the labour movement to women in positions of authority—ministers of state, public servants, judges—who simply found themselves called upon to act for women and rose to the occasion with surprise, with pride, with a deal of help from the movement, and often with success.

Turning first to the influence of 'foreign' ideas, eight of the 13 women had trained or lived or worked abroad, including two who were born outside the West Indies. On the other hand two of these eight had been active campaigners for women before they went to the West, and simply resumed their work when they returned. One of the women born abroad became active only after she came to the West Indies. She sought the help, support and friendship of a local colleague with similar objectives and an equal lack of knowhow in establishing a shelter. Although they had international contacts there turned out to be no international blueprints. Only one woman appeared to be using her overseas training and experience in a direct way, to create an organization to prevent child abuse through public education. However, she had formed an alliance with two local NGOs. Their relationships with the press and other workers in the field as well as their local knowledge were shaping the organization as powerfully as her own professional and campaigning experience abroad.

The evidence, however, is of a lot of western contact. I wish to explore this further in relation to the resources available to the organizations before turning to the evidence that we have here a case of interactive globalization, rather than hegemony or acceptance by the women of an occidentalist denial of difference.

In St Lucia I contacted three women in connection with their NGO work. The least formal of these groups came into being by phoning around when a key issue affecting women's vulnerability arose. One such occasion was when a man who had raped and killed a girl was convicted of manslaughter rather than murder because of an evidential flaw. In another case I attended a memorial march for a more recent victim supported by this group but organized by the Crisis Centre. Such alliances are common. The group, Cry for Justice, depends on ad hoc funding and volunteer help. Its sole activity to date is campaigning.

An alliance was also foundational in the establishment of a new campaigning group called Say No To Child Abuse. Leaders of two well established NGOs in alliance with a concerned social worker established this organization. The group seeks to reduce child abuse by raising public awareness and by education in communities. Children with disabilities, known to be especially vulnerable, and boys as well as girls, are the objects and subjects of concern. One of the three leaders is a man. The group is raising funds in an ad hoc way (they do not call it 'begging' in St Lucia as they do in Trinidad), and the established NGOs give it some solidity as regards places to meet and telephone lines.

More firmly established organizationally in St Lucia is the Crisis Centre, commonly known as 'Rape Crisis'. The organization is able to access foreign funds through Catholic Social Action, and the government has supplied office accommodation and land on which to build a shelter. A particular problem with fundraising has been male domination of the main potential donor groups. The Centre serves 'families', said its founder, not women, and provides a walk-in service, a hotline, and a counselling service. Since the establishment in 1997 of the Family Court the Centre as first point of call is also active in giving advice about referral. As already indicated, the Centre is also involved in issue-specific campaigns. It maintains a database and acts as a continuous pressure group in relation to the national government. Notably, only one of the groups working in St Lucia might be described as feminist (Cry for Justice). The child abuse group could be so described in terms of its practice, but said nothing about it, while the founder of the Crisis Centre explicitly distanced herself from feminism while maintaining a strong focus on the plight of women in particular.

The situation in Trinidad is very different. Here I interviewed four NGO organizers, two of whom worked with the same group. One group had past connections with the labour movement and all three NGOs were comfortable with a feminist perspective. Their strategies evidenced the much deeper history of feminism in Trinidad, from the labour movement of the 1930s (Reddock 1988, 1998), to the emergence of 'new wave' feminist groups (encouraged by the UN Decade of Women) in 1975 (Nicholas 1990).

The three organizations contacted specifically for this study, and perforce excluding the many others that I know about or, in one case, belonged to, were The Shelter (North) and the National Coalition Against Domestic Violence (of which the founder of the north shelter is now the chair), the Rape Crisis Centre (founded and run by Rape Crisis Society), and Working Women for Social Progress or 'working women'. This gives an ethnic and geographical bias to my data for Trinidad— more African than Indian descent, and more north than south.

Founded in 1986 the 'north' shelter survived in its early years by begging, ad hoc donations, and a plot of land donated by the government. Nearly 15 years on, the organization employs three people and is supported both by a subvention from the national government and also by project-specific funds from foreign governments. These projects usually involve capital expenditure. In addition the organization is 'still begging'. It provides a shelter, a counselling service for residents and, importantly, outreach education to groups. It has formed alliances with the national Coalition Against Domestic Violence and with the Community Police, for whom it provided a fully funded training programme. Four hundred officers received domestic violence awareness training in 1998.

The Rape Crisis Committee which became the Rape Crisis Society in 1986, was initially supported by the Catholic and Anglican churches, which provided accommodation. This office is known as the Rape Crisis Centre. In a second phase its resources came predominantly from UNIFEM. Today it receives a subvention for running costs from the national government and project specific funds from three foreign states. In addition to counselling the organization runs outreach programmes to schools, organizations and, in a new venture, to men in either ad hoc or formal groups. It also does campaigning work in relation to relevant legislation, although this aspect of its work has reportedly slowed down (Babb, 1996 and interviews.

The third NGO that I contacted in Trinidad was formed as part of a breakaway from a group that was perceived to be too narrowly focused on violence. The initial group has now dispersed, but there is evidence of some rapprochement in analysis. A former member of the original group argued in a local feminist newsletter in 1990 that domestic violence cannot be understood if the context is not given due weight (Mohammed 1990).

Be that as it may, Working Women for Social Progress (the breakaway group) seeks to improve the condition of women, making special efforts to reach poor women by direct community involvement as well as by campaigning and public education. Hands on activities have ranged from building a vegetable garden in a school—an early one off event—to adult literacy classes as part of a Language for Empowerment programme, and community workshops on violence against women. Campaign and public education work, not really distinguished by this group, include regular celebrations and demonstrations on International Women's Day and a Day Against Domestic

Violence. More specific campaigns have been organised on a broad range of issues: a campaign against government plans for free trade (or export processing) zones where it was feared that women would be employed at low wages and without trades union protection, a campaign in support of the Sexual Offences Bill, and in particular for the reinstatement of a clause on marital rape which was left out of the final draft; and the highlighting of women's role in the anti-apartheid movement.[24] A new campaign, organized through the Working Women School for Alternative Education, and moving against the tide of popular culture, is opposed to the beating of children in schools and in the home. Discussions focus on the development and adoption of non-violent methods for disciplining children. Workshops around the country with teachers and people from the communities are focusing attention on the issue and building a grassroots foundation for the campaign. The organization depends upon local funding, and has secured its position by the purchase of an organizational headquarters.

What can be made of these data? First of all local funding has proved a more stable source of money than project-specific international funding. However, national governments will support only organizations offering a service to fulfil a need which they have already come to recognize—the two 'rape crisis' organizations and the shelters. Understandably enough, governments do not want to resource campaigns of which their policies are the object. This means that campaigning and public education work either has to be reformulated into projects which international agencies can recognize and fund (eg conferences, workshops and training with specific groups) or resourced locally on an ad hoc basis. Creatively, the former can provide a secretariat and office space for the latter, but too much viring from project funds in support of general running costs can also land an organization in difficulty (Babb 1996). The women have to be imaginative in pursuit of their objectives. However, guided by a clear understanding of the need to empower the poor and the vulnerable, these women have kept their sights on what is important. They have not been seduced from their original objectives by the allurements of possible project funding. Indeed, it is possible to argue that subventions from national governments place more 'good behaviour' constraints on organizations than does international money. In both countries, as I hope to demonstrate,

[24] The Act which resulted from this Bill is now, as of 1999 subject to further amendment following a new round of consultations (interview 09/07/99; see also Reddock 1998).

serious constraints are avoided by the strength of that part of the movement that has no subvention. These are the groups breaking new discursive ground and effectively defining the issues for both governments
and for the semi-dependent groups.

Women's self protection in these two nations exemplifies interactive
rather than dependent globalization because of the deep tradition of
alternative theorizing in the region alluded to in my discussion of orientalism, and because this tradition has been developed further within
the women's movement. Paradoxically, it was a western organization
(the Institute of Social Studies in The Hague) which provided support
for women and Development Studies Groups, established in 1982 to
enhance research, teaching and outreach in relation to Caribbean
women, on the three campuses of the University of the West Indies.
Under their auspices a number of regional seminar series for the purposes of theoretical development were held. This development was
paralleled by the development of academic teaching (resourced by the
University). Now each campus staffs a Centre for Gender Studies offering undergraduate courses and postgraduate programmes, curriculum
development support, and a homebase for visiting feminist researchers.

The second reason that Caribbean feminists have been able to adopt
an instrumental rather than a deferential stance in relation to global
feminism is what might be described as the organizational depths of the
movement. Already well versed in traditional male politics, having historic and contemporary ties with both spiritual organizations and the
labour movement, the groups display both organizational capacity and
inventiveness of method. One example of the latter involved sitting in
the gallery of the Trinidad and Tobago Senate in 1993 dressed from
head to toe in black, to hear the debate on the Sexual Offences Bill.

Thirdly, the movement is located in a society where women have, in
some limited senses, been stronger for longer: that is to say, displays of
being silent and secondary, which ambitious western women must
both engage in and transcend, are not required at least of Caribbean
women of African descent. The complexities of different engenderings
have no place in this essay, however. What is clear is that four of the
women I spoke to held senior positions in government or the public service: two had been responsible for staff work, maintaining close relationships with the movement while providing their ministers (whether
male or female) with both data and arguments. One, as Attorney
General, negotiated an accommodation between government and feminist women, pushing through a great deal of legislation pressed for by

the Women's Desk during her tenure. One, still a Minister of State, has held consultations with the NGOs as well as professional groups prior to revising the Domestic Violence and Sexual Offences Acts.[25] The point is that having allies in strategic positions is important if the locally informed debate is to be embodied in legislation.

Finally, the theoretical strength of the movement combined with its organizational and campaigning capacity has enabled the more ideologically vulnerable groups to be supported. Crucial here too has been the pan-Caribbean dimension and the role of CAFRA. While global voices may sound more loudly in St Lucia, where the theoretical and organizational traditions of feminist work are weaker, the voice of CAFRA creates the opportunity for dialogue. Two of my Lucian respondents spoke of CAFRA contacts, and I learned later that a third respondent also had CAFRA connections. And while some organizations may be pulled in a relatively traditional direction by subventions from national governments, the close knit network among all activists for women, the strength and experience of the leadership as a whole, and the culture of non confrontation and inclusiveness, enable these groups to continue campaigning work while providing the services for which the government pays.

This extended example is intended to reveal in a different way the paucity of both orientalist and occidentalist approaches, including that version of occidentalism which while acknowledging difference can see it only as resistance. These women are starting from their own unique place for their own reasons: they want to achieve fullness of life and equality for Caribbean peoples and in particular for Caribbean women. They have their own historical experience, their own theoretical frameworks, and their own priorities, as well as their own international knowledge and resource networks. They have made some mistakes, no doubt, and they still have a long way to go.

It would not enhance understanding to compare them with, say, English or other western feminists, for the global and local networks are in dialogue, in interaction, whereas *comparison* as a method is static, and polarizing. Comparison too tends to be based on empirical generalization and 'recognition' of sameness and difference, whereas what is needed if we are to make use of Caribbean experiences and vice versa is not generalization but abstraction. In the West, for example, we

---

[25] The Domestic Violence Bill was in draft at the time of my visit in July 1999, and then under revision. The Sexual Offences Bill was at an earlier stage, on the point of being circulated for consultation.

could draw lessons about how to achieve inclusiveness without losing direction, about the central role of theory in sustaining practice, about getting beyond domination and submission as a useful model for understanding women's politics.

What are the lessons specifically for criminology? The most important is that if we are studying citizens' self protection we must not stay pegged to concepts of 'neighbourhood' and 'community' the genealogy of which lies in a sentimental attachment to police patrolling methods in the days before the dominance of the mobile patrol. Even if the past had indeed been golden,[26] there is no good reason for thinking that *self* protection and *police* protection are or should be geographically bounded in the same way. In short, if we can avoid both orientalism and occidentalism we might learn to see citizens' self protection in terms of more meaningful collectivities than communities.

In Conclusion: a Reflective Footnote

The paragraph above embodies my most important conclusion. However, because of the hegemonic form, it is necessary to reflect further on alternatives to that problematic methodology. The advantages and difficulties of comparative work and, more simply, of international work have recently been addressed in two important collections (Mawby 1999; Bayley 1999). Certainly a cultivation of myopia, or what Bayley (p. 5), calls 'the elevation of parochialism to a scientific principle', has nothing to be said for it. On the other hand, it has been the argument of this paper that comparison from within either an orientalist or an occidentalist mindset can do more harm than good. Orientalism these days perhaps does most harm to the orientalist, now that the Other has made a joke of being 'othered'. Occidentalism, however, can lead to the misapplication of both aid and internal resources: to fight a non-existent juvenile crime problem and in the process perhaps to create one; to legitimate over-policing of the poor on the spurious grounds of their greater vulnerability to crime; to distort (perhaps, but I am hopeful here) some promising developments in community self protection into an anglo-saxon model of community policing. Why am I hopeful in this last case? Because once again of an increasingly theoretically grounded (Mohammed 1998) capacity of Caribbean fem-

---

[26] My own work on policing in 1962 and 1963 (Cain 1973), and Brodgen's discussions with officers patrolling in the 1930s (Brogden 1991), demonstrate the absence of the golden age of policing.

inists to be inclusive of Caribbean men—in this case policemen—
enabling them to respond as an alliance to the increasingly obvious
need to protect women and children in the domestic sphere. Hear this
from a Chairwoman of the National Coalition Against Domestic
Violence:

> I tell you they [the police] were *so hostile*[27] . . . but now we have the commu-
> nity police it's started to change from within . . . [The Superintendent has] been
> interested in domestic violence. He was one of the few and yes, you are right,
> he was not supported because of it, but it was turning out to be one of the most
> damaging and high cost crime areas in the country, and he was there all along.

Now the community police are attempting to 'get men who are violent
together . . .' for counselling in their districts. The Coalition provides
materials.

> I tell you, I just felt like God had, you know, come back to us . . . you have no
> idea . . . one day I was cleaning the house and [my husband] said 'your feet
> haven't touched the ground!' . . . that was the day the first group [of commu-
> nity police] came up and asked if I could give them any material to help them
> with that . . . They're really making a difference . . .

On his side, the Superintendent reported the considerable help he had
received from the Coalition on a day-to-day basis, as described, and
also in designing and finding staff for a formal training programme for
the new Community Police.

> Supt: [The Chair of the Coalition] is doing a tremendous amount of
>   work for us.
> Maureen: For you! Supt: Yes.
> Maureen: She says you do a tremendous amount of work for her.
> Supt: Well—I would say both ways then.

If this doesn't sound like the UK, it isn't. There is a huge potential here,
hence my fears about the possibly malign influence of standard POP
(problem oriented policing). But there is also a strength in a newfound
professionalism, in having found a niche which was unfilled in a crime-
related area of police work, and in a supportive alliance with the community, as represented by the women's NGOs.
  So plainly my initial occidentalist response: 'beware the seductive
strategy of community policing and POP' was a nonsense. In a society

---

[27] To be fair, the NCADV chairwoman also said that when the north shelter was
founded good personal relationships between staff of the shelter and the local police station had ensured the safety of the shelter's residents and workers.

where 'community' is interpreted differently, where progressive collectivities are strong, community policing has the potential, paradoxically, to work exactly as a POP handbook might prescribe, with the
problems being formulated by the victim group.

This is why I dared, in the previous section, to hint that a community
police officer in the specific setting of Trinidad and Tobago might be
the person to suggest to a group of residents that one of the problems
they might like to consider addressing could be that of domestic violence. All is not rosy: there have been frequent organizational changes,
and both senior officers of the CP division with whom I discussed the
matter indicated that the standard marginalization by so-called 'mainstream' police officers remains. But an opportunity has been created.

The lessons for criminology in the new millennium then are:

(i)   avoid orientalism in both its negative and its romantic guises,
      for it will lead to false policies for the 'here';
(ii) avoid occidentalism, both in its denial of difference and in its
      self regarding interpretation of all difference as resistance, for it
      will lead to unhelpful and possibly damaging exports of theo-
      ries and resources;
(iii) avoid comparison, for it implies a lurking occidentalist stan-
      dard and user, and focuses on static and dyadic rather than
      dynamic and complex relations;
(iv) encourage the capacity to see the Other as her own subject; use
      other people's writings about their situation to feed into
      improved abstractions; if there are not enough such writings
      then choose carefully your allies among the others, for other
      societies are no more innocent than ours, and you cannot learn
      from everybody; remember that other people need your help no
      more than, and as much as, you need theirs. If the enterprise is
      theory building then every experience counts as one, only.

References

Annual Statistical Digest (1997), Trinidad and Tobago: Government Printery.
BABB, C. (1996), *Taking Action Against Violence: A Case Study of the Rape
   Crisis, Society of Trinidad and Tobago*. Barbados: The UNIFEM Caribbean
   Office.
BAYLEY, D. (1999), 'Policing the World Stage', in R. Mawby, ed., *Policing
   Across the World: Issues for the 21st Century*, 3–12. London: University
   College Press.
BAYLEY, D. and SHEARING, C. (1996), 'The Future of Policing', *Law and Society
   Review*, 30/3: 585–606.

Beckford, G. (1972), *Persistent Poverty: Underdevelopment in Plantation Economies of the Third World*. New York: Oxford University Press.

Bennett, T. (1990), *Evaluating Neighbourhood Watch*. Aldershot: Gower.

Best, L. (1968), 'Outlines of a Model of Pure Plantation Economy', *Social and Economic Studies*, 17/3: 283–324.

Birju, A. (1998), *A Crime Victim Survey of St James, Trinidad 1992–1994: Understanding the Hidden Dimensions of Crime*. Thesis submitted for the degree of Master of Philosophy, St Augustine, Trinidad: University of the West Indies, Department of Behavioural Sciences.

Braithwaite, F. (1996), 'Some Aspects of Sentencing in the Criminal Justice System of Barbados', in M. Cain, ed., *For a Caribbean Criminology: Caribbean Quarterly* 42/2, 3: 113–30.

Braithwaite, J. (1989), *Crime, Shame, and Re-Integration*. Cambridge: Cambridge University Press.

Braithwaite, J. and Mugford, S. (1994), 'Conditions of Successful Reintegration Ceremonies: Dealing with Juvenile Delinquents', *British Journal of Criminology* 34/2: 139–71.

Brogden, M. (1991), *On the Mersey Beat: Policing Liverpool Between the Wars*. Oxford: Oxford University Press.

Brogden, M. (1999), 'Community Policing as Cherry Pie', in R. Mawby, ed., *Policing Across the World: Issues for the Twenty-first Century*, 167–86. London: UCL Press.

Brown, S. (1998), *Understanding Youth and Crime*. Buckingham: Open University Press.

Cain, M. (1973) *Society and the Policeman's Role*. London: Routledge.

—— (1985/1989), 'Beyond Informal Justice', *Contemporary Crises*, 9/4: 335–73. Reprinted in R. Mathews, ed., *Informal Justice*. London: Sage.

—— (1995), 'Labouring, Loving, and Living: On the Policing of Culture in Trinidad and Tobago', in L. Noaks, M. Levi and M. Maguire, eds., *Contemporary Issues in Criminology*, 84–107. Cardiff: University of Wales Press.

—— (1996), 'Developing a Juvenile Justice Policy: Anomalies of Theory and Practice in Trinidad and Tobago', in M. Cain, ed. *For a Caribbean Criminology: Caribbean Quarterly*. 42/2, 3: 29–41. Jamaica: UWI Press.

Cain, M. (2000) 'Through Other Eyes: On the Limitations and Value of Western Criminology for Teaching and Practice in Trinidad and Tobago', in D. Nelken, ed., *Contrasts in Criminal Justice*. Aldershot: Dartmouth.

Carlen, P. (1996), *Jigsaw: a Political Criminology of Youth Homelessness*. Buckingham: Open University Press

Christie, N. (1977), 'Conflicts as Property', *British Journal of Criminology*, 17/1: 1–15.

Clegg, I. and Whetton, J. (1999), 'UK Government Assistance to the Police in Developing Countries', paper presented at the British Criminology Conference, Liverpool, July 1999.

COBB, S. (1997), 'The Domestication of Violence in Mediation', *Law and Society Review*, 31/3: 397–440.

DANZIG, R. (1973), 'Towards the Creation of a Complementary, Decentralized System of Justice', *Stanford Law Review*, 26/1: 1–54.

DFID (1998), *Eliminating World Poverty*, White Paper. London: HMSO.

DIGNAN, J., SORSBY, A. and HIBBERT, J. (1996), *Neighbour Disputes: Comparing the Costs of Mediation and Alternative Approaches*. Sheffield, UK: The University of Sheffield Centre for Criminological and Socio-Legal Research.

FINEMAN, M. (1988), 'Dominant Discourse, Professional Language, and Legal Change in Child Custody Decision Making', *Harvard Law Review*, 101: 727 ff.

FRANK, A. G. (1967/1970), *The Sociology of Development and the Underdevelopment of Sociology*. New York: Zenit Reprints (pamphlet). First published in *Catalyst*, 3, Summer.

—— (1967), *Capitalism and Under-development in Latin America*. New York: Monthly Review Press.

HARRIOTT, A. (1996), 'The Changing Social Organisation of Crime and Criminals in Jamaica', in M. Cain, ed., *For a Caribbean Criminology: Caribbean Quarterly*, 42/2 and 3: 113–30.

HEBDIGE, D. (1996), 'Postmodernism and the "Other Side" ', in D. Morley and K. H. Chen, eds., *Stuart Hall: Critical Dialogues in Cultural Studies*, 174–200. London: Routledge.

JONES, H. (1981), *Crime, Race and Culture*. New York: Wiley.

LEA, J. and YOUNG, J. (1984), *What is to be Done About Law and Order?* Harmondsworth: Penguin.

MAWBY, R. (1999), 'Approaches to Comparative Analysis: The Impossibility of Becoming an Expert on Everywhere', in R. Mawby, ed., *Policing Across the World: Issues for the 21st Century*, 13–22. London: University College Press.

MERRY, S. (1982), 'The Social Organisation of Mediation in Non-Industrial Societies: Implications for Informal Community Justice in America', in R. Abel, ed., *The Politics of Informal Justice*, vol. 2, 17–45. New York, Academic Press.

MILLER, E. (1991), *Men at Risk*. Kingston: Jamaica Publishing House.

MOHAMMED, P. (1990), 'The Women's Movement: Violence Against Women', *CAFRA News*, 34–45.

—— (1998), 'Towards Indigenous Feminist Theorising in the Caribbean', *Feminist Review*, 59: 6–33.

NICHOLAS, E. (1990), *Patriarchal Power and Women's Resistance in Trinidad*, paper submitted in partial fulfilment of the requirements for obtaining the Degree of Master of Arts in Development Studies, The Hague, Institute of Social Studies.

REDDOCK, R. (1988), *Elma Francois: The NWCSA and the Workers' Struggle for Change in the Caribbean*. London: New Beacon Books.

—— (1994), *Women, Labour, and Politics in Trinidad and Tobago*. London: Zed Books.

—— (1998), 'Women's Organisations and Movements in the Commonwealth Caribbean: The Response to Global Economic Crisis in the 1980's', *Feminist Review*, 59: 57–73.

Rios, J. (1995), 'Rio de Janiero, Brazil', in U. Zverkic and A. del Frate, eds., *Criminal Victimisation in the Developing World*, no. 55, ch. 10, pp. 233–74. Rome: UNICRI.

Robinson, W. (1996a) *Promoting Polyarchy: Globalization, US Intervention, and Hegemony*. Cambridge: Cambridge University Press.

—— (1996b) 'Globalisation: Nine Theses on our Epoch', *Race and Class*, 38/2:13–31.

Royal St Lucia Police (1993), *Review of the Force as at 1st July 1992*. Castries: Ministry for Home Affairs.

Said, E. (1978), *Orientalism*. New York: Pantheon Books.

Sampson, J. (1994), *Report of the Cabinet Appointed Committee to Examine the Juvenile Delinquency and Youth Crime Situation in Trinidad and Tobago*. Port of Spain, Trinidad: Ministry of Social Development.

Schneider, E. (1994), 'The Violence of Privacy', in M. Fineman and R. Mykitiuk, eds., *The Public Nature of Private Violence*, 36–58. New York: Routledge.

Smith, R. T. (1956), *The Negro Family in British Guiana*. London: Routledge and Kegan Paul.

West, D. (1982), *Delinquency, its Roots and Careers*. London: Heinemann.

5

Dangerization and the End of Deviance

The Institutional Environment

Michalis Lianos with Mary Douglas

In recent years risk and danger have moved from the edge to the centre of theorizing about contemporary capitalist societies. The world, natural and social, seems to have become a much more dangerous place than ever before. This probably reflects a new high level of risk-awareness that is directed to the potential dangerousness of other people. This chapter is about how public perception of danger is sharpened and directed. It focuses particularly upon the expectation of social dangers. Instead of helping us to overcome primitive fears of otherness, contemporary trends encourage us to redefine and dread the Other. The argument will be that this new attitude to deviance is a side effect of new forms of social regulation.

The majority of criminologists tend to use one of two models of social influence. Both focus on the social production of deviance. Self-control theories (Hirschi 1969; Gottfredson and Hirschi 1990) focus more on the existence of an inherent evil within individuals that socialization tames, instead of trying to explain the differential amount and content of socialization (Bernard 1995: 81). Empirical research in support of these theories (e.g. Farrington *et al.* 1988a, 1998b) associates the probability of offence with low self-control and low individual capacity to delay gratification; it then attributes both to the control exerted by the family and other institutions during childhood and youth. To argue that failures in socialization are at the origin of deviant behaviour is a sound and useful affirmation but it is also a tautological one.

The other model focuses on how definitions of deviance are constituted and how they change according to collective priorities.[1] Every community establishes its own idea of what is deviant according to how it establishes its norms. It is futile to analyse rule-breaking without having some idea of the processes that produce the rules. In fact, the introduction of preventive legislation is an admission of the failure of informal prescription. For this model, deviance is that behaviour which seems dangerous for the configuration of social relations, and note that it *seems dangerous*, without necessarily being so.

Adopting either of these approaches does not, however, resolve the central criminological question which, we think, must be asked anew: who are the deviants today? They are not the moral incorrigibles of the past and they are known to be disadvantaged. They are not to be morally condemned but they are to be contained. They are not to be patronisingly 'treated' but they are to be avoided, even though without value judgements. They are not detestable but they are disposable. They are simply 'dangerous', 'suspicious', 'aggressive, 'threatening', 'dodgy'. They do not need to break rules to be excluded. Their committing an offence is a matter of secondary importance to those parts of society that define what deviance is, a matter to be dealt within the social and geographical spaces where the deviants are concentrated. What is important is their perceived probability of being dangerous and this can even be associated with completely legal behaviour, like that of adolescents gathering together at the entrances of buildings in which they live. Such behaviour is a major cause of fear of crime even though it is open to observation. It is almost as if poor young people should pretend that there is a job waiting for them in the morning and go to bed early, and children from the housing estates should 'keep out of trouble' by staying indoors as if they had departed on a language exchange scheme abroad.

What are the norms that govern this new amoral assessment of the Other? How are they produced and reinforced? We can assume today that only in pre-modern societies norms were created spontaneously and informally, through immediate proximate interaction. On the foundation of this proximate norm, modernity built the formidable tool of massive, detailed legislation. The law is present enough today

---

[1] The major works in this direction include Rusche and Kirchheimer (1939), Melossi and Pavarini (1981) and Foucault (1977). Garland's (1990) critical overview of our understanding of penality reconstructs the premises of this approach. Melossi (1998) argues for its internal Marxist coherence.

for us to know its organizational influence, but what is its social basis, if there is one? For one thing, it is not a legal understanding of deviance that urges the middle classes to drive faster at the sight of a housing estate. Is this a new norm of distance rather than proximity, or perhaps the vacuum left by the decline of the evaluative norm? There is a large question mark behind the origin and the content of contemporary social regulation which cannot be dealt with, we think, through readjusted Foucauldist arguments on the transition of forms of social control at the emergence of modernity.

Nowadays spontaneous norms respond to prior changes in sociotechnical environments and to the laws which maintain these environments. Electronic information technology designs ways of organizing. These can be anything from magnetic gates at shops and password-protected computer networks to automatic turnstiles and image analysis systems. Anyone familiar with Foucault's analyses and the ensuing discussions on the dispersal of control (Mathiesen 1983; Cohen 1985; Marx 1987) and the 'electronic panopticon' (Lyon 1994; Sewell and Wilkinson 1992) will perhaps frown. It has all been said before. Technologies of control have not been invented in the last decades, they will say. Basically all technology is made for ordering the world and reproducing it. Modernity has applied these ordering techniques to humans, under the general category of discipline. It has produced its own masterpiece: the rational subject biographically, socially and politically modern. So, what is new? Basically, several things.

Automated Control

The continuing increase of technological mediation in human relations is not instigated by the police. It is generated by the economy and promoted by the state as a limitless field for capitalist competition and, accordingly, as a means of perpetuating existing social structures and the supremacy of the First World. To reduce contemporary technology to a set of disciplining devices is to miss the point twice: in terms of the wider importance of technological mediation in human societies and in terms of the qualities of contemporary forms of social control. We will make four suggestions in order to propose an alternative thesis on the relevance of technological applications for the study of social control. We will focus on the contact of some technological systems with individuals and crowds and, more particularly, on what we will call, for lack of a better term, Automated Socio-Technical Environments (ASTEs).

These are technology-based contexts of interaction that regulate, organize or monitor human behaviour by integrating it into a pre-arranged environment, built upon a conception of 'normality' or 'regularity' that all subjects are expected to reproduce. As it has been often pointed out, we come across such automated environments today in most of our contacts outside the domestic sphere.

1. ASTEs, once made, do not involve active human participation. Their internal workings are impenetrable for the user who only receives their responses. It is meaningless to try and establish what is wrong with the magnetic band of an underground ticket, with the PIN of our bank card or with the password for reading our e-mail. In fact, when we are refused access we are by now trained enough to know that the system is precise and reliable and that we ourselves have probably disregarded the parameters that the ASTE has set for us (we have typed for example our password in capital letters or inserted our ticket face down). When the ASTE rejects a contact the user can essentially do one of three things: either find what the error is on his/her side and put it right, or refer to that level of organization where a human contact can be established, or quit the attempt (for example by buying a new ticket or by using a second e-mail address). All these options lead to different interesting results; the fundamental point, however, is that the user cannot negotiate with the system.

What is involved here is a transformation of culture[2] so radical that it amounts to denial. Negotiation is the prime constituent of culture. The cultural process involves essentially the mutual understanding of communication and the development of mental skills that promote it. In that sense, cultural production is an elaborate reflection of social interaction. The deeper and sharper knowledge about the most effective strategies in each context of interaction comes from situations where we have to convince others about what we are and what we can, or cannot, do. Being calm and articulate improves our chance of convincing the ticket collector that we have really lost our ticket. Of course, this has nothing to do with the truth. But it has to do with cultural bias. This is why we use and simulate recognizable skills in order to pursue our aims, and in doing so we reproduce and sharpen our cultural dexterities as such. But negotiating with an ASTE is by definition impossible. The limits of interaction are set in advance and the whole existence of the user is condensed into specific legitimizing signals

---

[2] We use 'culture' here in its sense as the socially conditioned cognition.

which are the only meaningful elements for the system. *ASTEs radically transform the cultural register of the societies in which they operate by introducing non-negotiative contexts of interaction.*

2. Values emerge as prescriptive beliefs for social interaction through collective reinforcement. Automated environments transform the reproduction of values. Approval or disapproval of the acts of other individuals, groups or institutions seems to be the fundamental element of value judgement and the practices which result from it. ASTEs are built to place their user in a binary environment, in the sense that there is a clear distinction between the positive and negative answer to each specific request. This does not depend upon the behaviour of the user but upon the validity of the single element of mediation that the system recognizes. In other words, for the system there are no good and bad, honest and dishonest—or, for that matter, poor and less poor—individuals. There are simply holders or non-holders of valid tokens for each predetermined level of access. The space which was before open to doubt, this major value incubator, is now merely experienced and judged as loss of time. Legitimization and action fuse within the automated context: what simpler way is there to know if you are allowed to use your ticket than to put it in the slot and wait for the system's acceptance or rejection?

Automated environments undermine the social processes of value reproduction and reinforcement not only through their increased reliability but through their focusing on one discrete aspect of the world. To a telematic server one is a 'caller', or more precisely a valid caller number. One is a ticket-holder in car parks, a 'press to cross'-button-pusher in pedestrian crossings, a 'too-fast-walker' in shopping malls scanned by an image analysis system. Only those parameters that the ASTE is built to evaluate are relevant and in that sense the social universe is inevitably and progressively subjected to new configurations according to new managerial priorities. An integrated, coherent self is not necessary for dealing with an automated system because the system has its own unshakeable coherence into which it incorporates the acts of its user on a strictly delineated domain; the rest of the user's identity is simply meaningless each time. The fact that ASTEs are one-faceted, monosemic environments turns their users from coherent actors into mere fragmentary 'activators'. This results in value erosion. Values pertain to self-identity because they are projected into social interaction through a *coherent* line of attitudes (and coherence exists only in the interpretation of these attitudes by others). Far from having only one facet at a time, human interaction is polysemic: it co-assesses all visible elements of individuals or collectivities to which it ascribes meaning. Even when there is a main task to be completed in human interaction, there are as many ways of completing it as there are degrees of politeness. It is not because we can do a particular job that our way of speaking or dressing becomes irrelevant when doing it. In fact, we are continuously assessed from all angles that others can develop, to a point that recognizable ways of speaking and dressing make us good or bad candidates for that job. Values emerge and reproduce as patterns of conformity that polysemic social interaction creates through time.

Automated environments corrode the evaluative foundations of conformity by abolishing the distinction between value-based human performance and the good function of an automated system. There is a virtual identification between the activation and the reaction of the system, both in terms of time and of meaning. *What we are witnessing here is a structural tendency towards the replacement of the law-abiding citizen with an efficient user.* On the level of norm production there is a corresponding shift. Rules in polysemic human interaction must respond simultaneously to all registers of evaluation in order to become established. This allows for a coherent spectrum of normativity across each society, part of which can be formalized as law. In automated interaction there is no distinction between what is normative and what is practicable. All that works is norm and all that does not is deviance. In an efficient socio-regulating package, deviance becomes impossible and the norm becomes a technical rule of action, a neutral parameter independent of decisions and values. This is probably the most important transformation in the area of social control ever, at least outside exceptional periods of massive change in social regulation, such as wars, revolutions or major disasters.

3. It is the first time in human history that we have the opportunity to experience forms of control that do not take into account any category of social division. Age, sex, race, beauty and attire are irrelevant and, what is equally important, guaranteed to be so. We stand in the middle of a massive development of egalitarian processes which cannot even be suspected to discriminate among their users. This assertion is not an attempt to brush aside the fact that stratifying parameters can be inserted in the settings of ASTEs, eg credit cards that offer different levels of service. The point is not that automated environments abolish other vehicles of class (in this case money) but that they cannot discriminate among users on other grounds than their quality as users.

The attendant of a car park may be readier to suspect you of having stolen the car you are driving to the exit if you are a young black male rather than an old white female—and you may suspect him more readily of suspecting you—but all this complicated socio-cultural mechanics becomes redundant before the ticket-operated barrier. You either insert the right ticket or you do not. ASTEs are the only egalitarian devices of control because they are not programmed to co-assess multiple factors of human sociality. The question for the students of deviance would, therefore, be to decide whether the propagation of ASTEs is a reason for rejoicing. After all, every criminological theory views criminalized deviance as dependent to some degree upon the perception of stratifying social factors. In that sense, spreading the use of automated environments for crime prevention might be, contrary to conventional wisdom, a real crusade for non-discriminatory measures to which criminologists should adhere without delay. Why simply leave this development to those who are mostly preoccupied with efficiency and cost effectiveness of preventive measures when the major positive effects are actually to be found in the decrease of social stratification? I will argue further on in this paper that ASTEs displace rather than eliminate class distinctions.

4. ASTEs self-evidently owe their existence to the development of information technology. The availability of a certain technology is only a prerequisite but not a reason for the applications that it will find. A prominent exponent of the 'situational crime prevention' approach can help us trace the origin of such applications: '[Fare evasion] was considered a particular problem at certain suburban stations serving the more economically disadvantaged parts of the metropolitan area. Two of these stations were Brixton and Stockwell, where ticket collectors regularly complained that *large numbers of passengers pushed past without a ticket and without offering to pay an excess fare*' (Clarke 1993: 123; added emphasis). The installation of automatic gates in these two stations led to a reduction of fare evasion by two thirds, meaning that the cost was recovered within only two years. The interest of the automated system here seems to be that it orders the world in a precise manner at an affordable cost. The essential point, however, behind the installation of automatic gates is that human sociality, before being 'treated' by the automated system, is problematic for the institution involved (in this case, the Underground).

It would be too expensive to deploy several surveillance agents permanently, but it would also lead to perceiving the underground station increasingly in terms of security and deviance rather than in terms of transport. Machines are different. They are fast and effective while being perceived at the same time as neutral, administrative devices. They isolate users and control their influx while they offer valuable feedback information at the same time. They process the prospective user with their mere existence, with the knowledge that there is no possibility of avoiding control. They are not there to normalize individuals and train their souls but to order the external world in an optimal manner for the institution. This optimal manner involves 'regularized' behaviour: in approaching the gate the user takes out the ticket, inserts it into the machine, takes it back and passes through; all that while probably thinking about something else. The process is the same for opening an e-mail or vocal mail box, accessing a database, getting a reserved plane or train ticket delivered by a lounge machine or withdrawing money from a cash point. A *regulatory procedure* is in many ways the 'good morning' of an efficient, computerized world to those who participate in it and it soon becomes a constitutive element and a recognized sign of efficiency as such. A world of underground ticket collectors waiting in their booth trying to take a rapid view of each ticket, and failing to do so in rush hours, already looks obsolete. Mainprize (1996: 17) associates the performance of 'smart machines' to Foucault's notion of 'action upon action' as a constitutive element of a relationship of power (Foucault 1983: 220). This is an attempt to transpose Foucault's comments on 'modes of action' to the area of automated control. These are, however, two radically different environments. Machines do not exert power, they are not perceived as beings but as tools, even when they impose constraints; *but nonetheless they favour specific relationships of power*. Automated regulatory procedures are not simply procedures of control. They are general management instruments for adapting the social world to the aims of the institution that uses them. Their purpose is to eliminate all those aspects of social interaction which prevent the institution from achieving its set targets. This is why automated environments operate on the basis of suspected potential dangers caused by their users.

Suspicion and Dangerization

Dangerization is the tendency to perceive and analyse the world through categories of menace. It leads to continuous detection of threats and assessment of adverse probabilities, to the prevalence of defensive perceptions over optimistic ones and to the dominance of fear and anxiety over ambition and desire. Dangerization concerns all areas of experience in contemporary societies as a direct repercussion of the dominance of institutional action over collective social interaction. Because postindustrial institutions are guarantors of safe, uninterrupted delivery of goods and services in every field of human action, individuals become concerned and vulnerable outside a context of institutional coverage. Dangerization applies to the natural and technical world, eg in the form of worries about food quality or car safety. But it also applies to the social world as a tendency to continuously scan and assess public and private spaces in terms of potential threats by other people. In an era where the dominant, democratic, civil society imposes its highly institutionalized, formally egalitarian model of social coexistence, difference and otherness can only be established in terms of dangerousness. Where atomized individuals mostly exist in each other's world as employees or users of institutions, new distinctive signs of social stratification have to be invented. The supermarket shopper, carpark user, tenant, or motorway driver next to us cannot any longer be socially constituted and assessed through what we know by now to be mere causes of prejudice, such as race, appearance or visible signs of wealth. Such collective assessments are socially banned and, in the case of race and sex, formally sanctioned. Judgement upon others must, therefore, be withheld except if it concerns particular individuals in particular circumstances. In potential dangerousness postindustrial citizens find the ideal way of reconciling the contradictory demands between ignoring identifiable collective characteristics and assessing unknown individuals. They build their old lines of bias on the new legitimizing basis of danger and by doing so they resolve the conundrum of non-discrimination. Far from an objective condition, presumed dangerousness is the major postindustrial criterion for distinguishing between those who should be avoided and those who can approach.

'Security' is now a major consideration at all levels, from choosing a neighbourhood to live in, to driving the children to their school, from following specific preventive strategies when walking home to not using underground transport after a certain hour or in specific areas. The findings of studies of fear of crime show a deep awareness of vulnerability (Ferraro 1995; Roché 1993) with victimization often being the most important concern of postindustrial citizens (Hough 1995). The unknown other who does not live in the same area, does not have

access to the same institutions, does not possess the same external signs
of appearance (wears different clothes and often has different skin
colour), does not use the same micro-codes of interaction (such as few
body movements, low voice, individual isolation) will continue to be as
segregated as ever. A postindustrial society has a postindustrial lower
class: heterogeneous, multicultural and relatively well educated. It is
the deepest rooted western cultural duty to demonstrate the clear historical break with feudalism, colonialism and industrial capitalism and
with their hegemonic visions of a stupid, savage or immoral lower stratum that, accordingly, deserved to be abused, enslaved or punished. It
is therefore impossible to assign to today's 'underprivileged communities' degrading structural qualities that justify their place. For the first
time, however, those masses of peripheral individuals dispose of an
option: either accept their exclusion from institutionally managed
spaces of stratified access as a neutral technical element of contemporary society, or refuse to do so and develop distinctive signs of difference. Because stratifying parameters are now managed by this 'third
party' that the institution appears to be, social divisions between strata
become a matter of visibility of difference, rather than difference *per se*.
Assimilation into the dominant model of behaviour is expected from
all. Territories managed by institutions introduce the obligation of
simulating equality both for those who can participate in the game and
those who cannot. Specific combinations of age, sex, race, clothing and
attitude re-emerge as indicators of dangerousness proven by, and leading to, exclusion from the smooth institutional environment. ASTEs
should be seen as risk management devices, through and beyond their
structural controlling properties.

From a social sciences point of view, risk is better analysed as the
elaboration of danger through probability, that is, a defensive cultural
structure indicative of a society's organization and antagonisms
(Douglas 1966, 1992; Douglas and Wildavsky 1982). Contemporary
accounts of late modernity (Giddens 1990, 1991) suggest that risk is
instrumental for understanding the process of reflexive modernization
(Beck 1992; Beck *et al.* 1994; Lash *et al.* 1996). It is a matter of observation to claim that risk issues are ubiquitous in late modernity, but it
remains to be shown where they come from, how they develop and why
they persist. Deviance is a perfect domain for exploring risk and danger because it refers directly to mutual perception of groups and individuals. The transition towards automation greatly affects the
construction and treatment of deviance in terms of risk. The fact that

ASTEs handle their users equally does not necessarily mean that such handling is positive. On the contrary, it is clear that automated environments treat all prospective users as potential offenders. In this they differ greatly from the usual human processes of social control which attend to eliminating exceptions. Non-automated polysemic social control focuses on surveying a socially meaningful space to see if all is as it should be—just like an animal surveys its territory—and on intervening only to suppress, or flee, threatening exceptions.[3] Automated environments and regulatory procedures do not operate on that basis. Instead of controlling for variance they verify conformity. This process of anticipatory *inspection* which will be discussed below, integrates control into an administrative institutional activity and for this reason completely dissociates it from the social bond.

Inspection trivializes suspicion. There has always been the world where social stratification is also reflected in presumptions about others: would anyone think that a man in an expensive suit with a briefcase and the *Financial Times* under his arm is likely to mug them for cash? But there is now another world where institutionally delivered suspicion falls equally upon everybody. This suspicion is simply pre-embedded in systemic parameters. It is not selective, therefore from a social viewpoint it is meaningless; but it has a real effect at another level since it both makes all users aware of the fact that there is a danger and identifies those who are excluded as dangerous. Closed circuit television, one way doors and gates, or magnetic tags on all items of a store insert a constant, visible security component into a wide range of spaces and activities. Despite the great diversity of techniques used, all automated environments converge upon introducing a consideration of danger. Instead of developing control structures and associations of beliefs, often leading to presumption and prejudice, collectivities are now atomized and injected with a specific type of danger awareness, peculiar to the institution and its interests. The projection of menace is at a small scale a defensive tactic but at a large scale it becomes a contemporary way of building institutional legitimacy.

Danger-based legitimacy currently becomes part of normality, from shopping to starting one's car. *The awareness of deviance is therefore dissociated from the direct or indirect experience of deviant behaviour and incorporated into the norm through continuous, small doses of automated control.* Instead of experiencing victimization or learning

[3] In fact, this is probably the process from an ethological point of view (Archer 1992).

about it, thus perceiving it inevitably as exceptional, the user is individually experiencing the omnipresent *probability* of victimization. This is the case with all visible measures of crime prevention: they are reminders of dangerousness. While in exclusively human environments safety measures take a frustrating quality when they become meticulous, as Shearing and Stenning (1985) have described it, in sociotechnical environments safety and security are inserted as parts of the system's competence (Davis 1990: 221–63). To a great extent, it is exactly this competence that legitimizes the regulatory procedure as a whole, as it is the case with security control in airports which have now spread to boarding lounges and locker rooms in train stations. The probability of a terrorist attack reigns every day over the millions of passengers who walk through detecting gates. As technology becomes cheaper, faster and more precise, ASTEs expand over all those who take the underground every day, go to big stores and supermarkets, buy their newspaper at the shop around the corner or pay a visit to their friends. This has already happened with CCTV and magnetic gates. It will certainly happen in the future with a series of other systems that the police will recommend and insurance companies will promote. A safety device available at a reasonable price which does not hinder the client's movement cannot but meet with commercial success. We are caught in a dynamics that increasingly colonizes the life-world through safe, controlled spaces and defines all non-monitored territories, and those who are in them, as dangerous.

Unintended Control and Inspection

There are two interconnected tendencies that traverse these developments. One has to do with the proliferation of awareness of dangers related to deviance; the other with the restructuration of what could until now be called without hesitation 'social' control and which increasingly takes automated asocial forms. These are fundamental transitions for human societies, although they are being introduced in a way that leads us to take them immediately for granted; they call for a conceptual and theoretical context capable of accommodating them meaningfully into wider social developments and can be used as building blocks for an analysis and interpretation of the contemporary social condition. Fragmentation of identities, erosion of values and tendencies of individualization are commonplace in contemporary sociology and political science (eg Aronowitz 1992; Inglehart 1990; Bell 1974;

Gane 1993). But they are often seen as intrinsic qualities of current social organization and this allows for symptoms being mistaken for causes. In the domain of social control for example, it is the mediation of the social world by institutions that causes the atomization of individuals, which is often recognized as a parameter of contemporary sociality. The capacity of the institution to centralize focused human behaviour around it gives rise to a new territory for preventive control. *Unintended control* seems to be an appropriate term for this form of ordering human behaviour, particularly because it helps to emphasize that there is no socially generated intention behind the application of control, no attempt to enforce prescriptive deontological categories upon the social bond, no interest in promoting values. Such outcomes, to the degree that they exist, are simply perverse effects of an administrative *dispositif* seeking to create its environment in its own image. To state this inversely, while non-conformity, in the past, mostly challenged dominant belief systems, it now challenges operational efficiency. It is not the Bible or the Constitution that defines what is deviant today, but increasingly the policy paper and the balance sheet.[4]

Most of us consider obvious the difference between a security officer and a cashier, but who differentiates between a magnetic tag, which is clearly a crime prevention device, and a bar-code label, which mainly helps to manage product flow? The reduced social content of methods and devices of control allows for the integration of distinct social roles into a managerial totality which creates its own institutional categories, peculiar to the osmosis between practices and values. Paradoxically, this is often done through the application of boundaries, limits and thresholds. In the architectural manipulation of space for example, the institution seeks to become distinct, to mark its own area. But in doing so, it creates a boundary. Depending on the activity involved, this can be done in different ways varying from access control systems to a distinctively cleaner part of the pavement in front of a department store. But in all cases, this is a technique for creating a threshold of legitimization. Behaviour within the set limits is monitored and assessed according to operational standards. This makes it

---

[4] It is the indirect cost of specific types of dangerous deviance that can damage the image and the rhythm of the institution. This is particularly visible with big retailers, whose first priority is to maintain a safe, agreeable ambience before dealing with other forms of deviance (eg shoplifting). The direct cost of crime, however, is not negligible. Estimations based on the British Crime Survey report £780 million for the retail sector in the UK and £275 million for the manufacturing sector (Mirrlees *et al.* 1995). The insurance industry, profitably, faces a great part of this cost.

often impossible to distinguish between control and service. Even human interaction can become part of this assimilation: take for example the case of a department store employee who approaches a client looking at the floor guide for longer than usual. The stereotypical question 'may I help you?' is at the same time an examination of the client's legitimacy and an opportunity for the latter to get faster where he or she wants. The purpose of the act is to secure an optimally smooth context for business without disruptions and bottlenecks.

Control becomes accordingly an unintended effect of the continuous processes of inspection that the institution applies to its activity. Knowing as many details as possible about its field of operation allows the institution to plan its action more efficiently. CCTV is installed 'for our safety' in almost every institutional space open to the public. Its purpose is not to invade privacy, although it can do so (Lyon 1994; Lyon and Zureik 1996), but to supply useful information for management purposes. In such conditions of increased transparency, the institution is able to analyse its domain of activity and develop processes for the prevention and suppression of 'incidents'. From this point of view, there is no difference between traffic congestion, frost and joy-riding in terms of motorway CCTV monitoring. All three situations belong to the category 'must be dealt with'. The data, in this case images, are not being gathered as part of an attempt to exert general control upon human beings but as a detailed map which can supply answers to elaborate inquiries directed at improving institutional operationality (Mosco & Wasco 1988). Detailed data are therefore to be obtained as a principle, since it is widely established that they allow for ever-deeper analysis and finer targeted action. To give another example, the reason why each consumption item is individually identified by the use of a bar-code is not related to credit card fraud, but rather to a continuous series of business administration issues. However, the identification of each article allows also for building and applying 'profile' techniques to identify *potential* fraudulent credit card holders which the information system can isolate in fractions of a second while simultaneously alerting the security personnel. Detailed automated information permits the following sequence: (1) to ascertain that fraudulent card users often buy a small number of expensive items, (2) to isolate such cases in real time, (3) to observe and record the behaviour of the 'potential offender' through CCTV, (4) to activate at the time of payment a change of cashiers in order to delay the transaction and confirm data about the credit card, (5) to store the offender's car registration number and warn the police (Masuda 1993). It is impossible to argue seriously that any of the technologies involved has been developed against credit card fraud but they are all very effective in dealing with it when used for that purpose. The amount of examples reflecting such use of socio-technical systems is high and expanding fast in postindustrial environments. It is enough to watch a 'crime inquiry' television programme in order to see at what rhythm the cases of suspects recorded on CCTV multiply. In the same vein, it is not difficult to grasp how precise a credit card account statement is about the holder's movements and habits, or what information a satellite-guided car direction system contains, or how many security services can be interested in the data of air travel reservation systems. Yet, none of these devices has been built to serve inspection purposes.

The development of unintended control involves institutionally managed territories (physical or virtual). 'Managed territory' means in this context the space where the institution, in order to promote its interests, monitors and integrates human interaction into its activity to a degree that seriously affects sociality as such. Atomized 'users' are encouraged to interact exclusively with the outlets of institutional activity which can take any form, from employees behind counters to open access refrigerators packed with food, from video game screens to cyber-sites. From there, things take their natural course as in all processes that involve perverse effects. As Giddens puts it in a critical discussion of Merton's classic positions, 'the unintended consequences are regularly "distributed" as a by-product of regularized behaviour reflexively sustained as such by its participants' (1984: 14).

Managed territories are the exemplary fields of dominant institutional action over inter-subjective or inter-group interaction. At the same time, they constitute in postindustrial societies the majority of spaces where individuals unknown to each other may meet. The coincidence of these two factors leads to a very particular outcome: the social bond becomes redundant since the whole environment is configured to replace it completely by the atomized interaction with the institution. On the other hand, this general tendency of isolation between proximate non-interacting individuals takes on a specific meaning as it favours the conscience of a generalized suspicion, under the institution's all-encompassing management.

Sociality, Dangerization, Deviance

The more actors are subjected to institutional processes of 'clearance', the more such processes become identified as the new coordinates of social belonging and, by the same token, of social stratification. There is, accordingly, a great conundrum to be solved in the context of contemporary capitalist societies: that of reproducing lines of social division despite the institution's homogenizing intervention. The well-ordered world of polysemic class reproduction is currently being transformed to a new aggregate where stratification is directly judged by the capacity of admission to various, more or less excluding, institutional contexts. This does not mean, of course, that processes of class reproduction simply fail. On the contrary, as happens in all eras, they adapt to the new criteria and project upon them the perceptual configuration needed to distinguish between strata. Race, age, gender and poverty are being recast in the mould of dangerousness, which now becomes the emerging category for legitimizing social exclusion. Chocolate bar wrappings and empty aluminium cans thrown in abandoned flower beds do not any longer signify the lack of education and the weakening of local community bonds; they indicate non-managed—therefore dangerous and lawless—territories. It is the same with closed down shops, graffiti-marked walls, rusty cars parked over stains of engine oil, and teenagers in track suits. As ever, it is ensured that what the lower classes do is unacceptable. That suspicion and danger are the contemporary vehicles of this social axiom, shows precisely the shift towards a new sociality which is not based on dominant values but on avoidable threats. It follows that visible qualities which can be associated with the lower classes—such as race or subcultural attitudes—become automatic indicators of dangerousness.

Dangerization does not ascertain the *existence* of dangers. It is rather a constant social skill of scanning the environment for perceptual indices of irregularity, which are then perceived as menacing. That is why only activities which are 'different' from those undertaken by the classes of institutional users can be dangerous. The concept of 'incivility' has surely managed to unconsciously internalize this condition into the research categories of criminology and other disciplines. Consider for example the following paradox: it is incivility to gather legally in a doorway but it is not to let your dog foul in a public place, despite the forbidding signs that inform everybody of the offence. All possible explanations for this puzzle return to the essential fact that it is people of different classes that engage in these two behaviours. It is not behaviour as such that is of interest in conditions of dangerization but the connotations assigned to behaviour in terms of social belonging. 'Zero tolerance' crime policies, for example, target precisely these connotations. By 'rehabilitating' inner city spaces and erasing the signs of peripheral excluded cultures, they reclaim space as managed territory where safety is guaranteed. Those who live indeed in a socially rundown context are made to conform to the external signs of an orderly world. 'Zero tolerance' is the answer to the impasse pointed at by a 16-year-old member of a gang: 'Gangs are never goin' to die out. You all goin' to get us jobs?' (quoted in Davis 1990: 265). The plain reply is no, but we will force you to operate in an institutionalized way which does not produce alarming indices. The distribution of the risk of deviance is even more unfavourable to the poorer sections of the society than that of other dangers which are not purely sociogenic, such as road accidents or industrial pollution. When it comes to deviance, those very sections are seen as *sources* of risk and suffer the consequences of defensive behaviour, independently of their own participation in the process.

In the context of the dangerized social world, deviance is to an overwhelming extent a mere instrument for perpetuating social division. It is increasingly dissociated from legal offences and connected to perceived probable threats. To those who suffer from it least, crime is mostly a category related to real estate investment, a 'quality of life' concept, rather than a legally punished type of behaviour. We are, therefore, faced with a new conceptual map that further increases the distance between crime and deviance. In all societies governed through the mediation of prescriptive values rather than through mere managerial efficiency, criminalized deviance can be seen as a reprocessing of social control through the more powerful strata of a society. But the postindustrial institution seeks power on its own account and inside its own activity without representing classes as collectivities. While the evaluative aspects of crime are peeled off, deviance emerges as an all-encompassing horizon for perceiving society at large. It supersedes both the limits of the legal system and the frames of opposed social interests in order to reach the level of a pervasive interpretation of otherness in terms of safety or possible threat. Satisfactory safety cannot be attained where the institution is not present. As a result, deviance, seen in the context of public social interaction, is essentially projected, not materialized; feared, not deplored; avoided, not confronted;

prevented, not suppressed. It is being transformed into a completely renovated socio-cognitive realm arising from the clear-cut boundary between managed territories and dangerous others.

The Safety Paradox

Deviance has become a category dominating public social interaction through institutionally mediated perceptions. It is now built on isolated facets of human activity rather than on comprehensive assessment of whole persons. These tendencies counter the long-fought-for distinction between legal and illegal behaviour, which guarantees the existence of margins for legal non-conforming behaviour. These margins become meaningless as dangerized perceptions disregard the difference between the unpleasant and the illegal. In this perspective there is currently an interruption in the consistent historical association between democracy and positive law which started with the publication of Beccaria's manifesto in 1764 and continued at least until the counter-culture movements of the 1960s and 1970s. This does not imply that there are tendencies to abolish legal processes and civil guarantees for defining, judging and punishing offences in postindustrial societies. The interruption of the process consists in the phenomenal takeover of sociality by institutional activity and the consequent dangerization of the social world. To state this differently, the legal treatment of deviance has simply become obsolete inasmuch as processes of social control are concerned. This is the deeper reason behind the emerging new model of justice and penality based on risk management that Feeley and Simon (1994) have described. Dangerousness is now the exclusive stake of social control and the justice system is simply bound to follow this pattern since its old tools, like values, responsibilities and duties have lost their social legitimacy and their relevance for social protection. The remedies of policing, committing to trial, judging, convicting, selecting and executing punishment are socially perceived as operational tasks which also help to identify avoidable urban spaces. This operational understanding of law enforcement allows for the liberal beliefs of the middle classes, who at the same time avoid 'high crime areas'. In fact, a degree of deviance that triggers a reaction from the justice system is already much beyond the limits of tolerability of a dangerizing culture and an ASTE dominated society. Proximity with such deviance is a social failure, a lack of capacity to access those spaces of interaction where managed territories follow each other without interruption, guaranteeing an acceptable, homogeneous behaviour by the participants. This condition does not simplify in the slightest degree the issues related to the legal definition and treatment of deviance but it reduces them to the level of a specialist subject. The debate field of 'law and order', increasingly exploited politically,[5] is more about order than law and even more about insecurity.[6] The governance of offenders and offences is now a separate subject from the management of dangerousness. The former is a field of public administrative competence, the latter a component of daily transactions and practices. There are, therefore, grounds to distinguish between 'illegal deviance' and 'dangerous deviance', which is not a sub-category thereof but a differently perceived ensemble.

Dangerization is not a static process, but a self-proliferating tendency which encompasses the entire life-world. As the institution supplies and guarantees control over a specific part of this world, dangerizing tendencies are being projected beyond the controlled sphere. Control generates new claims for predictability and certainty over new areas of experience. The existence of a standard quality of a specific product, let us say a box of cereals, available at a given place for a previously known price is not unrelated to a claim for trains that come on time and cars that start at will. A predictable world is a uniform cognitive entity with a structural centripetal tendency for more predictability over increasingly larger areas of human experience. In terms of social organization, this can be represented by a vicious circle: institutional activity → control → predictability → safety/certainty → vulnerability → dangerization → new claim for control → new institutional activity . . . and so on. Control delivered by institutional mediation is a product that incorporates its own demand. Safety is not attained as a result of bounding schemes of social interaction but is delivered to unrelated, atomized individuals who thus become aware of their dependent vulnerable position in a world denuded from the stabilizing effects of culture. It is among such 'under-cultured' individuals of the postindustrial era that the delivery of safety leads to demands for its increase. This apparent paradox today plagues all areas of postindustrial sociality in an endless series of knock-on effects. It is, however,

---

[5] This exploitation seems to spiral upwards, independently from specialist findings, with victimization dangers being used as ideal fields of governmental competence. It begins to seem reasonable under these circumstances to call for a constitutional ban on reference to violence during political campaigns (Jencks 1991).

[6] It is revealing that in countries like France, where 'order' carries a strong totalitarian connotation, the coded reference for the same field of debate is 'safety' (*sécurité*).

internalized to a degree that renders it invisible even for social and economic analysts, who do not seem to take on board that pre-modern forms of sociality did not give rise to safety cultures when they dealt, and continue to deal, with challenges to uncertainty much more threatening than those posed by globalization, modern daily experience, or current forms of victimization. The safety paradox is not a consequence of increased danger, but a corollary of treating danger asocially, through technical and thematic institutional channels. It also reflects a transition from the industrializing phase of modernity, where danger was rationalized as an object-to-object category, to late modernity, where danger becomes a society-to-object concept and involves the management of relations among individuals, collectivities and institutions.

What is the future of deviance within the context of the safety paradox? The crystal ball of the social theorist can always come up with one or two dystopias of its owner's preference. But societies are self-balancing mechanisms and do not tolerate disorder for long. Wars of all against all happen rarely; what is more, wars have winners and winners impose their own type of order. Given that we cannot worry, or rejoice, about 'social explosion' in the long run, we need to decipher the processes by which deviance is constituted as a part of the general universe of postindustrial sociality.

It is not among the purposes of this essay to proclaim the arrival of an utterly homogeneous society. If deviance ends, this will happen as with all distinct social domains: by dilution into new schemes of culture and action which correspond more closely to the dominant pattern of social relations. Institutions in late modernity have already developed entire settings of interaction that often make deviant behaviour meaningless and simultaneously transform it into a managerial constraint. A generalized application of such practices will necessarily isolate deviant behaviour to such an extent that it is immediately dealt with by punitive measures. No decision by the justice system is needed for the cash distributor to retain a bank card because of a high overdraft. In the same way, an electronically tagged 'inmate' could automatically be banned from certain spaces, or be monitored upon entrance by a close surveillance unit, and a convicted driver could be denied access to the motorway. If institutional coverage of society surpasses a critical point, interdependence of managed territories will become (and is already becoming) dense enough to detect profiles of 'undesirable' behaviour. There is no need to refer such data to any centralized Big Brother-like authority. Exclusion from each territory of institutional activity will suffice in most cases to regularize the occasional challenger, particularly for the reason that there will be very few alternatives. The current difficulty of large excluded minorities, like the unemployed, to invent any type of social 'elsewhere' is already an omen of the great institutional ascendancy over contemporary conditions.

In the context of an increasingly automated and homogeneous institutional environment, the study of social control and deviance will have to refocus its interests and methods. As the mediation of values recedes and criminal law becomes merely another field of expertise and administration, it is increasingly necessary to expose in detail the social aspects of perceiving deviance and dealing with it. In particular, shifts in sociality and their underlying causes, such as the development of institutional mediation, are among the first issues to explore from a point of view of social regulation. Criminology needs to reorder its findings so as to meet the criteria of analytical categories of social reception and social activity. This would also be a major step towards recognizing the crucial importance of social control and deviance in attempting to comprehend sociality and social organization in postindustrial societies.

References

Archer, J. (1992), *Ethology and Human Development*. Hemel Hempstead: Harvester Wheatsheaf.

Aronowitz, S. (1992), *The Politics of Identity*. London: Routledge.

Beck, U. (1992), *Risk Society: Towards a New Modernism*. London: Sage Publications.

Beck, U., Giddens, A. and Lash, S. (1994), *Reflexive Modernization: Politics, Tradition and Aesthetics in the Modern Social Order*. Cambridge: Polity Press.

Bell, D. (1974), *The Coming of the Post-Industrial Society: A Venture in Social Forecasting*. London: Heinemann.

Bernard, T. J. (1995), 'Merton versus Hirschi: Who is Faithful to Durkheim's Heritage?', in F. Adler and W. S. Laufer., eds., *The Legacy of Anomie Theory: Advances in Criminological Theory*, vol. 6. New Brunswick, NJ: Transaction.

Clarke, R. V. (1993), 'Fare Evasion and Automatic Ticket Collection on the London Underground', in R. V. Clarke, ed., *Crime Prevention Studies*, vol. 1. Monsey, NY: Criminal Justice Press.

Cohen, S. (1985), *Visions of Social Control*. Cambridge: Polity Press.

Davis, M. (1990), *City of Quartz: Excavating the Future in Los Angeles*. London: Pimlico.

DOUGLAS, M. (1966), *Purity and Danger: An Analysis of Concepts of Pollution and Taboo*. London: Routledge.
—— (1992), *Risk and Blame: Essays in Cultural Theory*. London: Routledge.
DOUGLAS, M. and WILDAVSKY, A. (1982), *Risk and Culture: An Essay on the Selection of Technological and Environmental Dangers*. Berkeley: California University Press.
FARRINGTON, D. P., GALLAGHER, B., MORLEY, L., ST LEDGER, R. J., WEST, D. J. (1988a), 'A 24-year Follow-up of Men from Vulnerable Backgrounds', in R. L. Jenkins and W. K. Brown, eds., *The Abandonment of Delinquent Behaviour*. New York: Praeger.
—— (1988b), 'Are there Any Successful Men from Criminogenic Backgrounds?', *Psychiatry*, 51.
FEELEY, M. and SIMON, J. (1994), 'Actuarial Justice: The Emerging New Criminal Law', in D. Nelken, ed., *The Futures of Criminology*. London: Sage.
FERRARO, K. F. (1995), *Fear of Crime: Interpreting Victimization Risk*. NY: State University of New York Press.
FOUCAULT, M. (1977), *Discipline and Punish: The Birth of the Prison*. London: Penguin.
—— (1983), 'The Subject and Power', in H. L. Dreyfus and P. Rabinow, eds. *Michel Foucault: Beyond Structuralism and Hermeneutics*, 2nd edn. Chicago: University of Chicago Press.
GANE, M., ed. (1993), *Baudrillard Live: Selected Interviews*. London: Routledge.
GARLAND, D. (1990), *Punishment and Modern Society: A Study in Social Theory*. Oxford: Clarendon.
GIDDENS, A. (1984), *The Constitution of Society: Outline of the Theory of Structuration*. Berkeley: University of California Press.
—— (1990), *The Consequences of Modernity*. Cambridge: Polity Press.
—— (1991), *Modernity and Self-Identity: Self and Society in the Late Modern Age*. Cambridge: Polity Press.
GOTTFREDSON, M. R. and HIRSCHI, T. (1990), *A General Theory of Crime*. Stanford: Stanford University Press.
HIRSCHI, T. (1969), *The Causes of Delinquency*. Berkeley, CA: University of California Press.
HOUGH, M. (1995), *Anxiety about Crime: Findings from the 1994 British Crime Survey*, Home Office Research Study 147. London: Home Office.
INGLEHART, R. (1990), *Culture Shift in Advanced Industrial Society*. Princeton, NJ: Princeton University Press.
JENCKS, C. (1991), 'Is Violent Crime Increasing?', *The American Prospect*, 4.
LASH, S., SZERSZYNSKI, B. and WYNNE, B., eds. (1996), *Risk, Environment and Modernity: Towards a New Ecology*. London: Sage,.
LYON, D. (1994), *The Electronic Eye: the Rise of Surveillance Society*. Minneapolis: University of Minnesota Press.

LYON, D. and E. ZUREIK (1996), 'Surveillance, Privacy, and the New Technology', in D. Lyon and E. Zureik, eds., *Computers, Surveillance, and Privacy*. Minneapolis: University of Minnesota Press.

MAINPRIZE, S. (1996), 'Elective Affinities in the Engineering of Social Control: The Evolution of Electronic Monitoring', *Electronic Journal of Sociology*, 2/2.

MARX, G. T. (1987), *La Société de sécurité maximale*, paper given at the 38th Cours International de Criminologie, 'Nouvelles tecnologies et justice pénale', University of Montreal, 21 August 1987.

MASUDA, B. (1993), 'Credit Card Fraud Prevention: A Successful Retail Strategy', in R. V. Clarke, ed., *Crime Prevention Studies*, vol. 1. Monsey, NY: Criminal Justice Press.

MATHIESEN, T. (1983), 'The Future of Control Systems: The Case of Norway', in D. Garland and P. Young, eds., *The Power to Punish: Contemporary Penality and Social Analysis*. London: Heinemann.

MELOSSI, D., ed. (1998), *The Sociology of Punishment: Socio-structural Perspectives*. Aldershot: Ashgate/Dartmouth.

MELOSSI, D. and PAVARINI, M. (1981), *The Prison and the Factory: Origins of the Penitentiary System*. London: Macmillan.

MIRRLEES-BLACK, C. and ROSS, A. (1995), *Crime against Retail and Manufacturing Premises: Findings from the 1994 Commercial Victimisation Survey*. London: Home Office.

MOSCO, V. and WASKO, J., eds. (1988), *The Political Economy of Information*. Madison: University of Wisconsin Press.

ROCHÉ, S. (1993), *Le sentiment de l'insécurité*. Paris: PUF.

RUSCHE, G. and KIRCHHEIMER, O. (1939/1968), *Punishment and Social Structure*. New York: Russell & Russell.

SHEARING, C. and STENNING, P. (1985), 'From the Panopticon to Disneyworld: The Development of Discipline', in A. Doob and E. Greenspan, eds., *Perspectives in Criminal Law*. Ontario: Aurora.

SEWELL, G. and WILKINSON, B. (1992), 'Someone to Watch over me: Surveillance, Discipline and the Just-in-Time Labor Process', *Sociology*, 26/2.

WACQUANT, L. J. D. (1992), 'Au chevet de la modernité : le diagnostic du docteur Giddens', *Cahiers internationaux de sociologie*, 43.

6

Statism, Pluralism and Social Control

PAUL HIRST

As we enter the twenty-first century it is appropriate to question whether social control through the legal order and institutionalized policing is now effective.[1] (One may question whether the remedies to contemporary social problems might *not* involve policy and institutional changes that are radical departures from the main line of development of social control in this century. That line could well be presented in classic whiggish fashion as the steady increase in social control through progressive legislation and social reform. It could be argued that by 1960 Britain and the USA had become relatively homogeneous societies, with growing equality in income distribution as an effect of full-employment and improved welfare provision, and that legal regulation had increased in scale and scope so that the old legacy of *laissez faire* had been replaced by a new liberal collectivism in which most major social activities were under effective public supervision or control. Obviously, this view could be, and was, challenged in detail: for example, by the Civil Rights movement in the USA, or by the campaigns for abortion and divorce reform, the decriminalization of homosexuality and for the abolition of the death penalty in the UK. But most reformers were themselves committed to the notion of a magnificent journey toward betterment, of which their own actions were perceived to be part.

[1] Social control is defined very broadly here to include not only criminal law, but the regulation of social affairs in a much wider sense. The supervision of social action to ensure certain outcomes, summed up in the eighteenth century notion of 'police', is thus the focus of this discussion. On the concepts of governance and social control see Rose (1999). The arguments in this chapter have been deliberately confined to the UK and USA.

Outline of a Crisis

It would hardly be possible to present such a view today. I raise the issue as to why with two events taken at random in the last week of May 1999. These sharply illustrate two major trends in policing and in state regulation that have arisen on the ruins of mid-century liberal collectivism. They are plucked from many similar events that could have been chosen instead and that are effects of a crisis in the relationship of the state to the wider society that is especially acute in Britain and the USA.

In Los Angeles a middle-aged black woman is shot and killed by police trying to determine whether the shopping trolley she was pushing was stolen.[2] The woman, a graduate who had lost a respectable job because of mental illness, appeared to challenge the police officers with a screwdriver. In England Summerhill School, a progressive school since the 1920s, is threatened with closure after a visit by central government school inspectors.[3] The reason for the school's bad report is its very *raison d'etre*: pupils can decide when, or if, they study. To accuse the school staff of weak leadership is to deny the school's educational philosophy any validity; government performance norms must be rigidly applied. For those who are not British, it is important to know that Summerhill is a private fee-paying school.

What these two cases exemplify is a last ditch attempt to make policing and legal regulation succeed as means of social control in circumstances that are increasingly ill-suited to such methods.[4] In the United States, and to a lesser extent the UK, the local adoption of zero tolerance policing strategies, the increasing use of custodial sentences and mandatory sentencing, and extensive prison building programmes are results of a populist political response to public fear of rising crime. The police are seeking to control an increasingly heterogeneous and unequal society, in which their effects bear almost exclusively on one part. At the same time, other pressures from rather different middle class constituencies, professionals and issue activists, extend the scope of legal regulation in order to protect citizens against an ever widening range of contingencies. The result is to create a rapidly growing volume of new legal norms and new public inspectorates to police them.

---

[2] See the *Guardian*, 29 May 1999, p. 21.
[3] See the *Times Education Supplement*, May 1999.
[4] I do not pretend to be a criminologist. For a survey of responses in policing and punishment see Garland (1996).

Litigation grows with each new law. Intervention by a growing army of public health inspectors, social workers, environmental agencies and financial regulators produces a complex web of control seeking comprehensively and consistently to enforce an ever growing body of norms.

Neither of these strategies is working, even in their own terms. Both are attempts to enforce hierarchical control in complex circumstances that render it ineffective, and on the contrary, that require more diverse, decentralized, and self-regulatory strategies.[5] At its worst, the new politics of policing and corrections amounts to a brutal war against the poor. Mike Davis has chronicled the various attempts to repress and contain outcast Los Angeles (Davis 1990, 1992, 1998). The inanities of the ultra-regulatory supervisory state have yet to find an adequate chronicler. If zero tolerance policing reaches its extreme in New York and Los Angeles, then state inspection reaches it apogee in Britain.[6] We now have regular crises and absurdities: from social workers hunting for imaginary satanic abusers in ways reminiscent of the early-modern European witch craze, to lunatic scrutiny procedures for prospective parents that prevent children being adopted, or to health regulations that forbid people willing to take the risks from eating beef on the bone or eating cheese made from unpasteurized milk. Such inanities are the result of two combined, if apparently contradictory, tendencies: 'one-size-fits-all' regulatory policies applied to diverse circumstances and to groups with different values; and the growth of administrative discretion on the part of regulatory professionals, which is an effect of the increasing complexity and inconsistency of the rules that result from trying to subject activities to ever more detailed central norms.

Zero tolerance policing is a contradiction in societies that apparently pride themselves on constitutionalism and limited government. For the strategy to be effective the poor and black have truly to be excluded, to become a distinct *de facto* status group outside of normal citizenship who can be stopped, searched, bullied, beaten, shot at and jailed at will. For this to happen, our societies would have to abandon their core values, to drop the belief in the equal worth of all citizens and the pretence of equality before the law. The cruel and unequal treatment that

[5] I discuss this issue of the growing problematicity of the prevailing models of governance in Hirst (1997, ch. 1).
[6] Some sense of the new inspection state can be gleaned by combining Jenkins (1996), Weir and Hall (1994), and, invaluably, Power (1997).

such strategies must inevitably tend to produce generates regular crises in the relation of the police to the public. The poor and the black have a sense of justice too. Occasionally it is heard, such as the Rodney King riots, or the Stephen Lawrence scandal in the UK, or the protests over the death of Amadou Diallo. Middle class citizens, however fearful of the excluded, know something is wrong when the police shoot at a harmless street seller forty-one times. It is not that harassment and neglect cease but that the periodic crises mean that they cannot be systematized; scandals interrupt such practices even if they do not eradicate them.

Zero tolerance policing inevitably criminalizes life on the street. Overlying widespread fears about the street is a dystopian vision of a 'Blade Runner' society that has gained wide currency as the model of our collective future. In this systematically unequal society a secure corporate elite lives a completely separate life in its fortified office towers and gated communities from an excluded, impoverished and brutalized mass.[7] Although there are obvious examples of such phenomena in the USA, this is an improbable general outcome for modern societies. In fact populist policing exists to satisfy the large middle class in between the small elite of the rich and the rising numbers of the poor. The middle class cannot afford total security, their kids go to public schools, and they regularly have to use the streets. That broad middle class is central to the existence and survival of modern capitalism. The office towers cannot survive without high mass consumption. The millionaires protected by armed response security in their luxury houses are a mixture of business executives and *rentiers*: they are rich because high mass consumption feeds into their own salaries, dividends and stock values. Social solidarity in values and *mores* may have broken down in the more brutalized parts of the USA, but the structured interdependence inherent in the complex division of labour in the advanced societies remains. To fuse the not so contradictory logics of Adam Smith and J. M. Keynes, it is not upon the benevolence of others but on their effective demand that we depend for our livings.

Many of the rich imagine that they live in a pure market society, in which they will pay for what they choose and that only includes the absolute minimum of public goods. But a market society is an impossibility, for the market is not a society but a series of exchanges. These exchanges are conducted between people whose attributes are not

---

[7] On the spatial dimension of this see the essays in Sorkin (1992) and for a revealing account of the film see Scott Bukatman's *Blade Runner* (1997).

wholly constituted in or by exchanges.[8] Current public policy in the USA seems determined to ignore this fact—it appears to imagine that responsible social agents can be either created by the market or coerced into existence. It has, through its tax policies and cuts in welfare and other public services, abandoned investing in building the citizens of a sustainable social order. Regressive tax policies have allowed income inequalities to run riot. The social security net, thin to begin with, no longer pretends to protect the weak against the contingencies of market forces (Pierson 1994). The major growth areas in public spending are those concerned with repression. The result of such policies is fear and insecurity and demands for greater social control. The same tendencies have been evident in the UK on a lesser scale, as are the fears about a breakdown in social order and social control.

It will be obvious to most readers that the issues central to social control are not mainly social control issues at all. Rather they are the following: does the economic and welfare system create and maintain a rigid boundary between the middle classes and the poor? How are the poor treated? How many of them are there? None of these issues can be settled by policing, they are matters of social organization. Insofar as they are subject to policy intervention, then it is economic and welfare policy which is at stake. I shall argue that the crucial issue in welfare in the 'Anglo-Saxon' countries is to counter tax aversion and to build common institutions that both the middle classes and the poor will use. A pauper welfare state will never achieve the aim of lifting the poor out of poverty. Targeted at the poor alone and paid for by the middle classes who hope they will never use it, it will always be provided at a level below that which could possibly integrate the poor into society. I shall argue that an associative welfare system could go some way to unlocking this problem (Hirst 1998).

Intensified normatizing regulation by a new class of supervisory professionals is also self-defeating and contradictory in its effects. Again a dystopian vision has been constructed on the basis of the proliferation of such regulation, that of a 'surveillance society' in which every aspect of social life is subject to control by inspection.[9] This is frequently seen

---

[8] This point has been obvious to sociologists since the days of Durkheim, but such voices are seldom heard in the economic liberal circles to which the rich pay heed. Paradoxically, as economic liberal policies have sought to strip mine the social foundations of a market economy, socio-economists have given a new saliency to the notion that market economies can only function with appropriate nonmarket institutions—for an example see, Rogers Hollingsworth and Boyer (1997).

[9] This is usefully discussed and criticized in Rose (1999: 240–6).

in terms of the new potentialities of electronic eavesdropping, but the more real threat is of auditing as the central tool of top-down central control in combination with centralized discretionary funding. The school inspector, the social worker and the accountant are more concrete sources of such control than are super-computers. As we shall see, such strategies of inspection and control are the combined result of new and multiple demands on government and a crisis of the means of governance of complex activities that threatens to undermine centralized authority. Such strategies are an attempt to assert hierarchical control in a world of strong pressures towards decentralization and autonomy.

The growth of regulatory agencies and of professionals supervising ever wider aspects of social life in ever greater detail has become an object of concern in circles far wider than traditional civil rights liberals and *laissez faire* conservatives. Such tendencies to control lead to what Carl Schmitt called 'motorized legislation', in which the quantity and complexity of primary and delegated legislation increases exponentially (Schmitt 1990). This is especially obvious in a country like the UK, where the executive runs the legislature and makes it a tool of government. The principal danger of such intensified regulation by the state is that is undermines the rule of law. This is firstly by the sheer volume of rules produced, which baffles even specialist lawyers. Laws cease to be a guide to action in any normal sense, they are rather the empowering of governmental agencies. Laws do not aim at the citizen, but at officials in their capacities as regulators of citizens' activities. It is secondly because such complex and overlapping norms inevitably give professionals great discretion as to whether or how to use and to interpret them. The result is a tendency to undermine rule-bound government. Government ceases to be limited, it is everywhere, despite all the talk of the 'retreat of the state'. It also ceases to be calculable; enforcement becomes something of a lottery. Limited government is the foundation of a liberal society, in which there is a distinct private sphere lightly regulated by law. The new regulatory state is in danger of creating a post-liberal society, in which government becomes ubiquitous and arbitrary and rule application an arcane process. One might call this a *nouveau ancien regime*.[10]

---

[10] This notion is intended to capture the points made by Enlightenment critics like Cesare Beccaria of the *ancien regime* system of justice and police, that it was inconsistent and arbitrary, opaque to the citizen and, therefore, unable to regulate conduct in a moral way. Beccaria's *On Crime and Punishments* repays reading not as a historic text but as a form of contemporary social criticism.

The United States may have cut back on welfare and social spending, but it too has produced its own variant of the supervisory state, nor has public spending as a percentage of GDP fallen, despite reduced entitlements for the poor. In the UK, however, the combination of a highly centralized governmental system in the hands of the core executive and the demolition of countervailing powers has produced an extreme version of this strategy of government by regulatory surveillance. Indeed, the central feature of this system is the attempt to achieve control by promoting uniformity, standardizing the activities regulated according to detailed performance norms.

The result of this new regime is not in fact systematic surveillance but caprice, and a clash between standardized definitions of norms and the widely different values groups of citizens bring to issues like health-care, education, environmental protection, public health and moral conducts. Adoption, abortion, the consumption of cigarettes, alcohol and recreational drugs, the limits of pornography and of adults' relations with children, and many other issues, become politically explosive conflicts, in which groups contend over the scale and scope of state regulation. The problems with surveillance based on norms are that norms are contested and increasingly so. The problem is that in a centralized sovereign state with a single legal system someone must win and someone must lose in such contests over the content of law. This conflict can be somewhat limited by the centrality of constitutionalism and the scope for differing legislation by the states in the USA. This shifts the conflicts to the Supreme Court and the state legislatures but it does not eliminate it. Similarly, the US is sufficiently large that to some extent a *de facto* separation into different regulatory regimes takes place on a state and municipal level. Yet clashes continue between Federal Agencies like the FBI and ATF and value-based groups as diverse as deep ecologists and Christian fundamentalists.

How Did We Get Here?

In 1960 Britain and the USA were still living in the afterglow of wartime solidarity and the reforms of 1945–51 and the New Deal and Eisenhower's Cold War Keynesianism respectively. Both were societies substantially made up of manufacturing sector employees and manual workers generally, mostly employed by large corporations. In both the UK and the USA manufacturing employment has fallen to less than a quarter of the labour force and services predominate. Companies have changed radically, especially in the USA. Many have reinvented themselves as more flexible and less formally bureaucratic organizations. The collapse of standardized mass production in the 1970s produced a serious crisis for manufacturing in both countries (Piore and Sabel 1984). It shattered hitherto unassailable companies, like US Steel. It also undermined the power of trade unions and the prevailing forms of institutionalization within companies of labour rights and work norms in both economies.[11] Companies have been largely rebuilt on a radically different basis, one in which managers have acquired the power to manage and the capacity to divert a significant portion of the income stream from companies to themselves (Roe 1994). The result has been growing inequality of incomes in the USA since 1973, both pre- and post-tax, and the growth of the working poor.[12] Full employment in the US has been achieved in the 1990s on a very different basis from the 1960s.[13]

This has undoubtedly undermined the economic foundations of social solidarity. The USA has very high rates of job turnover and geographical mobility. Jobs are less and less the foundation of ordered lives in stable communities. It has also made it harder to provide welfare through work, as unionized job security has declined, and private health insurance is increasingly cut back by employers. The weak welfare safety net in the USA is less and less compensated by private occupational welfare.

The upshot is that the economy is harder to regulate, whether that regulation is by a series of localized contracts between corporations and organized labour, or else by the macro-economic management of the central government. Something analogous happened in the UK where the highly imperfect corporatist agreements between industry, labour and the state collapsed at the end of the 1970s and were rejected in principle thereafter.

The result in both countries has been a relative disembedding of the market economy from the social institutions that form and stabilize it, giving greater effect to market forces. The institutions at the level of the

[11] For a valiant attempt to look at such institutionalization see Storper and Salais (1997).

[12] See David Gordon (1996). In 1996 the top 5 per cent of income earners took 20.3 per cent of the national income and the top 40 per cent 70 per cent—*Historical Abstract of the United States* (1998, table 747, p. 473).

[13] Full employment conceals a vast amount of job 'churning' in which workers rotate through jobs and jobs are regularly abolished and created, workers often losing income when they are re-employed—see Farber (1997: 55–142).

firm and at the level of the major social interests in the national economy that had regulated work and the distribution of national income
between different groups have largely broken down. The result has
been a dislocation in the relationship of the state and the wider society
in respect of the economy. It would be a mistake, however, to imagine
that the new economic liberalism is just a return of the old *laissez faire*,
for that to be the case the state would have to spend less than 10 per
cent of national income. In both the UK and the USA general government total expenditure has risen from 32.2 per cent and 27 per cent
respectively in the supposedly high spending Keynesian welfare 1960s
to 42.5 per cent and 36.1 per cent in 1995. Public expenditure on social
protection remained relatively constant in the 1980s despite the ideological climate of Reaganism and Thatcherism: at 21.3 per cent in the
UK in 1980 and 22.3 per cent in 1990, and for the USA 14.1 per cent in
1980 and 14.6 per cent in 1990 (Hirst and Thompson 1999, tables 2.2,
2.3). The UK and USA have become bigger spenders, but not on social
security. On what then? In part on demands to meet new needs like
environmental protection, in part on the growth in other forms of
social spending—like health and education, but also on an increase in
regulation. With the decline of self-regulation between firms and
unions, and the breakdown of wider institutions of economic management, so the state has been forced to substitute control through
legislation and regulation. Law and inspection has grown as the countervailing power of unions and the scope of negotiated social governance has declined.

If the economy underwent major changes so did the bundle of services that successful citizens in work expected to receive from central
and local governments. Until the 1960s welfare was still emerging from
the period of what might be called 'basic' services that provided for contingencies and offered a bare minimum. Thus workers and their families were to receive unemployment insurance and basic pensions, help
with the doctor's bill, and services like mass public housing or elemen-
tary education. Now services are conceived on a very different basis. In
the UK higher education has become a normal expectation for about a
third of families, even the poor expect access to organ transplants, and
the stably employed have shunned public housing, benefiting from state
subsidies for mortgages, and have also supplemented inadequate public
basic pensions with private and occupational schemes.

In the 1970s growing demand for new extended services was
combined with the effects of widespread unemployment and social

dislocation, which put an increased demand on the more basic services. Hence the tendency to try to contain social spending throughout the 'Anglo-Saxon' world, irrespective of initial ideology. Thatcher's and Reagan's policies were echoed by the complete conversion of the New Zealand Labour Party and the partial conversion of the Australian one to economic liberalism. Equally, there were serious problems of the governance of the new extended welfare states. Such services were difficult to control, unlike the old basic ones. The latter could easily be provided by centralized government bureaucracies disbursing insurance entitlements or discretionary payments, and basic services were easy to deliver locally and to inspect since they were relatively homogeneous and standardized. The problem comes with extended services that rely mainly on professional labour forces. Universities, hospitals, social services departments all employ large numbers of professionals whose competence requires a large measure of autonomy in making judgements about given cases. This is also true of the regulatory personnel in new departments created by the need to meet and control new contingencies. Yet the centralized delivery of such services to national or local common standards is problematic. Professionals are not easy to regiment and they have an inherent tendency to seek more resources for their services. Hence the combination of the desire to contain spending and to reimpose hierarchical controls and impose common 'standards'.

Welfare states and companies have faced analogous problems of control. More flexible and customized methods of production demand a substantial measure of autonomy from shopfloor workers; without it they cannot accomplish the localized problem solving inherent in such methods. Some companies in the US have followed the logic of this productive flexibility, relaxing supervision regimes and involving workers in decisions (Sabel). Others have gone in the opposite direction, seeking to micro-manage from above and having more technician grade workers and supervisors to control the process in detail (Gordon 1996). Central government in the UK is engaged in an equivalent strategy of micro-management for the public sector. Seeking to regulate every last detail of the curriculum and teaching methods in schools, and attempting to set standardized performance norms for surgical procedures, are part of a strategy of delivering a standardized service with the least possible expenditure.

The problem with such micro-management is that two other social changes are working against standardization. It appears that inspection regimes can only discover the variability inherent in complex services, when such services were 'frozen' absolutely to a set of given standard performances, but in that case improvement, innovation, and competence based on learning would have be abandoned. Even if inspection regimes could standardize outcomes it is not clear that such outcomes are welcome to citizens.

First, most western societies have become more and more heterogeneous. This is especially true of the large cities. Los Angeles, New York, Toronto, London and Sydney, for example, have a vast range of different ethnic, religious and lifestyle groups. Such groups have different ideas about not only broad social values but also the specific content of services. Gays want services sympathetic to their concerns. Many middle class people would like various alternative therapies— from osteopathy to homeopathy—to be available through public health agencies. Ethnic groups in the US want their own university courses. Asian families often resent the intrusion of social workers in what they see as matters of private governance through family and community. One can extend the list indefinitely, and there is little prospect of a new homogenization.

Secondly, societies throughout the western world have become more individuated and more demotic. Widespread tertiary education and the growth of middle class occupations as a proportion of the labour force have led to a better educated population that possesses the material preconditions of personal autonomy. As mass consumption has become a dominant leisure activity, so people have become more used to choosing goods and services according to their own preferences. Equally, in all groups of the population, deference to and trust in elites has declined—people do not automatically believe officials and professionals know what is best for them. In that sense the age of guardianship, a central prerequisite of one-size-fits-all welfare, is over. Automatic obedience to collectivities like unions, parties and churches has declined too and most political collectivities are in severe decline both of numbers of members and the commitment of those members. Of course the USA is full of fanatical 'believers', Born Again Christians, radical ecologists, and so on, through a vast list of contemporary enthusiasms, but the difference is that they have *chosen* to believe and often change beliefs. The result of this growth in consumerist, non-deferential, and person-centred attitudes is that attempts to impose hierarchy and standardization are working against fundamental changes in society that are unlikely to be reversed.

How might we resolve the problems of social control and social welfare?

I have tried to show that the problems of social control, legal regulation and welfare are linked. The problems in each area stem from a common crisis in the relation of state to society. How might this be resolved? I will claim that the answer is associative democracy, in which publicly funded services are devolved to self-governing voluntary associations, and as many social institutions as possible, including private corporations, are mutualized and made answerable to the major interests affected by them—through the representation of those interests in the institutions' governance.[14]

Associationalism faces the fact that the institutions of representative democracy were invented in the eighteenth century to govern largely self-regulating societies in which the role of government was strictly limited. Such representative institutions are ineffective at rendering accountable modern ramified public service states, since the government plays the contradictory roles of service provider and the source of accountability for such services. Societies are no longer self-regulating. The notion of a 'civil society' of competing individuals and associations, in which authority is widely dispersed and easily counteracted, is no longer the case. In its place we have an 'organizational society' of state bureaucracies, quasi-governmental agencies, corporations and large bureaucratized bodies in the non-profit sector like charities, cultural foundations and universities.[15] Against such bodies individuals or small voluntary associations do not exercise effective countervailing power. Since the creation of representative government the modern corporation has come to dominate the economy and, increasingly, much of the wider society through its provision of marketed services and commodified leisure. Conceived as an association of private persons, the corporation has become a source of largely unaccountable hierarchical authority. Government has grown in scale and scope in part to aid and in part to restrain such corporate bodies that are best conceived as autocratic private governments. The problem of accountability of such private governments has become acute since the economic changes of the 1970s and the governmental changes of the 1980s.

[14] This is more fully developed in Paul Hirst (1994). See also Joshua Cohen and Joel Rogers (1996).

[15] Robert Presthus's *The Organisational Society* (1965) is still a valuable guide to this continuing growth and proliferation of bureaucracy.

Indeed one could argue that the effect of the latter, privatization and the growth of semi-autonomous agencies, has been to blur the division between state and civil society. Private companies now perform many public functions and have been granted public powers under law to do so. Public agencies are managed as if they were private companies and are encouraged to behave in a market-oriented way. Private companies are also now harder to control and to regulate. Hitherto unions exercised a substantial measure of countervailing power. The companies of the era of standardized mass production were large, but they tended to be highly centralized and their operations were relatively predictable, and, therefore, they were easier for public bodies to regulate.

It could be said we live in a 'post-liberal' order in the sense that the architecture of a liberal society—a limited representative government and a self-regulating civil society—has ceased to describe our main social institutions. Yet we persist in behaving as if representative democracy and a competitive market were the essential features of our social system. Because they are not, we are forced to create endless makeshifts that dig us deeper into the hole—more laws, more regulation, more inspectorates, more agencies, and less accountability. The only way to deal with the organizational society is to face the fact of its existence and the blurring of the public-private divide. Private and quasi-public governments need to be made more directly accountable to those whose interests they affect—a new principle of 'no impact without representation' needs to be introduced into our democracy. Private governments need to be seen for what they are, and not as something beyond the political system. Corporations and their property rights were the product of nineteenth century legislation, they are not natural institutions (Roe 1994; Alborn 1998). The advantage of associationalism is that it faces the fact of the organizational society; it places welfare back in the hands of citizens, by giving them public entitlements but the choice of how those services should be provided, and it treats all organizations whether public or private as governments in which members of the public should have a say if their specific interests are seriously affected.

Undoubtedly, a full-blown associationalist democratic supplement to the existing institutions of representative democracy, organizational power and the market remains in the realm of political ideas. However real our present problems, they have become opaque to most citizens as our societies have grown more complex. The prospect of democratizing the governance of companies is at present utopian, however real the need for such governance might be. The advantage of associationalism is that it does not involve a simultaneous and once and for all societal transition, like socializing a market economy or marketizing a socialist one. It can be introduced iteratively and piecemeal. If the associative principle gains ground in certain spheres, then it may be possible subsequently to extend it elsewhere. The advocacy of an associative reform agenda needs to start with the issues of out-of-control regulation and common services being imposed upon a heterogeneous society with disparate values. Thus the associative principle, of governance through voluntary organizations, can tackle three related issues:

1. conflicting community norms, through community self-government;
2. an over-extended regulatory state—through the growth of institutions that set decentralized and democratic norms, binding on their members alone;
3. by combining citizen choice and public provision in welfare, thus bridging the public and private sectors in welfare, and, thereby, reducing tax aversion and encouraging the middle classes and the poor to share common institutions.

Three points need to be made before we proceed further. These points stem from the fact that modern associationalism is based on the principle of individual choice and not on the belief of many traditional associationalists in our natural propensity to fellowship. It thus fits better with modern individuation than do many competing political doctrines. The first point follows from this, associative democracy is not a variant of communitarianism. In essence the communitarian movement seeks to rebuild social solidarity by an act of will, reinventing norms and values that we all supposedly share (Etzioni 1995). It also seeks to use this remoralization to compensate by citizens' self-action for tax aversion and thereby serve to prop up failing institutions. Associationalism accepts that there is a thin common morality, that most groups in society oppose murder, theft, lying and fraud. But beyond that they may conceive the social world very differently, and it is their specific normative programmes and desires for services of a certain type that lead them into conflict. A thin common morality means, however, that associationalism is a possible principle of social organization, that a society organized around distinct social groups will not descend into barbarism. The second point is that the groups in question are principally communities of choice not of fate. Individuals are free to join and to leave associations. Hence groups will not solidify into tribes: there will be circulation between them and also overlapping memberships—people will belong to different groups for different purposes.[16] Thirdly, the principal constraint on groups in an associationalist system is not voice but exit: individuals can leave and, with publicly-funded services, can periodically choose to move their formula-funded entitlements. Associationalism does not depend on a generalized principle of active citizenship. For those who want to be active, to build participative institutions, they are free to craft the forms that they wish. Most associations will, however, be representative democracies in which members have a right to vote for the governing body, but the main democratic constraint will be the fear of the loss of funds if policies are followed that prove contrary to many members' interests. It is the coexistence of competing organizations and the option of exit that provide the most effective check to organizational oligarchy.

Self-Governing Communities

If society is splitting into communities of choice then maybe we should accept that fact. We can see that in a heterogeneous society rules for one group about acceptable conduct will seldom agree with another— Born Again Christians and gays will disagree seriously about many aspects of how people should lead the good life. Imagine we decide to accept the existence of plural groups with different values as the foundation of rule making. How might they coexist and yet keep their own values? Certainly, not as at present fighting to come out on top in the representative democratic system and define central state legislation. A possible strategy is by a mixture of micro-governance, that is, special zones where different rules apply, and by mutual extra-territoriality, that is, the parallel existence of self-governing communities sharing the same space but applying rules in matters of community concern to their members alone.

Elements of such strategies exist already. If the Danes found they could, with difficulty, tolerate the anarchist enclave of Christiania in Copenhagen, then to everyone's surprise it has become almost normal, indeed, quite *bourgeois*. In the more liberal major cities like Sydney or Manchester we now have gay villages, not merely tolerated but

[16] In chapter 3 of *Associative Democracy* I have discussed how the various rights of inclusion and exclusion of individuals in and from associations might be justified on associationalist principles.

welcomed for the high-spending business they bring to town. In the Netherlands, the policy of deliberately not enforcing the law and accepting marginal zones or 'uiterwaarden' where prostitution and soft drug use are tolerated, has proved relatively successful (van der Horst 1996). To those who imagine there can only be one set of rules, one has only to counter with the example of religious tolerance that developed in Holland in the seventeenth century. The original meaning of religion, *religio*, is to follow a rule. Sixteenth and seventeenth century Europe was riven with religious civil wars in the aftermath of the Protestant schism, as rival religious groups sought to prevail. One might say modern American is riven with various low intensity 'social wars', in which whole communities are criminalized in the pursuit of the War on Drugs, and abortion clinics are firebombed by religious fanatics. The United States is the most religious of the advanced countries, yet religious toleration has been one of the founding principles of the Republic. Almost nobody questions the right of Catholics or Jews to worship at they wish—well, imagine we extend the principle to social conduct?

This is not an argument against law, it is an argument for less state regulation and more community self-regulation and internal arbitration. Basing modern societies on such self-governing communities of choice would reduce the load of central inspection and rule making. This would check central state rule proliferation and allow different groups to manage their own affairs.[17] Laws could be simplified and applied to a thinner core of common social life and, in consequence, could be more effective. Far from undermining formal law, community self-regulation could restore public confidence in it. People would not be criminalized for matters of value choice—remember when homosexuality was a crime in the UK? In consequence they would not come to hold the whole apparatus of law in contempt. For that core of common offences, agreed by all, the police would enjoy greater cooperation and respect. Social control within communities and over the common law between them might well be more effective than now. Individuals could escape excessive and unwelcome community regulation by choosing to leave and the formal law would have to protect this right vigorously. The advent of greater community self-control would in the

---

[17] The principles and practice of informal arbitration and community self-regulation are well known to criminologists. The point of associationalism is to link them in with a wider doctrine of economic and social governance in which they cease to be exceptions to the mainstream.

long term tend to reduce inter-community friction. Individuals could govern their own affairs as they wished and would not feel threatened that moral minorities would gain control of legislation and threaten their lifestyle through the temporary fact of an artificial political majority.

Imagine cities clearly divided into permissive and restrictive zones with regard to drug use. Imagine that if the rich can live in gated communities with security guards, that the metaphorical 'ghettos' of the USA became more like real ones, with their own boundaries and their own local policing. Tell that to the LAPD? But the cost of their rule is immense, including the cost of riots, and its results ineffective.

It may be objected that such proposals are utopian because no societies have ever been organized like this. On the contrary, it is modern nation states with culturally homogeneous populations and single systems of law and values that are the exceptions. Moreover, within many such nation states there have been extensive elements of such group pluralism. The classic example is the 'pillars' system in the Netherlands where much of education and welfare, and social associations generally were organized on a confessional basis between the main religious communities.[18] If we take two examples of our main models, micro-governance and extra-territoriality, then we can see that such pluralistic systems have been moderately effective and have persisted over long periods. The most durable example of the former is the Ottoman *millet* system in which the different religious/ethnic communities enjoyed a substantial measure of self-governance, subject only to taxation by and the ultimate authority of the representatives of the Sublime Porte.[19] Thus a city like Damascus was divided into distinct closed quarters, the members of which were subject to their own customary law, and communities shared only certain common spaces in the city, like the main bazaar. This system made Muslim rule just about acceptable to tolerated religious minorities like Jews and Christians, at the price of extra taxation and certain civil disabilities. Indeed, in its heyday, the Ottoman Empire compared favourably with the religious intolerance and persecution of Europe. Extra-territoriality has a bad reputation because of its association with imperialism, but it makes the point that parallel legal systems are not impossible. Thus in the period of *de facto* foreign rule in Egypt after 1881 Europeans enjoyed extra-territoriality,

[18] On the pillars system see Arend Lijphart (1975).
[19] On the *millet* system and the issue of relations between the different religions in the Ottoman Empire generally see Braude and Lewis (1983).

but so did Ottoman citizens. British, French and Egyptian legal systems coexisted, as did the customary law of multiple religions and ethnic groups within their own communities such as Jews, Greeks and Copts.[20]

I am not advocating copying such arrangements, not least because these were based on traditional communities in which membership was by birth and tended to be for life. Even the Dutch pillars system has broken down to a considerable degree. Few people will tolerate the rigidity of such arrangements, or the tendency toward multiplication of associations simply because every confessional group must have one, as in Hans van der Horst's wonderful mock example of the Roman Catholic Goat Breeders Association (van der Horst 1996: 51). However, an associative system does not have to be either rigidly confessional or traditional in its membership. Many people would, for most purposes, choose to join 'neutral' associations, like clubs, for the benefits of membership. For every community of Hassids or Black Muslims, with a thick script of customary conduct, there would be large numbers of people happy to enjoy the silence of the laws and lead unobtrusive private lives.

Self-regulation

Much of the substance of the issue of self-regulation has been covered by the above discussion, but some points need to be made about prudential rather than value standards. Much health and safety, environmental protection and public health legislation exists because the state tries to compensate for bodies, like companies, in which affected interests have no say and over which there is no countervailing power. It is also elaborate because it is created by bodies like the US Federal Government or the European Union, that apply rules to large areas with very diverse circumstances. The answer to such regulation is to build communities that internalize risks, either by localization or by mutual interest. Thus, for example, a company in which the workers had a substantial say and in which company policy affecting workers' interests was subject to the check of mutual consent between management and employee represen-

[20] On the extra-territorial system in Egypt see Cannon (1998). Supporters of the theory of 'plural societies' like J. S. Fumival and M. G. Smith assumed that such distinct communities were pre-modern forms supplanted by the nation state, yet in a society returning to heterogeneity they may be the only way to preserve liberal representative government. See Smith (1974).

tatives, could evolve its own local safety standards and underwrite them with its own insurance scheme. Again, provided members accept the risks and public agencies publicize the perceived dangers, members who join food clubs that supply foods for which there is public concern, like beef on the bone, or certain cheeses, should be free to do so. Many regulations about product definitions and standards are needlessly complex due to an excessive concern to prevent non-trade rules acting as trade barriers under EU or WTO free trade rules. However, the chief concern here is that large bodies may practice protectionism by the back door, like nation states. Centralization is the key source of the problem. If local communities or associations ban or refuse to consume certain products they should be free to do so. Localized regulation and self-regulation would reduce the complexity and scale of the rules to be made and, therefore, contain the tendencies toward 'motorized legislation' and capricious and intrusive enforcement.

Associative welfare

An associative welfare state would be based on the dual principles of competing voluntary self-governing providers chosen by citizens and formula-based entitlements from public funds received proportionate to membership. It would give everybody choice, something that is at present largely confined to the upper echelons of the middle classes, who shun public welfare. Most people cannot afford to pay their taxes and also pay for private education, health insurance and pensions. In an associative system one would receive one's public entitlement only if one joins an association open to all. The well-to-do could then 'top-up' the public provision available and the poor would receive basic entitlements. This would encourage the better off to stay with the public welfare system and to share the same institutions with others. Getting back part of what they paid for in taxes, they may become less averse to supporting the system and its entitlements, and, indeed, to increasing the basic publicly funded formulas. In effect associative welfare would merge the public and private systems. This would put pressure on private providers, who often offer poor or very variable terms for such services as pensions and insurance, and who take substantial profits from them. It would also give poor citizens the option to choose providers, rather than to be given paternalistic welfare.

The effects of associationalism would be to challenge the bifurcation of welfare provision but also to allow a radical divergence in its content. Education, health and social services could differentiate into competing styles of provision as groups and individuals seek to craft packages to suit themselves. Parents who want progressive education could have it. Muslims could establish their own schools. People could use public money to build their own conception of health services, based, for example, on the fusion of conventional and alternative medicine and a more equal partnership between patients and doctors. Such ability to lock into public funds and develop distinct community facilities would strengthen the system of community self-government, since groups could provide more for their members. In turn such groups would become active defenders of the associationalist principle in welfare and supporters of its extension. Religious groups would have a basis to unite rich and poor in common collective services, but not only such groups—one can envisage the extensive development of, for example, gay and feminist associations strengthened by welfare provision.

In such a system provision would be devolved to groups, as would the first line of standard setting. Beyond that, however, liberal democratic representative government would remain. It would be the source of public funds and its institutions would set their level. It would set minimum common standards and enforce them. It would protect individuals against abuse by groups and groups against abuse by one another. As the association of associations it would come close to being that limited but virtually necessary public power envisaged by the creators of the idea of modern representative government in the eighteenth century. Such devolution of provision and self-regulation would restore the liberal state rather than weakening it, by giving it tasks its institutions can accomplish. Those who fear a more limited government would be powerless before the fact of continuing corporate power should think of how much more constraint an active and empowered civil society would place upon corporations' activities. Those who fear for the core values of liberalism in a society of competing communities and associations should remember that greater self-governance may make people more able to tolerate others and aware of those common values essential to preserve their own autonomy. The example of religious toleration is once again apposite here. The advantage of pluralistic social provision is that we can 'depoliticize' social and community standards, stopping the fight as to whose size will fit all. Liberalism and associationalism are not in conflict. Associationalism does not seek to supplant representative government but to supplement it, so that it can do the job for which it was envisaged.

References

ALBORN, T. (1998), *Conceiving Companies—Joint Stock Politics in Victorian England*. London: Routledge.

BECCARIA, C. (1995), *On Crimes and Punishments*, Richard Bellamy, ed. Cambridge: Cambridge University Press.

BRAUDE, R. and LEWIS, B., eds. (1983), *Christians and Jews in the Ottoman Empire*, vol. 1. New York: Holmes and Mayer.

BUKATMAN, S. (1997), *Blade Runner*. London: British Film Institute.

CANNON, B. (1998). *The Politics of Law and the Courts in Nineteenth Century Egypt*. Salt Lake City: University of Utah Press.

COHEN, J. and ROGERS, J. (1996), 'Secondary Associations and Democratic Governance', in E. O. Wright, ed., *Associations and Democracy*. London: Verso.

DAVIS, M. (1990), *City of Quartz*. London: Verso.

—— (1992), 'Fortress Los Angeles "The Militarisation of Urban Space" ', in M. Sorkin, ed., *Variations on a Theme Park—The New American City and the End of Public Space*. New York: Farrar Strauss Giroux.

—— (1998), *Ecology of Fear—Los Angeles and the Imagination of Disaster*. New York: Metropolitan Books.

ETZIONI, A. (1995), *The Spirit of Community*. London: Fontana.

FARBER, H. S. (1997), 'The Changing Face of Job Loss in the United States 1981–95', Brookings Papers on Economic Activity: Microeconomic.

GARLAND, D. (1996), 'The Limits of the Sovereign State—Strategies of Crime Control in Contemporary Societies', *British Journal of Criminology*, 36/4: 445–71.

GORDON, D. (1996), *Fat and Mean—The Corporate Squeeze on Working Americans and the Myth of Managerial Downsizing*. New York: Martin Kessler Books/The Free Press.

HIRST, P. (1994), *Associative Democracy*. Cambridge: Polity Press.

—— (1997), *From Statism to Pluralism*. London: UCL Press.

—— (1998), 'Social Welfare and Associative Democracy' in N. Ellison and C. Pierson, eds., *Developments in British Social Policy*, No. 1. Basingstoke: Macmillan.

HIRST, P. and THOMPSON, G. (1999) 'Globalisation—Frequently Asked Questions and Some Surprising Answers', in Peter Leisink, ed., *Globalisation and Labour Relations*. Cheltenham: Edward Elgar.

JENKINS, S. (1996), *Accountable to None: The Tory Nationalisation of Britain*. London: Penguin.

LIJPHART, A. (1975), *The Politics of Accommodation: Pluralism and*

Democracy in the Netherlands, 2nd edn. Berkeley, CA: University of California Press.

PIERSON, P. (1994), *Dismantling the Welfare State?* Cambridge: Cambridge University Press.

PIORE, M. and SABEL, C. (1984), *The Second Industrial Divide*. New York: Basic Books.

POWER, M. (1997), *The Audit Society*. Oxford: Oxford University Press.

PRESTHUS, R. (1965), *The Organisational Society*. New York: Vintage.

ROE, M. J. (1994), *Strong Managers Weak Owners*. Princeton: Princeton University Press.

ROGERS HOLLINGSWORTH, J. and BOYER, R., eds. (1997), *Contemporary Capitalism: The Embeddedness of Institutions*. Cambridge: Cambridge University Press.

ROSE, N. (1999), *Powers of Freedom*. Cambridge: Cambridge University Press.

SABEL, C. (1991), 'Moebius Strip Organisations and Open Labour Markets: Some Consequences of the Integration of Conception and Execution in a Volatile Economy', in P. Bourdieu and J. S. Coleman, eds., *Social Theory in a Changing Society*. Boulder, CO: Westview Press.

SCHMITT, C. (1990), 'The Plight of European Jurisprudence', *Telos*, 83: 35–70.

SMITH, M. G. (1974) 'Institutional and Political Conditions of Pluralism', in *Corporations and Society*. London: Duckworth.

SORKIN, M., ed. (1992), *Variations on a Theme Park—The New American City and the End of Public Space*. New York: Farrar Strauss Giroux.

STORPER, M. and SALAIS, R. (1997), *Worlds of Production*. Cambridge, MA: Harvard University Press.

VAN DER HORST, H. (1996), *The Low Sky—Understanding the Dutch*, 118–26. The Hague: Scriptum Books.

WEIR, S. and HALL, W. (1994), *Ego Trip: Extra-Governmental Organisations in the UK and Their Accountability*. London: Charter 88 Trust.

7

Changing Representations of the Criminal

DARIO MELOSSI

In this paper I intend to present a way of connecting views of the criminal which have been developing in public opinion as well as in criminological discourse, with the fracturing, breaking down and recomposition of the social orders within which those views were produced and reproduced. As far as penality and social control are concerned, I submit that two ideal-typical situations may obtain, between which modern societies have been oscillating. In one, a fragmented and rapidly changing society conceives of itself, through its thinkers, as a plural and conflictual entity. Herein the concept of deviance, or indeed of crime, is relative to the standpoint of the one who is talking, and the representation of the criminal is a fundamentally controversial and contested representation, where some criminals at least play more the role of innovators and heroes than that of villains. Examples of this kind of society are Europe and North America at the turn of the century and then again in the 1920s and in the 'extended' 1960s. These periods are also characterized by declining imprisonment rates and by a public rhetoric of discourse centred around social innovation, experimentation and change.

These types of societal period usually respond to—and are at the same time followed by—periods when the fragmentation has reached 'intolerable limits', at least from the perspective of elites, and the need for a re-establishment of unity, authority and hierarchy (even if under a somewhat changed balance of power) seems to impose itself. These periods suggest theories of social order which are characterized by an idea of unity and cohesion (I would call them 'monist' theories) where the basic normative order is consensually shared and where the image of the criminal is one of 'the public enemy', to use the FBI's 1930s label. The criminal is now a morally repugnant individual (as described by criminologists as well as in 'the public opinion' or in fiction) and is in any case the one who brings a deadly threat to society's moral order. The causes of such a threat, if at all relevant, are to be found within the criminal himself, or herself, and not in social relationships. Examples are the periods when national states were first established in the nineteenth century, the worldwide Depression in the 1930s, and the period after 1973 till today, that Eric Hobsbawm has very aptly dubbed 'the crisis decades' (Hobsbawm 1994: 403–32). During these periods imprisonment rates tend to increase, and the public rhetoric is one re-emphasizing the value of the collectivity around concepts such as 'the state', ' the nation', 'the community'.[1]

In order to explore these hypotheses, I rely on the one hand on Kai Erikson's insight that representations of crime and punishment in the public arena are projections of deeper social and cultural concerns (Erikson 1966) and on the other hand I am following Georg Rusche's pioneering lead in conceiving the condition (and, I would add, the *representation*) of the criminal as tied to the fate of the most marginal sectors of the working class (Rusche 1933; Rusche and Kirchheimer 1939). Criminologists usually refer to social control as a 'response' to deviance, and particularly to legally sanctioned deviance, 'crime'. I believe such connection between social control and crime is a contingent matter which depends on the specific nature of what is meant by 'social control' and 'crime' in a given socio-historical situation (Melossi 1994). Increasingly in contemporary societies the control of crime is subaltern to social practices that are largely based on the construction of consensus (Melossi 1990) and are directed to controlling the generality of the public rather than the few who are responsible for what is officially defined as 'crime'. This was also the view of many 'classical' social theorists, most notably the view clearly expressed by Durkheim:

[Punishment] does not serve, or else only serves quite secondarily, in correcting the culpable or in intimidating possible followers. From this point of view, its efficacy is justly doubtful and, in any case, mediocre. Its true function is to

---

[1] What follows is basically a research programme. I do not claim that the chronology and the impact of events are the same in all societies and cultures, or even all societies and cultures of the same type. There are time lags and there are specific cultural traditions that should be emphasized and taken into account in a more developed study (cf. e.g. Nelken 1994; Savelsberg 1994; Melossi forthcoming).

maintain social cohesion intact, while maintaining all its vitality in the common conscience . . . We can thus say without paradox that punishment is above all designed to act upon upright people, for, since it serves to heal the wounds made upon collective sentiments, it can fill this role only where these sentiments exist, and commensurably with their vivacity.[2] (Durkheim 1893: 108–9)

These concerns in criminological research speak to social theory in a number of ways. The emergence of a preoccupation with the field of 'culture' goes back to a deep dissatisfaction social theorists have increasingly expressed, in the 1970s and 1980s, with the mechanistic view traditionally encapsulated in the Marxist-derived distinction between 'structural' determinants of social action and 'superstructural' ideological forms. Such dissatisfaction took the direction of an emphasis on a more *autonomous* role of cultural forms and on the feedback of such autonomy on traditional 'structural' variables, such as economic variables. In the field of criminology, for instance, theorists manifested a similar dissatisfaction with the relationship between social structure and penality as this had been most classically expressed in Georg Rusche and Otto Kirchheimer's *Punishment and Social Structure* (Garland 1990; Melossi 1980; Foucault 1975). This is why I am emphasizing here the theme of changing *representations* of crime and criminals. By 'representation' I mean the descriptive portrayal of criminals in criminological discourse, in the public opinion or in aesthetic discourse, as a distinctive 'type' presenting identifiable moral, physical and social characteristics according to specific locales of time and space (Leps 1992; Rafter 1997; Sparks 1992; Fritzsche 1998). Each cultural environment in fact produces a given 'knowledge' of the criminal that spans different discursive forms, from scientific tracts to newspapers, from televised media to fictional accounts. Such representations perform a work in society which consists, among other things, in orienting public morality. This work of representing and giving moral orientation can be accounted for, according to a concept of the relationship between social structure and culture which is one of 'elective affinity' between social practices that are usually ascribed to 'structure' and social practices usually ascribed to 'culture' (Weber 1904–05; Howe 1978). As we will see more specifically below, if rates of punishment, for instance, seem to 'respond' to changes in the economy (Chiricos and DeLone 1992; Melossi 1998a) this is not because of some

---

[2] A paper by Bruce DiCristina (1998) drew my attention to this passage. Similar remarks can be found in George H. Mead (1918).

kind of homeostatic 'blind' mechanism—even if in such a guide it could be described by social theorists—but because ideas expressed in a publicly available language about where 'the economy' is going, what a 'social crisis' is, what causes it and who is to blame for it etc, appear to change, in society, together and in a tight cultural exchange with, publicly available ideas about crime, punishment, and responsibility. Even if the social theorist's description is simply a *reduced form* description, ultimately the connection between such disparate aspects of social life is a work performed by discourse, ie by that discursive interaction which makes social coordination and therefore social practices possible (Marx and Engels 1845–46; Mead 1934; Smith 1976; Melossi 1985a).

This kind of approach is bound to be eminently 'reflexive'. Whereas, what is usually called a 'positivistic' attitude, has powerfully contributed, especially in the last 15 or 20 years, to obscuring a 'reflexive' view in criminology, sociological theory has instead tried to come to terms, for instance in the work of authors such as Anthony Giddens (1984), with the concept of reflexivity—with the challenge, that is, brought to a science of society, by the scientist's awareness of the necessary implication of his or her ideas, with the material that he or she strives to describe by means of those ideas. Not so in criminology. Or rather: the pronounced reflexivity of the works that appeared in the late 1960s and early 1970s such as Matza's (1969) or Taylor *et al.*'s (1973), has brought the field too close to what one might call a kind act of euthanasia to be tolerated within the boundaries of a social science whose fate has always been intimately linked with the issue of political legitimation.

The Penal System between 'Exclusion' and 'Inclusion'

It is customary today to think of the penal system as a system of exclusion (Steinert 1998). This may be perceived as its 'real' function and outcome but certainly, especially in its very beginnings, it was not imagined as pursuing such a goal. On the contrary, the prison especially was thought of as a mechanism of in-clusion, or in-corporation, I would say, into a social contract. This was particularly the case in republican or proto-democratic societies, such as the United States in its beginnings (Thomas Dumm (1987) on de Tocqueville (1835–40), following Foucault (1975)).

The post-structuralist, critical thinking of 1970s culture pointed out that prisons and 'ideological state apparatuses' in general had been 'invented' with the aim additionally of 'creating subjects' (Matza (1969), Althusser (1970), and Foucault (1975) have all said quite similar things about this) or, in the more direct and transparent language of North-American reformer Benjamin Rush (Dumm 1987: 88), of making 'Republican machines', citizens, that is, who know how to govern themselves, the necessary prerequisite to a system based on self-government. What I would like however to point out is that the terms of any such 'incorporation' into the social contract, into the social body, in fact, tend to respond to the specific juncture a society is going through and to the way in which, in that given society, social order is framed and conceived.

A number of 'classic' commentators, from Beaumont and Tocqueville (1833) to Rusche and Kirchheimer (1939), have pointed out the affinity between the main features of the penal system in a given society in a given period and the consideration that society gives its citizens and especially its *labouring* citizens: whereas the valorization of labour would typically be connected with an attitude of inclusion and incorporation, the *de*-valorization of labour—in a situation, for instance, of high unemployment—would be usually connected with a concept of the penal system as exclusion, as a system at most of 'warehousing' inmates. Whereas this way of thinking about relationships between the social structure and the penal system carries more than a grain of truth, I believe it is still too mechanistic because the definition of a given situation and of the policies required therein is never something objectively 'given' according to strict economic standards, but is the discursive product of hegemonic processes in which political and economic elites have a very important say. What is a 'social crisis', for instance, depends a great deal on the perspective of the one defining it (O'Connor 1987; Hall *et al.* 1978; Sparks 1992: 55–77). From the perspective of social elites, a crisis is first and foremost an assault on their power, whether political or economic.

I would therefore submit that two situations may obtain from the standpoint of penality.

In the exclusionary penal mode, society is (successfully) described as being in a state of 'crisis', where order needs to be re-established and the social fabric mended and brought back to unity after having been lacerated and torn apart. Here, it is often the metaphor of the state to appear: Leviathan as a purveyor of order and unity or better, of unification (*reductio ad unum*) and hierarchy—as David Matza explained very nicely (1969). Because one of the main powers of the state is the power to punish (Beccaria 1764), penality is particularly apt to be used to define powers and boundaries of sovereignty. In such situation, the task which is characteristic of the system of criminal justice is described as one of bringing society to unity by eliminating fragmentation and anarchy.

In the inclusive situation instead, social order is perceived as suffocating and unfair, and social change as necessary. The task which is conceived as characteristic of the system of criminal justice becomes then one of allowing for experimentation and 'innovation' (in the Durkheimian sense).

How can we sociologically explore such oscillations? From a *quantitative* perspective, one could show, for instance, that the productivity of a penal system increases in situations of moral panic and crises (particularly when such crises are perceived by elites as threatening the dominant form of social relations, ie their power). We can see that incarceration rates tend to increase in situations of crisis (economic and/or political) (Melossi 1985b and 1998a). *Qualitatively* however, we can observe that the representations of the criminal offender change too, ie the representations that society produces, and that criminologists produce for society, about the criminal.

The two perspectives, quantitative and qualitative, are related: the devaluation of the person who is at the centre of the penal system's attention, either as a criminal or as an inmate (usually conceived by the public as synonyms), is related to a rise in the number of such persons. There is, once again, an *affinity* between those social processes that increase the number of inmates and those that change the representation of the criminal. Or rather: it is the same social process, in which the changed representation—in orienting social action—makes it possible for the numbers to go up or down, and the numbers' seesaw in turn affects the quality of the representation.

I have previously (Melossi 1993) advanced the hypothesis that the sphere of penality, in its quantitative and qualitative variability, constitutes a sort of 'gazette of morality' by which more or less pressure is exercised on the generality of the public (given that, as I already mentioned, I follow Durkheim—and, for that matter, the classical theorists—in conceiving the main function of the penal system as being one of controlling the public much more than the criminals, who should actually be regarded as the 'useful' 'bearers' of such control (Foucault 1975)).

Here we come finally to the primary focus of this paper. In the situation characterized by a tendency to exclusion, we may observe in fact that criminologists (*as well as* public opinion *and* 'aesthetic' productions) assume an attitude of distance/antipathy toward the criminal: the deviant is himself seen as the producer of evil (whether he wants it or not), social order is represented as a *given* order which is to be established or re-established, and the representations of the criminal are under the constellation of the *monstruum*, the monstrosity, far removed from any common experience and hence from the possibility of empathy.

In the situation characterized instead by a drive to include, criminologists (as well as public opinion and fictional accounts) tend to assume an attitude of vicinity/sympathy toward the criminal: the deviant is seen as in some sense a victim of society, social order is represented as justly or at least reasonably contested, and the representations of the criminal are located under the constellation of innovation when not of a heroic striving against the dictatorship of fate or social conditions.

In order to offer a less abstract sense of what I mean, a few illustrations follow, taken mainly from the history of criminology.

The Italian Positive School

Cesare Lombroso's position cannot be separated from the historical context of Italian Unification in 1861 and the subsequent annexation of large provinces, especially southern provinces, in the ten years that followed, when Piedmontese ('Italian') army troops engaged in a bloody repression against peasant bandits who were portrayed as instruments of the previous regime and the Church (Molfese 1964; Hobsbawm 1959, 1969; Adorni 1997). This is the not irrelevant backdrop to Lombroso's story. Lombroso himself had been for a short period, in 1862, a medical officer in the Piedmontese army in the southern region of Calabria. He was impressed with the different culture of its inhabitants, a difference that he also tried to explain on the ground of 'race' (Lombroso 1862; Baima Bollone 1992: 43; Teti 1993: 13–14, 158–65). The skull of Villella, studying which less than ten years later he had the famous revelation of the theory of the born criminal (Rafter 1997), belonged to a peasant from Calabria, incarcerated till his death for being a thief and a brigand (Baima Bollone 1992: 114–25). There's a certain bitter irony in this. Let us listen however to Lombroso's famous summing-up of his theory:

Many of the characteristics found in savages, and among the coloured races, are also to be found in born criminals. These are: thinning hair, lack of strength and weight, low cranial capacity, receding foreheads, highly developed frontal sinuses, a high frequency of medio-frontal sutures, precocious synosteosis, especially frontal, protrusion of the curved line of the temporal, simplicity of the sutures . . . darker skin, thicker, curly hair, large or handleshaped ears, a greater analogy between the two sexes . . . indolence . . . facile superstition . . . and finally the relative concept of the divinity and morals. (Lombroso 1876: 435–36)

It is hard not to see, in Lombroso's theory, a sort of somatic transfiguration of a cultural difference so deep[3] that could not be understood on its own terms but had to be racialized in the difference between North and South, between Europe and the Mediterranean, between normality and atavistic pathology (Teti 1993).[4] Indeed many of the physical characters that were identified by Lombroso in criminals were also ascribed to southerners. The deep historical difference between industrial northern masses that had already been 'processed through' the machine of modernity and were therefore ready for self-government at the same time that they were ready to enter the gates of factories and offices, and southern masses who were tied to a particularly backward type of rural life, finds its roots in history (Putnam 1993). At the time, it was still so deep, however, that it had to be represented in the myth of the heritage of human evolution as this connected with races and individual dispositions. In 1926, Gramsci would note, in his famous essay on La questione meridionale (the southern question):

It is well known what kind of ideology has been disseminated in myriad ways among the masses in the North, by the propagandists of the bourgeoisie: the South is the ball and chain which prevents the social development of Italy from progressing more rapidly; the Southerners are biologically inferior beings, semi-barbarians or total barbarians, by natural destiny; if the South is backward, the fault does not lie with the capitalist system or with any other histor-

---

[3] Revealed however in that closure, 'the relative concept of the divinity and morals . . .'

[4] In his remarkable article, 'Why Is Classical Theory Classical', Robert Connell (1997), juxtaposes a 'colonization' model for social theory's origins to the usual 'modernization' one; it seems to me the Italian case shows that such juxtaposition is unfounded and that the two insights strongly imply each other. In other words: the 'civilizing gaze' that eventually was directed at non-'Western', 'colonized' people, in all European countries was first experienced and developed toward domestic and mainly rural lower classes (notice also that the concept of 'Western' or even 'European' is far from being an intelligible, homogeneous one: English-speaking authors (such as Connell), usually refer to English-speaking societies and more rarely German- or French-speaking ones as representative of 'Western' or 'European' cultures: how should the quite different Catholic/Southern European traditions be characterized? (The Italian and, especially important on a worldwide scale, the Spanish. See Salvatore and Aguirre (1996), for similar themes about Latin America and Melossi (forthcoming), about Italy).

ical cause, but with Nature, which has made the Southerners lazy, incapable, criminal and barbaric—only tempering this harsh fate with the purely individual explosion of a few great geniuses, like isolated palm-trees in an arid and barren desert. The Socialist party was to a great extent the vehicle for this bourgeois ideology within the Northern proletariat. The Socialist party gave its blessing to all the 'Southernist' literature of the clique of writers who made up the so-called positive school: the Ferri's, Sergi's, Niceforo's, Orano's and their lesser followers, who in articles, tales, short stories, novels, impressions and memoirs, in a variety of forms, reiterated one single refrain. Once again, 'science' was used to crush the wretched and exploited; but this time it was dressed in socialist colours, and claimed to be the science of the proletariat. (Gramsci 1926: 444)

It is usually pointed out that Enrico Ferri, a leading Socialist politician and Lombroso's follower, innovated on the theory of his mentor by introducing a more sociological consideration of criminal 'tendencies'. I believe however that the shift of emphasis in the Positive School, from Lombroso's theory of the born criminal to the more sociologically oriented position of Enrico Ferri, should be traced back also to a change of protagonists or *personas* in criminal representation and correspondingly to strata and types of working class population expressing different 'criminal' figures.

Ferri, before being a prominent Socialist, was a very successful lawyer and criminal law professor, at least as famous for his scientific theories as for his legal defences, being an orator of great success.[5] Born in the northern rural district of Mantua, one of the very first rural areas where in northern Italy a working-class movement made its appearance due to the more advanced level of 'capitalist' land tenure and agriculture, one of his first defences was that of a group of peasant agitators from that area. The Mantua peasants had been engaged in a wider movement of northern rural masses called *la boje*[6]—a movement that demanded better conditions for the agricultural daily workers and better wage levels. In Enrico Ferri's defence in court, one gathers that the vicinity of the orator to the 'criminals' he is defending could not be greater, a vicinity which is first geographic, then cultural and political. The mode of his defence turns around concepts of innovation, social justice, social causes of crime, if indeed one can speak of 'crime' in this case. Indeed, for Ferri, these men are close to heroes:

[5] See Radzinowicz's recollections of his encounter and apprenticeship with Ferri (Radzinowicz 1999: 1–25).
[6] From the rallying cry used by the peasants, in their dialect, *'la boje, la boje, e deboto la va de fora!'* (it boils, it boils and soon it will boil over!) (Sereni 1948: 386).

As a student of social pathology, I am given to the observation of criminals in prison and in free life, and following the steps of my teachers, I have noticed their moral and physical characteristics which, together with the social environment, drive them to fight the inexorable struggle for existence through the means of crime.

Now, as a professor of criminal sociology, I am very happy to state that from this trial my anthropological studies did not profit a bit, because I had to come to the conclusion—a reassuring one for the lawyer—that no trace of criminality can be found in these defendants. On the contrary, I have to declare that we know from the laws of psychology that heroic souls like Siliprandi and honest people like his colleagues will never be able to become common wrongdoers. These are monstrosities, that can be imagined only by those who do not know the laws of the human heart or who are blinded by passions or personal resentments (*applause*).

And I desire to state that I would always be proud to shake hands with these men whether they will come back to being free men or, by absurd hypothesis, might go back to wearing the prisoner's uniform (*burst of applause*).

But if the professor has idly opened his books of criminal anthropology for this trial, the student and the lawyer together have had to gaze into another page of the great book of life, marred by other pains and other sighs; with patient and painful anatomy, he has had to dissect the poverty that hopelessly oppresses the workers of his native province. (Ferri 1886: 9)

Tens and tens of pages follow in which Ferri reconstructs the just causes of the complaints raised by the peasants 'of his native province' by analysing the economic and social conditions of the Region. The rhetoric is one of social change: those who have been unjustly charged with crime are actually the pioneers of a new world, more just and more humane. They are not criminals, they are indeed 'our' heroes. How far are we from the harsh southern mountains where the brigand Villella had been fighting his own primitive and uncivilized struggle!

One might however object that we are talking of very different types of crime here, according to a distinction similar to the one that at the time another leading Positivist author, Baron Raffaele Garofalo, famously dubbed as the distinction between 'natural' and 'artificial' crimes (1891). However, I believe that the choice of which type of crimes criminologists (as well as the courts, the media, etc.) focus upon, is indeed part of our *explanandum*, because our orientation toward specific 'facts' of analysis, knowledge, entertainment etc. is inscribed within and directed by historically variable sets of values (Weber 1904). One could even dare suggest that the criminals themselves are not immune to the prevailing social discourse on criminality, ready to confirm it with their own actions and in their own self-images. Criminals too belong in a web of social and historical relationships: the particularly cruel character of their deeds or, in other circumstances, their sophistication and innovation depend at least in part on the environment within which they find themselves thrown. According to Dane Archer and Rosemary Gartner (1984), for instance, a society like the US—one which encourages violence as an important resource to solve conflicts—will very probably end up fostering a higher violent crime rate. The opposite will happen in a society in which violence is shunned but cunning and fraud are more benignly considered, such as, for instance, Italian society (Melossi 1994).

In other words, we cannot really understand Lombroso's and Ferri's different emphases, on the 'born delinquent' or on 'social conditions'[7] without considering the specificity of Italy's dualistic socio-economic development, which meant very different types of economic growth, rates of unemployment, types of working class in the North and in the South. The incorporation of a more developed and combative working class in the North brought to a more inclusive and sympathetic attitude toward the kind of problems—even criminal problems—that were emerging there. At the same time a more exclusionary attitude prevailed toward the poor peasants in the South, whether such attitude meant semi-starvation in the fields or outright expulsion through emigration. After Unification, in 1861, the already high imprisonment and unemployment rates in the whole country were even higher in the South. Between 1880 and World War One however, in Italy as in the rest of Europe, the betterment in the conditions of the working class in the North, together with the massive migration from the South, corresponded to generally declining imprisonment rates (Sutherland 1934; Rusche and Kirchheimer 1939: 138–65; Pavarini 1997; Melossi 1998b).

Chicago: an attitude of 'appreciation'

The children of Villella and others like him, tired of having to deal with the arrogance of northern army officers and local *massari*—the rural middle strata that will be connected with the emergence of *Mafia*—moved *en masse* toward the ports of Naples and Palermo to look for fortune in the New World. Vito Teti, in his reconstruction of the debate on the Southern Question (1993), points out how emigration

---

[7] Which does not mean of course that Ferri shied away from the determinism (also *anthropological*), of his mentor (Garland 1985).

was seen by the southern masses as well as by their enemies, the south-ern gentry and the northern elites, as a 'substitute' for brigandage and crime, a gesture of revolt against a situation that was perceived as not changeable.[8] The emigrants, the 'Americans', as they were called, were seen as deviant, non-integrated, traitors to their customs and their land. 'Escaping to America' was equivalent to 'escaping to the moun-tains' (the choice of becoming brigands). This imagery fuelled at the same time the contemporary panic about immigrants' crime that was developing in those years on American shores, from the streets and alleys of New York to those of Buenos Aires (Teti 1993: 24–25; Salvatore and Aguirre 1996).[9]

Southern Italians were of course not the only ones; together with them, driven by similar circumstances, were Russian Jews and various Eastern European peoples, replacing the Irish and the Germans who had crowded Ellis Island's barracks earlier on. Chicago, even more than New York, was a big draw for these men and women. With its fac-tories, its stockyard, its rail- and river-ways in a privileged position in the mid-West of America, migrants were flocking to Chicago by the tens of thousands, the fastest growing city in America in those years. And in Chicago it was therefore natural for the newly founded Department of Sociology, of the newly founded University, to find the central metaphor of the social process in the issue of migration, in the same way in which many Chicagoans found reasons for their own mil-itancy and advocacy in migrants' causes.[10] Jane Addams's Hull House—the leading experience of the settlement movement in the US—was a vital centre of these interests, where the likes of John Dewey, George Herbert Mead and William I. Thomas would congre-gate, discuss the events of the day, converse with the migrants, and gen-erally understand 'the social process' as this was taking place in Chicago (Addams 1910; Bulmer 1984; Deegan 1988; Lindner 1996). Many volumes have been written about the experience of the Chicago School. The point that I would like to emphasize however is what

[8] In fact, mass migration in 1890–1913 might have been a not irrelevant cause for decreasing imprisonment rates in Italy in the same period.

[9] Paul Federn, in a Freudian-inspired essay, noted at the time that there was a deep psychological affinity between the cultural ethos of Bolshevik revolutions and that of the United States, both types of societies being likened by their Utopian attempt at building 'fatherless' societies, i.e. societies without authority, hence—a criminologist might note—'anomic' (Federn 1919–20; Melossi 1990: 72–91).

[10] Many of the sociologists and criminologists here mentioned were themselves, in dif-ferent ways, also outsiders.

David Matza later called an attitude of *appreciation* by the Chicagoans toward the deviant worlds they were describing: the immigrants, the hobos, the taxi-dancers, the prostitutes, the juvenile delinquents. Such appreciation had its roots in a vicinity of the sociologist to his object that in some cases was simply coming from a feeling of political and moral solidarity, in other circumstances from the researcher having shared at least part of his subjects' experiences, as was the case for Nels Anderson (1923) or Thorsten Sellin. The connection between such vicinity and the particular methodology used by the Chicagoans, an ethnographic approach that involved the need for talking to, living with, getting to know the people they were writing about, seems self-evident enough.

The concepts of social order and social control that emerged from Chicago could only reflect such attitudes: social control was a matter of interaction in a world sharply divided along lines of language, culture, religion, class, ethnicity, an eminently *relative* and plural concept where the official definitions of social control and therefore of deviance were in the worst case due to brutal suppression of opposition and in the best case to that democratic process that 'the Chicagoans' valued so highly. Never was social order however conceived as given or crystallized. On the contrary, Pragmatist thought, the overarching philosophical expression of the Chicago *Zeitgeist*, stressed the fluid becoming of social life, and ideas such as those of 'the social experiment' and 'the social laboratory', applied particularly to the Settlement movement and Hull House (Dewey 1931; Addams 1910). This Chicago 'ethos' was the quintessential expression of Progressivism and later on of the spirit of the 1920s, 'the jazz age', an era of ruthless capitalist development that was to last until the rough awakening of the 1929 great crash. This was a period of optimism and experimentation, powerfully captured for instance in Scott Fitzgerald's prose:

It ended two years ago, because the utter confidence which was its essential prop received an enormous jolt, and it didn't take long for the flimsy structure to settle earthward. And after two years the Jazz Age seems as far away as the days before the War. It was borrowed time anyhow—the whole upper tenth of a nation living with the insouciance of grand ducs and the casualness of chorus girls . . . Now once more the belt is tight and we summon the proper expression of horror as we look back at our wasted youth . . . (Fitzgerald 1931: 21–2)

In fact, after an increasing trend in incarceration rates during the nineteenth century, quite typical of a country that in many ways was still

taking shape, the period between the 1890s and the 1920s presented the
clearest decline in the history of US incarceration rates (Cahalan 1979;
Berk et al. 1981). This was to change after 1929, when the unprecedented unemployment of the Depression was accompanied by a sharp
rise in imprisonment, even if not wholly proportional to the extremely
sharp upward lift of unemployment (Jankovic 1977). Even if the
rhetoric of the 'public enemy' championed by J. Edgar Hoover, Chief
of the newly formed Federal Bureau of Investigation, was created during these years, the generalized character of economic misfortunes in
the Depression kept at least the level of *relative* frustration lower than
might otherwise have been, and the progressive tinge of political solutions kept open the possibility that 'public enemies' were not all chosen
from the lower classes.

Edwin Sutherland's criminology was probably the best representation of such a progressive stance, exposing the criminal undercurrents
present in so much of official society (and connecting that view to the
quintessential pluralist theory of social control and deviance, differential association theory). This he did most famously of course in *White
Collar Crime* (1949), *the* criminological tract belonging in F. D.
Roosevelt's 'New Deal', but if one considers his previous *The
Professional Thief* (1937), an attitude of benevolent indifference
toward the thief Chic Conwell goes together with a thinly veiled contempt for the hypocrisy of official society. In his conclusions, discussing
'the profession of theft' from the perspective of differential association,
Sutherland writes:

[The thief] receives assistance from persons and agencies which are regarded as
legitimate or even as the official protectors of legitimate society. In such persons and agencies he frequently finds attitudes of predatory control[11] which are
similar to his own. The political machine which dominates the political life of
many American cities and rural districts is generally devoted to predatory control. The professional thief and the politician, being sympathetic in this fundamental interest in predatory control, are able to co-operate to mutual
advantage. This involves co-operation with the police and the courts to the
extent that these agencies are under the control of the political machine or have
predatory interests independent of the machine. The thief is not segregated
from that portion of society but is in close and intimate communication with it
not only in his occupational life but in his search for sociability as well. He finds

---

[11] Note the changing fortunes of the term 'predator' that the revanche criminology of
the 1970s–90s would of course reserve to the *lumpen* element ('the underclass');
Sutherland (1937: 208), has a footnote thanking A. B. Hollingshead for suggesting the
term 'predatory control'.

these sympathizers in the gambling places, cabarets, and houses of prostitution, where he and they spend their leisure time.[12] (Sutherland 1937: 208–9)

The 'Neo-Chicagoans': sympathy for the devil

After a period, spanning the New Deal, the war and then the 1950s cold war, of social recomposition, best expressed, in sociology, in the systemic aspirations of Talcott Parsons' structural functionalism,[13] an attitude of appreciation of deviance re-emerged of course in the 1960s at the end of one among the most sustained positive trends in economic history and in conjunction with another decade of declining imprisonment rates (Cahalan 1979; Berk et al. 1981). Such an attitude went to the point of seeing the deviant as a sort of hero or saint, and reached its climax with the theory of the social reaction, or labelling approach. Stanley Cohen (1972) has written of 'folk devils' in his landmark essay about the Mods and the Rockers in 1960s UK. Indeed, borrowing from another icon of the 1960s, one can actually speak of 'sympathy for the devil' for the kind of attitude shared both by many young people at the time and by the kind of sociology produced by some of these young people. In his reconstruction of the 'making' and 'unmaking' of the New Left (specifically the SDS) during those years, Todd Gitlin (1980) devotes a few pages to 'the aestheticizing of violence in films'. Probably the first and the most famous among such films was *Bonnie and Clyde*:

Arthur Penn's *Bonnie and Clyde* was the most skilled, the most provocative, and probably the most popular; it launched not only new fashions but a hero cult; it stylized violence in living colour. Though Penn's heroes lived during the Depression and started robbing banks to help out (or make a gesture toward helping out) dispossessed farmers, they were not the creatures of economic ruin. Unlike the characters in 1937 and 1949 movies based on the same real-life Bonnie Parker and Clyde Barrow, Penn's characters were free-standing angels, children of the sixties set three decades back. Their doomed life of crime began as a lark, an escapade of sexualized bravado up against boredom and impotence[14] . . .

---

[12] Still in the late 1970s Cressey (1978), would define white collar criminals as 'subversives'.

[13] The postwar desire for ethical stability brought about also a revival of interest for natural law theories to which Parsons was no foreigner (Parsons 1970: 67; Pound 1960; Fuller 1964; Sciulli 1986).

[14] On the issue of 'youth problems' during the pre-1960s cf. Albert K. Cohen (1955), and Paul Goodman (1956).

At the Hollywood premiere, I heard, someone in the audience stood up at the end and yelled, 'Fucking cops!' He got the point. The spirit of Bonnie and Clyde was everywhere in the movement—and in the larger youth culture surrounding it—in the summer and fall of 1967 and on into 1968. (Gitlin 1980: 197,199)

American sociology of deviance went from Howard Becker's 'appreciation' of his friends jazz musicians smoking dope (Becker 1963) to a 'Romantic' heroization of the outlaw or maybe we should say 'sanctification' in the case of Jean Genet and his *Journal du voleur* (1949), Jean-Paul Sartre's 'Saint Genet' (1952), whose presence looms large in Matza's *Becoming Deviant* at the same time that Genet was touring American campuses showing support for the 'Black Panthers'. It is especially and most powerfully in David Matza's *Becoming Deviant* that this attitude, which is at the same time moral, cultural and political, emerged most clearly. In this classic piece of anarchist literature, an old polemic argument that finds its roots deep in Enlightenment thought,[15] was presented anew: how can Leviathan, whose hands have spilled the blood of thousands or indeed, during the century that is coming to a close, of millions, dare to judge who is and who is not a criminal? More specifically (at that time), how can the government of the United States, engaged in a war against the civilian population of Vietnam, dare to jail those of its citizens who have engaged in what is officially defined as 'crime'? Let's hear it however from the sharp and unusual prose of Matza, in his conclusions:

In its avid concern for public order and safety, implemented through police force and penal policy, Leviathan is vindicated. By pursuing evil and producing the *appearance* of good, the state reveals its abiding method—the perpetuation of its good name in the face of its own propensities for violence, conquest, and destruction. Guarded by a collective representation in which theft and violence reside in a dangerous class, morally elevated by its correctional quest, the state achieves the legitimacy of pacific intention and the appearance of legality— even if it goes to war and massively perpetrates activities it has allegedly banned from the world. But, that, the reader may say, is a different matter altogether. So says Leviathan—and that is the final point of the collective representation. (Matza 1969: 197)

Notice the date: 1969. Not only were those the years of a generalized turbulence in North America and Europe, of the working classes' unprecedented strength (Boddy and Crotty 1975), of a new progres-

---

[15] Most eloquently in a short tract by none else than the Marquis de Sade within *La philosophie du boudoir* (1795), entitled 'Yet Another Effort, Frenchmen, if You Would Become Republicans'.

sivism and experimentalism in all sectors of social life, but also, consistently, of a generalized, harsh criticism of traditional ways of penality and especially of the prison. It is no accident that in these years we find concentrated: prison protests and riots in all industrialized countries, continuous calls for penal reform that in some cases came close to asking for the outright abolition of the penitentiary, the emergence of a revisionist history and sociology of punishment that culminated in Michel Foucault's *Discipline and Punish* in 1975, and finally a decreasing trend in imprisonment rates in many western countries.[16] In the United States in 1973 the National Advisory Commission on Criminal Justice Standards and the National Council on Crime and Delinquency went as far as recommending a moratorium on prison building and the use of imprisonment as an extremely limited last resort device (Zimring and Hawkins 1991: 65–6, 87). However, the orientation of authoritative recommendations was soon to change very decisively.

A 'Revanche' Criminology

The tide of penality (as well as of many other social processes) turned around this same year 1973, the year of the oil and energy crisis, the start, according to historian Eric Hobsbawm, of the 'crisis decades' (Hobsbawm 1994). If until then the history of western economies had been one of unparalleled growth and development, and of tight labour markets that finally in the 1960s had encouraged workers' organization and defiance (a defiance, as we have seen, that would extend to many other aspects of social life), around 1973 everything started to change. One may suggest that Matza's work was as critical of his own times as well as foretelling of the future, not only because, as it has often been remarked, Matza's veering toward an anti-determinist position opened up to a future rhetoric of responsibility and retribution, but especially because the coupling of Leviathan and penal policies was to become tighter and tighter in the years to follow. Penal policies are implemented by the state—Matza wrote—in order to achieve one of the main features of the state and 'its' not least accomplishment: the representation of society as a unified (and hierarchically ordained) structure (Matza 1969; Melossi 1990: 155–68). A few years after the publication of *Becoming Deviant*, in the United States at least, the *ethos* that more and more prevailed was one of forceful unification of society after years

---

[16] Certainly among these the US (Cahalan 1979), and Italy (Melossi 1998b).

and years during which everything had been questioned, from the family structure to the supremacy of the white race, from the work ethic to a policy of moderation and temperance, from gender roles to chains of authority in all social institutions.

At that time, the conservative sectors of the establishment launched a pointed, self-conscious, purposive revanche that lasted at least from the Nixon to the Bush presidencies and found an international echo in Margaret Thatcher's policies in the United Kingdom.[17] Twenty and more years would follow of rising unemployment, deep restructuring of the economy and, together with this, of deep *disciplining* of the working class. At the same time, the most massive process of incarceration that ever happened in the West from the days of 'the great internment' in the seventeenth century, started taking place in the United States.[18] The total numbers of those in prison or under some kind of correctional control came quite close to a sizeable portion of the demographic groups at the bottom of social stratification, such as the Afro-Americans and the unemployed (Melossi 1993; Beckett 1997; Western and Beckett 1998; Tonry 1995; Miller 1997). The new tune was accompanied by a change in criminologists' mood. In a 1977 article endowed with remarkable foresight, Anthony Platt and Paul Takagi identified a new *realist* criminology: such criminology was to rediscover that the harm inflicted by criminals on individuals and communities was *real*; that criminals were often mean and/or inferior types of human individuals; that penality did indeed serve the positive function of protecting society from 'predators' of all kinds, people who are not deserving of our sympathy. It is in this sense that I would like to talk of a 'revanche' criminology, a criminology, that is, that took it upon itself not so much the task of criticizing and innovating, as it had been in the 1960s, but the opposite task of restoring and shoring up, contributing to the solidification, legitimation and complacency of a community of well-

---

[17] One may object to not including in such *revanche* Clinton's US or Tony Blair's UK but it seems to me that, by the mid-1990s, the conservative counterattack had become so successful that it constituted simply a new consensus, a new hegemonic received opinion that allowed 'Left' governments to build their own views on crime, order and security, *starting* from that consensus.

[18] This dramatic increase in imprisonment rates in the 1970s–1990s gave the lie to all the main explanatory mechanisms identified by the 1970s sociology of punishment: there was certainly no 'decarceration' at work here (Scull 1977), nor oscillations around a 'stable' level (Blumstein *et al.* 1977), neither a simple effect of unemployment (Jankovic 1977; Greenberg 1977—on the possible applicability of Rusche and Kirchheimer's model to the US 1970–92 period, see Melossi 1993).

behaved people who needed guidance and orientation after a period of deep tumultuous change.

The criminology of the period between the 1970s and 1990s certainly took many forms, different among themselves for theoretical inspiration, politics, criminal policy recommendations. Recently, David Garland has usefully made a distinction between a *criminology of the self*, 'that characterizes offenders as rational consumers', exemplified by the routine activity approach, and a *criminology of the other*, 'of the threatening outcast, the fearsome stranger, the excluded and the embittered' (Garland 1996: 461). Still, I would submit that what such different orientations have decisively in common is, as Garland himself points out immediately after having posited his distinction, 'an official criminology that fits our social and cultural configuration—one in which amorality, generalized insecurity and enforced exclusion are coming to prevail over the traditions of welfarism and social citizenship' (Garland 1996: 462). They express an attitude of distance, antipathy, even contempt, for their object of analysis. The general emphasis on 'predatory street crime' is particularly revealing, as Platt and Takagi had noticed more than 20 years ago. Routine activity approach (Cohen and Felson 1979) moved from the assumption that the predatory nature of criminals[19] was a given, not to be explained: only criminals' opportunity to commit crimes was to be explained. Genetic inferiorities should not be excluded and would often correlate with race (Wilson and Herrnstein 1985; Herrnstein and Murray 1994). An 'actuarial' penology rediscovered the value of the positivists' concept of 'dangerousness' (Blumstein and Cohen 1979; Blumstein 1983; Greenwood 1982—for a critique cf. Feeley and Simon 1992). And, according to Gottfredson and Hirschi's 'control theory':

Criminal acts provide *immediate* gratification of desires. A major characteristic of people with low self-control is therefore a tendency to respond to tangible stimuli in the immediate environment, to have a concrete 'here and now' orientation. People with high self-control, in contrast, tend to defer gratification.

Criminal acts provide *easy or simple* gratification of desires. They provide money without work, sex without courtship, revenge without court delays. People lacking self-control also tend to lack diligence, tenacity, or persistence in a course of action . . .

---

[19] The animalistic imagery of the predator, which can hardly be presented as a piece of detached scientific description, nicely fits with the 'evolutionary ecological' theoretical assumptions of this approach which harks back to Spencerian motifs and Hobbesian suggestions.

Recall that crime involves the pursuit of immediate pleasure. It follows that people lacking self-control will also tend to pursue immediate pleasures that are *not* criminal: they will tend to smoke, drink, use drugs, gamble, have children out of wedlock, and engage in illicit sex.[20] (Gottfredson and Hirschi 1990: 89–90)

And so on and so forth, in a long list of activities contradicting the usual middle-class, work ethic, American way of doing things. Gottfredson and Hirschi's prose carries more than an echo of Lombroso's list, especially of Lombroso's final item, 'the relative concept of the divinity and morals'. Even in more 'left-wing' accounts, less connected to established criminologies, such as Jack Katz's (1988), 'bad asses' are however real and dangerous 'bad asses'. Such homogenized portrayal of criminals, without distinction of 'right' and 'left', helps us coming to the core of the theoretical issue that is here at stake. The social transformations at work between the 1970s and the 1990s produced at the same time a historically rooted criminal phenomenology and an account of it that was reflected in criminologists' work. Both the types of crime and the criminological accounts were different from those characteristic of the previous period. The attitudes of 'distance/vicinity', or 'sympathy/antipathy' are not at all solipsistic, idealist, constructionist products of more or less ideologically inclined criminologists, but are socially produced attitudes, rooted in solid circumstances such as, in the 1970s–90s period, a higher unemployment rate, racism, a consumerist culture, a society fostering violence—circumstances at least in part different from those that had characterized the US society in a previous period. As Jonathan Simon has noted, the nineteenth-century spectre of the 'dangerous classes' reappeared in the 'underclass debate':[21]

The collapse of the power of the working class to demand improvements in their income and security, combined with the growing economic irrelevance of the urban poor, has driven a return to more exclusionary role for punishment.

---

[20] I was witness to a rather amusing scene during a panel of the American Society of Criminology in San Diego (1997), when a small group of European criminologists in the audience, eager for the session to finish in order to go take a smoke outside, were however trying to make the correlation between crime and smoking a bit more problematic *vis-à-vis* the position of two young American presenters, students of Hirschi, who defended the pristine validity of such correlation, completely oblivious to the humorous aspects of the situation.

[21] Indeed only a desire for terminological originality and the fear to be tinged with a socialistic vocabulary must have caused the participants in the underclass debate to shy away from using the identical but much older term *lumpenproletariat*.

Separated from the edges of the working class by hardened economic and geographical borders, those members of the underclass committed to state prison no longer provide a coherent target for the strategies of integration and normalization. (Simon 1993: 255)

What made of the criminology of this period what I am here calling a *revanche* criminology, therefore, lies in the ideological disconnection (Smith 1981) of the issue of crime from such circumstances, in focusing on the end-product of crime and criminals *naturalizing* it in ways not too dissimilar from what Lombroso had done almost a century earlier, without shedding light on the ways in which such end-products have been in fact socially produced. In doing so, criminologists powerfully contributed to the validation and reproduction of the overall redirection of social relationships in the US and other societies in the period considered. The representation of crime became a way in fact of talking about society and society's ills that went much beyond phenomena and types of behaviour legitimately identified as criminal by penal law. Rather, they addressed the moral value of society as a whole.

Once uprooted from its embeddedness in the complexity of social relationships, the question of crime became simply a question for moral edification. Hence the *revanche*: the main issue was one of combating the 'bad' morality of the 1960s by means of a new, 'good' morality. In the *revanche* movement the appreciative or agnostic stances of the previous criminology were often expressly evoked as having contributed to the fall—Charles Murray and his colleagues at the Manhattan Institute being as much concerned with the treasons and perversities of the intellectuals themselves as with the predations of the underclass.[22] In ways similar to what had happened in the late 1920s and 1930s when the rise to power of Fascist regimes in Europe had been accompanied by their also then successful polemic against the 'softness' of previous liberal regimes on crime,[23] the criminal was represented as a *monstruum*—a being whose features are inherently different from ours and shocking to the well behaved.[24] The criminal was once again portrayed as an incarnation of the ultimate sin of

[22] On the construction of a new 'penal commonsense' in the US and its subsequent worldwide diffusion, see Wacquant (1999).

[23] On the 1930s *leitmotiv* of the 'Weimar prison paradise' see Rusche and Kirchheimer (1939: 179).

[24] I do not know whether anybody has gone farther in this rhetoric than Bennett *et al.* in their *Body Count* (1996), where they talk of a 'new generation of street criminals', 'superpredators', 'the youngest, biggest, and baddest generation any society has ever known'.

breaking the fabric of society apart, somebody who had to be contained through incapacitation or death in order to restore the unity and order of society, ie in the colourful language of Matza, the power of Leviathan. These monstrosities were paraded around in the media too numerous all to be recorded here. Suffice to recall perhaps the most famous, or maybe the most politically useful, the case of 'Willie' Horton, 'a wonderful mix of liberalism and big black rapist', in the words of one of the producers of the political advertisement about Horton in the Bush campaign (Karst 1993: 73–4).[25]

The devaluation of the criminal went together with the collective devaluation of the social group to which criminals were seen as belonging, namely, a racially defined and demonized underclass. The devaluation of the *underclass*, however, went hand in hand with the devaluation of the *class* as such, that is of the working class as a whole, in the very literal sense of a 20-year long containment in weekly wages coupled with unprecedented increases in working time (Melossi 1993; Peterson 1994; Schor 1991). In the 1960s, crime had often been seen as innovative, sometimes as a challenge to unjust institutions, whether these were political or economic institutions. It was possible to identify with the lowest stratum of society because such stratum had not been described as sordid and shameful. Starting in the early 1970s, all this was to change. Crime was built to be a synonym for everything that was wrong in American culture. It was necessary to 'say no' to illicit behaviour, whether the consumption of illegal substances or the committing of crimes. There was nothing glamorous in crime and drugs, whether illicit or licit (the very successful campaign at vilifying tobacco smoke is a very good example of such strategies). Drugs were consumed by inferior, not glamorous, people, of lower-class, often ethnic, extraction (Reinerman 1979).

In short, the criminal was no longer a human being similar to us, as Sutherland had written, or whose destiny we can even appreciate, as Becker and Matza had proposed, let alone an innovator and a hero. Again in the 1970s, 1980s, 1990s, the spotlight of the criminologist, very much like the spotlight of police helicopters in the dystopian LA portrayed in Mike Davis's *The City of Quartz* (1990),[26] has been focusing

[25] Horton was the black Massachusetts convict who raped a white woman while on a furlough programme when Michael Dukakis was governor of the state and that became a favourite card of George Bush's 1988 presidential campaign against the same Dukakis, whose vice-presidential candidate was the African American leader Jesse Jackson!

[26] Reverting, in this sense, to pre-1960s times, before the time, that is, when, according to Bill Chambliss (1978: 14), criminologists had stopped looking at the outside of

on people who are not at all nice or charming. On the contrary, they are dangerous. They are either bad or saddled with some kind of personal deficit which makes them act as bad people.[27]

Very often, furthermore, *they* are very different from *us*, so different in fact that, even if one has to discount (but not everybody agrees on this[28]) some kind of constitutional anthropological difference of the Lombrosian or the more recent genetic varieties, one can however notice the different colour of *their* skin or the fact that *they* come from different, less civilized, places. There is no doubt that western societies have been hit, starting in the 1960s, with unprecedented amounts of crime that, at specific times and places, went together with a very deep destructuring of accepted ways of doing things, morality, values. This very deep cultural change has been responded to on the one hand by incorporating elements of the cultural revolution within the social control setting provided by a so-called 'consumerist' culture (especially those aspects having to do with the lifestyle choices of middle class men and women) and on the other hand, as we have seen, by a very extensive process of criminalization and the creation of new '*classes dangereuses*'. As it has always been typical of the way of functioning of the criminal justice system, the criminalizing response has mainly concerned the underclass, ie ethnic minorities in many countries and immigrants in others. This attitude repeated a century-long refrain. Already in 1833 de Tocqueville and de Beaumont, in their report *On the Penitentiary System in the United States*, had noted:

[I]f the statistical documents which we possess of Pennsylvania, should be applied to the rest of the Union, there are in this country more crimes committed than in France, in proportion to the population. Various causes of another nature explain this result: on the one hand, the colored population, which forms the sixth part of the inhabitants of the United States, and which composes half of the inmates of the prisons; and on the other hand, the foreigners pouring in every year from Europe, and who form the fifth and sometimes even the fourth part of the number of convicts. If we should deduct from the total number of crimes, those committed by Negroes and foreigners, we should undoubtedly find that the white American population commits less crimes than

police cars (*together with* the police), and had started looking *inside* police cars, *at* the police!

[27] The self-image of criminals was not immune from such deterioration: the 1980 New Mexico State prison riot, probably the most pointlessly bloodthirsty uprising in the rich history of North-American prison riots, took place exactly at the beginning of the new Reagan 'law and order' era (Morris 1983; Colvin 1992; Rolland 1997).

[28] Wilson and Herrnstein (1985), and Herrnstein and Murray (1994).

ours. But proceeding with this, we should fall into another error; in fact, to separate the Negroes from the whole population of the United States, would be
equal to deducting the poorer classes of the community with us [in France],
that is to say, those who commit the crimes. (Beaumont and Tocqueville 1833:
99; my emphasis)

The coloured, the immigrants, the poor are *those who commit the
crimes*. Many researchers have already told us that these people even
today are indeed those who commit the crimes, and that this is not a
product of discrimination toward them (Blumstein 1982; Tonry 1997;
Barbagli 1998) as if the issue of discrimination were disposed of once
ascertained that apparently it does not unfold within the criminal justice system. On the contrary, it seems to me that a more important question is about the relationship between economic, political, social and
cultural discrimination and a higher involvement with (officially perceived and labelled) criminal activities.

Whereas most of my references are to developments in North
American societies, I think one should add that in many societies, of
Europe and probably also, now, of Latin America, where a system of
social control mainly based on consensus has been established only
quite recently, the 'criminal question' has emerged there recently as
well. This process has unfolded together with the maturation of democratic forms of government that have put an end to very deep and divisive lacerations in civil society and have emphasized at the same time
the need for a process of social *unification*. In the same way in which a
rhetoric of the 'public enemy' emerged in the United States around the
time of the New Deal (that saw the incorporation of organized labour
within the system of government), so only today, with the coming to
maturity of a 'respectable' and non 'anti-system' Left in Italy, for
instance, and other European and Latin American[29] countries, is the
spectre of 'crime' (as opposed to that of 'political violence', whether
from governmental or non-governmental agencies) appearing in these
societies for the first time as a matter of public concern.[30]

[29] In Latin America this is probably true for a country such as Argentina.
[30] What I am submitting, in other words, is that 'crime' tends to emerge as a central
figure of social discourse and preoccupation only after certain historical conditions are
given and one of such conditions is the completion of a process of societal democratization and unification. On the more general argument and more specifically on the Italian
case, see Melossi (1990, 1997 and forthcoming); and Della Porta and Reiter (1996); on
Turkey, see Green (1998); on Spain, see Cid and Larrauri (1998); on France, see
Wacquant (1999); I believe that aspects of this argument may also apply to the current
situation in Northern Ireland.

Conclusions: Toward More Humane Representations?

Already in his 'Foreword' to Cullen and Gilbert's *Reaffirming Rehabilitation* (1982), Don Cressey protested vigorously against the 'neo-conservative' turn taken by 'American' government in penal matters, and called for 'renewed humanitarianism' (Cressey 1982). It seems to me that today, 17 years later, such change is overdue. The hegemony of the kind of society that was built by those who brought their *revanche* against the 1960s is now uncontested, probably more so than in their wildest dreams. Conservative criminologists are able to portray the recent decline in crime rates in the US, especially *violent* crime rates, as a measure of the unmitigated success of repressive policies, even if other mainstream criminologists call for caution about such judgements (Blumstein and Rosenfeld 1998). Once again, it is hard to discover any form of opposition on the horizon, except maybe for those forms of marginal upper-class eccentric art where cultural opposition takes refuge in periods like this. However, the very strong decline in unemployment rates—at least in the countries that have spearheaded this whole process, the US and the UK—may harbour an indication of changing times in penality also.[31] After one quarter of a century of 'reconstructing' moral stability, respect for authorities, work habits and profit margins, the time may be ripe again for questioning a suffocating, rigid and certainly 'repressive' moral and legal order. The case of ethnic minorities' and new migrants' crime could probably be one of the most obvious to try and look at in a different perspective from that of simple criminalization.[32]

Let us try and summarize finally the argument presented here. I have identified two 'typical' scenarios between which modern societies have found themselves: one, that sees a fractured, quickly changing, society expressing a concept of itself as a plural and conflictual entity, within which deviance, or indeed crime, is relative to the standpoint of the one who is doing the defining, and the representation of the criminal is an essentially contested representation: *some* criminals at least, play more the role of innovators and heroes than that of villains. One may find

[31] There is certainly a cyclical argument which is implicitly being presented here. In a previous work of mine I had referred to Kondratieff's idea of 'long waves' (Kondratieff 1935; Melossi 1985b). For an application of this type of (long) cyclical thinking to long-term social change cf. Zvi Namenwirth (1973), and Robert P. Weber (1981).

[32] The recent development of a 'cultural criminology' with its renewed sympathetic interest for all kinds of 'social deviance' might constitute a signal in this direction (Ferrell and Sanders 1995; Ferrell and Hamm 1998).

these kinds of societies in Europe and North America in the period between the end of the nineteenth century and the 1920s and, later on, in the 1960s–early 1970s. As we have seen, these periods are also characterized by declining imprisonment rates and by a public rhetoric of discourse centred around inclusiveness, social innovation, experimentation and change.

Such 'open' types of society follow or precede societal periods when, at least from the standpoint of elites, the fracturing and disorganization have reached 'unthinkable excesses', and the want for reinstituting a unity of authority, purpose and hierarchy (even if under a somewhat changed balance of power) asserts itself as a matter of social life and death. During such periods, predominant ('monist') theories of social order are characterized by an orientation toward unity and cohesion, the normative order is consensually shared and views about criminals are organized around the label of 'the public enemy'. Wrongdoers are now morally repugnant individuals, in the eyes of criminologists and the public alike, especially because offenders bring a deadly threat to society's moral order (different definitions of this threat can be found, for instance, in Beccaria (1764), Lombroso (1876), or Gottfredson and Hirschi (1990)). The causes of such a threat, if at all relevant, are to be found within the criminal himself, or herself, and not in any societal cause.[33] Periods when national states were first established in the nineteenth century, the reaction in the 1930s against the 'revolutionary' 1920s, and 'the crisis decades' after 1973 (Hobsbawm 1994: 403–32) are all good examples of such situations. As we have seen, at such point imprisonment rates tend to increase, and the public rhetoric is one re-emphasizing the value of the collectivity around concepts of 'the state', ' the nation', or 'the community'.

In orienting the activities of the many social institutions that frame the question of 'crime' and 'punishment', representations perform an essential work in connecting the main articulations of 'the social structure'. Beyond artificial and often parochial distinctions between qualitative and discursive analyses on the one hand and quantitative ones on the other, publicly produced and shared representations link the ways in which human agents perceive of and give accounts to themselves and others of phenomena of crime and punishment, with regularly changing 'structural' variables indicating specific aspects of the economy, the

---

[33] What appears to be a reference to 'societal causes', such as the fragmentation of the family, is anyway usually referred back to the weakening of the moral temper of the individual.

polity and society. It is in this sense that a few years ago I had advanced the idea of a 'grounded labelling theory' in which observation of the social activity of labelling should be connected with observation of more traditional structural aspects (Melossi 1985a). The present paper should be understood as a further contribution to that line of research and at the same time as a research programme to be further developed.

References

ADDAMS, JANE (1910/1998), *Twenty Years at Hull House*. New York: Penguin Books.

ADORNI, DANIELA (1997), 'Il brigantaggio', in L. Violante, 283–319.

ALTHUSSER, LOUIS (1970), 'Ideology and Ideological State Apparatuses', in L. Althusser, *Lenin and Philosophy*, 127–86. New York: Monthly Review Press.

ANDERSON, NELS (1923), *The Hobo*. Chicago: The University of Chicago Press.

ARCHER, DANE and GARTNER, ROSEMARY (1984), *Violence and Crime in Cross-National Perspective*. New Haven, CT: Yale University Press.

BAIMA BOLLONE, PIER LUIGI (1992), *Cesare Lombroso ovvero il principio dell'irresponsabilità*. Torino: Società Editrice Internazionale.

BARBAGLI, MARZIO (1998), *Immigrazione e criminalità in Italia*. Bologna: Il mulino.

BEAUMONT, GUSTAVE DE and TOCQUEVILLE, ALEXIS DE (1833/1964), *On the Penitentiary System of the United States and Its Application in France*. Carbondale: Southern Illinois University Press.

BECCARIA, CESARE (1764/1986), *On Crimes and Punishments*. Indianapolis: Hackett.

BECKER, HOWARD S. (1963), *Outsiders: Studies in the Sociology of Deviance*. New York: The Free Press.

BECKETT, KATHERINE (1997), *Making Crime Pay: Law and Order in Contemporary American Politics*. New York: Oxford University Press.

BENNETT, WILLIAM J., DiIULIO, JOHN B. JR and WALTERS, JOHN P. (1996), *Body Count: Moral Poverty . . . And How to Win America's War Against Crime and Drugs*. New York: Simon & Schuster.

BERGALLI, ROBERTO and SUMNER, C., eds. (1996), *Social Control and Political Order: European Perspectives at the End of the Century*. London: Sage.

BERK, RICHARD A., RAUMA, DAVID, MESSINGER, SHELDON L. and COOLEY, THOMAS F. (1981), 'A Test of the Stability of Punishment Hypothesis: The Case of California, 1851–1970', *American Sociological Review*, 46: 805–29.

BLUMSTEIN, ALFRED (1982), 'On the Racial Disproportionality of United States' Prison Populations', *Journal of Criminal Law and Criminology*, 73: 1259–81.

—— (1983), 'Selective Incapacitation as a Means of Crime Control', *American Behavioral Scientist*, 27: 87.

BLUMSTEIN, ALFRED and COHEN, JACQUELINE (1979), 'Estimation of Individual Crime Rates from Arrest Records', *Journal of Criminal Law and Criminology*, 70: 561–85.

BLUMSTEIN, ALFRED and ROSENFELD, RICHARD (1998), 'Explaining Recent Trends in U.S. Homicide Rates', *Journal of Criminal Law and Criminology*, 88: 1175–216.

BLUMSTEIN, ALFRED, COHEN, JACQUELINE and NAGIN, DANIEL (1977), 'The Dynamics of a Homeostatic Punishment Process', *Journal of Criminal Law and Criminology*, 67: 317–34.

BODDY, RAFORD and CROTTY, JAMES (1975), 'Class Conflict and Macro-Policy: the Political Business Cycle', *The Review of Radical Political Economics*, 7: 1–19.

BULMER, MARTIN (1984), *The Chicago School of Sociology*. Chicago: The University of Chicago Press.

CAHALAN, MARGARET (1979), 'Trends in Incarceration in the United States since 1880', *Crime and Delinquency*, 25: 9–41.

CHAMBLISS, WILLIAM J. (1978), *On the Take: From Petty Crooks to Presidents*. Bloomington: Indiana University Press.

CHIRICOS, THEODORE G. and DELONE, MIRIAM A. (1992), 'Labor Surplus and Punishment: A Review and Assessment of Theory and Evidence', *Social Problems*, 39: 421–46.

CID, JOSÉ and LARRAURI, ELENA (1998), 'Prisons and Alternatives to Prison in Spain', in V. Ruggiero, N. South and I. Taylor, 146–55.

COHEN, ALBERT K. (1955), *Delinquent Boys: The Culture of the Gang*. Chicago: The Free Press.

COHEN, LAWRENCE E. and FELSON, MARCUS (1979), 'Social Change and Crime Rate Trends: A Routine Activity Approach', *American Sociological Review*, 44: 588–608.

COHEN, STANLEY (1972/1980), *Folk Devils and Moral Panic: The Creation of the Mods and Rockers*. New York: St Martin's Press.

COLVIN, MARK (1992), *The Penitentiary in Crisis: From Accommodation to Riot in New Mexico*. Albany: State University of New York Press.

CONNELL, ROBERT W. (1997), 'Why Is Classical Theory Classical?', *American Journal of Sociology*, 102: 1511–57.

CRESSEY, DONALD R. (1978), 'White Collar Subversives', *The Center Magazine*, 11: 44–9.

—— (1982), 'Foreword', in Cullen and Gilbert, xi–xxiii.

CULLEN, FRANCIS T. and GILBERT, KAREN E. (1982), *Reaffirming Rehabilitation*. Cincinnati: Anderson Publishing Co.

DAVIS, MIKE (1990), *City of Quartz: Excavating the Future in Los Angeles*. London: Verso.

DEEGAN, MARY JO (1988), *Jane Addams and the Men of the Chicago School, 1892–1918*. New Brunswick: Transaction Books.

DELLA PORTA, DONATELLA and REITER, HERBERT (1996), 'Da "polizia del governo" a "polizia dei cittadini"? Le politiche dell'ordine pubblico in Italia', *Stato e mercato*, 48: 433–65.

DEWEY, JOHN (1931), 'Social Science and Social Control', *The New Republic*, 67: 276–7.

DICRISTINA, BRUCE (1998), 'Human Sympathy and Criminal Punishment: Another Durkheimian Irony', paper presented at the 50th Annual Meeting of the American Society of Criminology, Washington, DC.

DUMM, THOMAS L. (1987), *Democracy and Punishment: Disciplinary Origins of the United States*. Madison: The University of Wisconsin Press.

DURKHEIM, EMILE (1893/1964), *The Division of Labor in Society*. New York: The Free Press.

ERIKSON, KAI (1966), *Wayward Puritans*. New York: John Wiley.

FEDERN, PAUL (1919–20), 'Zur Psychologie der Revolution: die vaterlose Gesellschaft', *Der Oesterreichische Volkswirt*, 11: 571–4, 595–8.

FEELEY, MALCOLM M. and SIMON, JONATHAN (1992), 'The New Penology: Notes on the Emerging Strategy of Corrections and Its Implications', *Criminology*, 30: 449–74.

FERRELL, JEFF and SANDERS, CLINTON R. (1995), *Cultural Criminology*. Boston: Northeastern University Press.

FERRELL, JEFF and HAMM, MARK S. (1998), *Ethnography at the Edge: Crime, Deviance and Field Research*. Boston: Northeastern University Press.

FERRI, ENRICO (1886/1899), 'I contadini mantovani all'Assise di Venezia', in *Difese penali e studi di giurisprudenza*, 1–62. Torino: Bocca.

FITZGERALD, F. SCOTT (1931/1956), 'Echoes of the Jazz Age', in *The Crack-Up*, 13–22. New York: New Directions.

FOUCAULT, MICHEL (1975/1977), *Discipline and Punish*. New York: Pantheon.

FRITZSCHE, PETER (1998), 'Talk of the Town: The Murder of Lucie Berlin', paper presented at the Symposium 'The Criminal and His Scientists', European University Institute, Florence.

FULLER, LON L. (1964), *The Morality of Law*. New Haven: Yale University Press.

GARLAND, DAVID (1985), 'The Criminal and His Science', *British Journal of Criminology*, 25: 109–37.

—— (1990), *Punishment and Modern Society*. Chicago: The University of Chicago Press.

—— (1996), 'The Limits of the Sovereign State', *British Journal of Criminology*, 36: 445–71.

GAROFALO, RAFFAELE (1891/1914), *Criminology*. London: Heinemann.

GENET, JEAN (1949/1964), *The Thief's Journal*. New York: Grove Press.

GIDDENS, ANTHONY (1984), *The Constitution of Society*. Berkeley: University of California Press.

GITLIN, TODD (1980), *The Whole World Is Watching*. Berkeley: University of California Press.

GOODMAN, PAUL (1956), *Growing Up Absurd*. New York: Vintage Books.

GOTTFREDSON, MICHAEL R. and HIRSCHI, TRAVIS (1990), *A General Theory of Crime*. Stanford: Stanford University Press.

GRAMSCI, ANTONIO (1926/1978), 'Some Aspects of the Southern Question', in *Selections from Political Writings (1921–1926)*, 441–62. London: Lawrence and Wishart.

GREEN, PENNY (1998), 'Crime Control Without Criminal Justice: the Case of Turkey', paper presented at the Workshop on 'Criminal Policy in Transition', International Institute for the Sociology of Law, Onati.

GREENBERG, DAVID F. (1977), 'The Dynamics of Oscillatory Punishment Processes', *The Journal of Criminal Law and Criminology*, 68: 643–51.

GREENWOOD, PETER (1982), *Selective Incapacitation*. Santa Monica: Rand Corporation.

HALL, STUART et al. (1978), *Policing the Crisis: Mugging, the State, and Law and Order*. London: The Macmillan Press.

HERRNSTEIN, RICHARD J. and MURRAY, CHARLES (1994), *The Bell Curve*. New York: The Free Press.

HOBSBAWM, ERIC (1959), *Primitive Rebels*. New York: The Norton Library.

—— (1969), *Bandits*. London: Weidenfeld & Nicolson.

—— (1994), *The Short Twentieth Century 1914–1991*. London: Abacus.

HOWE, RICHARD H. (1978), 'Max Weber's Elective Affinities: Sociology within the Bounds of Pure Reason', *American Journal of Sociology*, 84: 366–85.

JANKOVIC, IVAN (1977), 'Labor Market and Imprisonment', *Crime and Social Justice*, 8: 17–31.

KARST, KENNETH L. (1993), *Law's Promise, Law's Expression: Visions of Power in the Politics of Race, Gender and Religion*. New Haven, CT: Yale University Press.

KATZ, JACK (1988), *Seductions of Crime*. New York: Basic Books.

KONDRATIEFF, N. D. (1935), 'The Long Waves in Economic Life', *Review of Economic Statistics*, 17: 105–15.

LEPS, MARIE-CHRISTINE (1992), *Apprehending the Criminal: The Production of Deviance in Nineteenth-Century Discourse*. Durham and London: Duke University Press.

LINDNER, ROLF (1996), *The Reportage of Urban Culture: Robert Park and the Chicago School*. Cambridge: Cambridge University Press.

LOMBROSO, CESARE (1862/1973), *In Calabria*. Reggio Calabria: Casa del libro.

—— (1876/1984), *L'uomo delinquente*. Milano: Hoepli.

MARX, KARL and ENGELS, FREDERICK (1845–46/1970), *The German Ideology*. New York: International Publishers.

MATZA, DAVID (1969), *Becoming Deviant*. Englewood Cliffs, NJ: Prentice-Hall.

MEAD, GEORGE H. (1918/1964), 'The Psychology of Punitive Justice', in G. H. Mead, *Selected Writings*, 212–39. Indianapolis: Bobbs-Merrill.

—— (1934), *Mind, Self, and Society*. Chicago: University of Chicago Press.

MELOSSI, DARIO (1980), 'Georg Rusche: A Biographical Essay', *Crime and Social Justice*, 14: 51–63.

—— (1985a), 'Overcoming the Crisis in Critical Criminology: Toward a Grounded Labeling Theory', *Criminology* 23: 193–208.

—— (1985b), 'Punishment and Social Action: Changing Vocabularies of Punitive Motive Within A Political Business Cycle', *Current Perspectives in Social Theory*, 6: 169–97.

—— (1990), *The State of Social Control: A Sociological Study of Concepts of State and Social Control in the Making of Democracy*. Cambridge: Polity Press.

—— (1993), 'Gazette of Morality and Social Whip: Punishment, Hegemony and the Case of the USA, 1970–92', *Social and Legal Studies*, 2: 259–79.

—— (1994) 'The "Economy" of Illegalities: Normal Crimes, Elites and Social Control in Comparative Analysis', in D. Nelken, 202–19.

—— (1997) 'State and Social Control *à la Fin de Siècle*: From the New World to the Constitution of the New Europe', in R. Bergalli and C. Sumner, 52–74.

—— (1998a) 'Introduction', in D. Melossi, ed., *The Sociology of Punishment: Socio-Structural Perspectives*, xi–xxx. Aldershot: Ashgate.

—— (1998b) 'Omicidi, economia e tassi di incarcerazione in Italia dall'Unità ad oggi', *Polis*, 12: 415–35.

—— (forthcoming), 'The Cultural Embeddedness of Social Control (or, of the Impossibility of Translation): Reflections on the Comparison of Italian and North-American Cultures Concerning Social Control, with a Few Consequences for a "Critical" Criminology', *Theoretical Criminology*.

MILLER, JEROME (1997), *Search and Destroy: African-American Males in the Criminal Justice System*. Cambridge: Cambridge University Press.

MOLFESE, FRANCO (1964), *Storia del brigantaggio dopo l'Unità*. Milano: Feltrinelli.

MORRIS, ROBERT (1983), *The Devil's Butcher Shop: The New Mexico Prison Uprisings*. New York: Franklin Watts.

NAMENWIRTH, J. ZVI (1973), 'Wheels of Time and Interdependence of Value Change in America', *Journal of Interdisciplinary History*, 3: 649–83.

NELKEN, DAVID (1994), 'Whom Can You Trust? The Future of Comparative Criminology', in D. Nelken, ed., 220–43.

——, ed. (1994), *The Futures of Criminology*. London: Sage.

O'CONNOR, JAMES (1987), *The Meaning of Crisis: A Theoretical Introduction*. Oxford: Basil Blackwell.

PARSONS, TALCOTT (1970/1977), 'On Building Social System Theory: A Personal History', in *Social Systems and the Evolution of Action Theory*, 22–76. New York: Free Press.

PAVARINI, MASSIMO (1997), 'La criminalità punita: processi di carcerizzazione nell'Italia del xx secolo', in L. Violante, 981–1031.

PETERSON, WALLACE G. (1994), *Silent Depression: The Fate of the American Dream*. New York: Norton.

PLATT, ANTHONY and TAKAGI, PAUL (1977), 'Intellectuals for Law and Order: A Critique of the New "Realists" ', *Crime and Social Justice*, 8: 1–16.

POUND, ROSCOE (1960), 'Natural Natural Law and Positive Natural Law', *Natural Law Forum*, 5: 70–82.

PUTNAM, ROBERT D. (1993), *Making Democracy Work: Civic Traditions in Modern Italy*. Princeton: Princeton University Press.

RAFTER, NICOLE H. (1997), *Creating Born Criminals*. Urbana and Chicago: University of Illinois Press.

RADZINOWICZ, SIR LEON (1999), *Adventures in Criminology*. London: Routledge.

REINERMAN, CRAIG (1979), 'Moral Entrepreneurs and Political Economy: Historical and Ethnographic Notes on the Construction of the Cocaine Menace', *Contemporary Crises*,3: 225–54.

ROLLAND, MIKE (1997), *Descent into Madness: An Inmate's Experience of the New Mexico State Prison Riot*. Cincinnati: Anderson.

RUGGIERO, VINCENZO, SOUTH, NIGEL and TAYLOR, IAN, eds. (1998), *The New European Criminology: Crime and Social Order in Europe*. London: Routledge.

RUSCHE, GEORG (1933), 'Labor Market and Penal Sanction', *Crime and Social Justice*, 10: 2–8.

RUSCHE, GEORG and OTTO KIRCHHEIMER (1939), *Punishment and Social Structure*. New York: Russell & Russell, 1968.

SADE, MARQUIS DE (1795/1965), 'Philosophy in the Bedroom', in *The Complete Justine, Philosophy in the Bedroom, and Other Writings*, 177–367. New York: Grove Press.

SALVATORE ,RICARDO D. and AGUIRRE, CARLOS, eds. (1996), *The Birth of the Penitentiary in Latin America: Essays on Criminology, Prison Reform, and Social Control, 1830–1940*. Austin: University of Texas Press.

SARTRE, JEAN-PAUL (1952), 'Saint-Genet comédien et martyr', in J. Genet, *Oeuvres Complètes*. Paris: Gallimard.

SAVELSBERG, JOACHIM (1994), 'Knowledge, Domination, and Criminal Punishment', *American Journal of Sociology*, 99: 911–43.

SCHOR, JULIET B. (1991), *The Overworked American*. New York: Basic Books.

SCIULLI, DAVID (1986), 'Voluntaristic Action as a Distinct Concept: Theoretical Foundations of Societal Constitutionalism', *American Sociological Review*, 51: 743–66.

SCULL, ANDREW T. (1977), *Decarceration: Community Treatment and the Deviant—A Radical View*. Englewood Cliffs, NJ: Prentice-Hall.

SERENI, EMILIO (1948), *Il capitalismo nelle campagne (1860–1900)*. Torino: Einaudi.

SIMON, JONATHAN (1993), *Poor Discipline: Parole and the Social Control of the Underclass, 1890–1990*. Chicago: The University of Chicago Press.

SMITH, DOROTHY E. (1976), 'The Ideological Practice of Sociology', *Catalyst*, 8: 39–54.

—— (1981), 'On Sociological Description: a Method from Marx', *Human Studies*, 4: 313–37.

SPARKS, RICHARD (1992), *Television and the Drama of Crime: Moral Tales and the Place of Crime in Public Life*. Buckingham: Open University Press.

STEINERT, HEINZ (1998), 'Critical Criminology and the Short Career of "Social Exclusion", paper presented at the 50th Annual Meeting of the American Society of Criminology, Washington, DC.

SUTHERLAND, EDWIN H. (1934/56), 'The Decreasing Prison Population of England', in A. Cohen, A. Lindesmith and K. Schuessler, eds., *The Sutherland Papers*, 200–26. Bloomington: Indiana University Press.

—— (1937), *The Professional Thief*. Chicago: The University of Chicago Press.

—— (1949), *White Collar Crime: The Uncut Version*. New Haven: Yale University Press, 1983.

TAYLOR, IAN, WALTON, PAUL and YOUNG, JOCK (1973), *The New Criminology: For a Social Theory of Deviance*. London: Routledge.

TETI, VITO (1993), *La razza maledetta: origini del pregiudizio antimeridionale*. Roma: Manifestolibri.

TOCQUEVILLE, ALEXIS DE (1835/1961), *Democracy in America*. New York: Schocken.

TONRY, MICHAEL (1995), *Malign Neglect: Race, Crime and Punishment*. New York: Oxford University Press.

——, ed. (1997), *Ethnicity, Crime, and Immigration: Comparative and Cross-National Perspectives*. Chicago: The University of Chicago Press.

VIOLANTE, LUCIANO, ed. (1997), *La criminalità. Annali 12, Storia d'Italia*. Torino: Einaudi.

WACQUANT, LOIC (1999), 'How Penal Common Sense Comes to Europeans', *European Societies*,1.

WEBER, MAX (1904), ' "Objectivity" in Social Science and Social Policy', in *The Methodology of the Social Sciences*, 49–112. New York: The Free Press.

—— (1904/1958), *The Protestant Ethic and the Spirit of Capitalism*. New York: Scribner's.

WEBER, ROBERT P. (1981), 'Society and Economy in the Western World System', *Social Forces*, 59: 1130–48.

WESTERN, BRUCE and BECKETT, KATHERINE (1999), 'How Unregulated Is the U.S. Labor Market? The Penal System as a Labor Market Institution', *American Journal of Sociology*, 104: 1030–60.

WILSON, JAMES Q. and HERRNSTEIN, RICHARD J. (1985), *Crime and Human Nature*. New York: Simon and Schuster.

ZIMRING, FRANKLIN E. and HAWKINS, GORDON (1991), *The Scale of Imprisonment*. Chicago: The University of Chicago Press.

8

Government and Control

NIKOLAS ROSE

Governing Conduct[1]

Analysts of control practices often seem to suggest that we are in the midst of a shift into a radically novel epoch, whether this be a post-disciplinary society, an electronic panopticon, risk society, actuarial justice or a society of control. Others, however, suggest that the picture is more complex, that current control practices manifest, at most, a hesitant, incomplete, fragmentary, contradictory and contested metamorphosis, the abandonment of some old themes, the maintenance of others, the introduction of some new elements, a shift in the role and functioning of others because of their changed places and connections within the 'assemblage' of control. Thus David Garland and Pat O'Malley have pointed to the fact that the contemporary discourse of crime control seems to combine incompatible specifications of the problem to be addressed, and cycle rapidly between different programmes for its solution (Garland 1996; O'Malley 1999). Proposals stressing the need for individuals and communities to take more responsibility for their own security, whether this be through schemes of 'target hardening' or by setting up neighbourhood watch, coexist with arguments for zero-tolerance policing. Demands for exemplary sanctions against offenders are accompanied by schemes for 'naming, shaming and blaming' focused on the relations between offender and victim. The prisoner is to be incapacitated, or the prisoner is to be taught life skills and entrepreneurship, or the prisoner is to be stigmatized and made to accept moral culpability, or the prisoner is to be helped to reintegrate into the community. The spread of community types of correction such as fines, probation orders, community service

---

[1] The arguments in this chapter are developed in more detail in Rose (1999a).

and so forth goes hand in hand with an inexorable increase in the prison population and the constant expansion of the prison building programme. Schemes of risk reduction, situational crime control and attempts to identify and modify criminogenic situations, portray the criminal as a rational agent who chooses crime in the light of a calculus of potential benefits and costs. Schemes for the retraining of offenders portray the prisoner as one who lacks the entrepreneurial skills to actualize himself in a competitive society. Proposals to increase the information, surveillance capacities and investigative skills of police divisions of criminal intelligence portray the criminal as an organized professional lacking normal moral controls who preys in a calculated manner upon the law-abiding. And so on.

In this chapter I would like to see what, if anything, recent analyses of 'governmentality' can contribute to our understanding of this complex and contradictory situation. Over the past few years, Michel Foucault's relatively brief published comments on governmentality have proved extraordinarily fruitful in generating conceptually rigorous, empirically rich and politically provocative studies of specific problem fields (Foucault 1991). Focusing upon the emergence and transformation of programmes, strategies and techniques for the conduct of conduct, such studies have described the rationalities and technologies underpinning a whole variety of more or less rationalized and calculated interventions that have attempted to govern the existence and experience of contemporary human beings, and to act upon human conduct to direct it to certain ends (useful introductions and overviews are provided in Barry *et al.* 1996; Dean 1999; Dean and Hindess 1998; Rose 1999a). They have demonstrated the historical variability and situational contingency of the *problems* that have seemed appropriate to be governed, the sites within which these problems come to be defined and delimited, and the diversity of authorities that have been involved in more or less rationalized attempts to address them. They have analysed the *languages of description* that have made these problems thinkable and governable and their dependence upon the concepts, explanations, arguments and theories of priests, philosophers, lawyers, doctors, statisticians, sociologists, psychologists and other experts. They have examined the different ways in which such strategies of government depend upon and disseminate certain conceptions and *models of the persons* to be subjected to government—as members of a flock to be shepherded, as children to be nurtured and tutored, as citizens with rights, as rational calculating individuals whose preferences are to be acted upon. They have mapped the different *spaces* opened up for government—the nation, the economy, the city, the community, the factory, the home, the global world itself. They have charted the assembly of complex and hybrid *technologies of government*, linking together forms of judgement, modes of perception, practices of calculation, types of authority, architectural forms, machinery and all manner of technical devices with the aspiration of producing certain outcomes in terms of the conduct of the governed—the technologies that we have come to know as the social insurance system, the schooling system, the penal system and so forth. And they have suggested that, at particular historical periods, there are family resemblances amongst the various ways of thinking and acting upon human conduct, that give them a kind of *strategic coherence*, as, for example, in the plethora of attempts over the twentieth century to understand and govern conduct from a 'social' point of view.

In focusing on practices of government, such analyses have reframed the role to be accorded to 'the state' in analyses of control and regulation. Centres of political deliberation and calculation have to act through the actions of a whole range of other authorities, and through complex technologies, if they are to be able to intervene upon the conduct of persons, activities, spaces and objects far flung in space and time—in the street, the schoolroom, the home, the operating theatre, the prison cell. Such 'action at a distance' inescapably depends on a whole variety of alliances and lash-ups between diverse and competing bodies of expertise, criteria of judgement and technical devices that are far removed from the 'political apparatus' as traditionally conceived. This generates an intrinsic heterogeneity, contestability and mobility in practices for the government of conduct. This mobility and contestability is intensified by the fact that 'the state' is neither the only force engaged in the government of conduct nor the hidden hand orchestrating the strategies and techniques of doctors, lawyers, churches, community organizations, pressure groups, campaigning groups, groups of parents, citizens, patients, survivors and all those others seeking to act upon conduct in the light of particular concerns and to shape it to certain ends. And mobility and contestability is further enhanced by the fact that contemporary strategies for the government of conduct, far from seeking to crush and eliminate the capacities for action of those persons and forces they act upon, on the contrary seek to foster and shape such capacities so that they are enacted in ways that are broadly consistent with particular objectives such as order, civility, health or enterprise. And what individuals, groups, factory workers, psychiatric patients and even prisoners are required to give, they are also empowered to refuse.

One can see such complexities in most historical periods and political contexts. However I have suggested that they become particularly significant within contemporary programmes, strategies and techniques for the government of conduct—forms of government that I have termed 'advanced' liberal (Rose 1999a). A number of elements are involved. There is a widespread recasting of the ideal role of the state, and the argument that national governments should no longer aspire to be the guarantor and ultimate provider of security: instead the state should be a partner, animator and facilitator for a variety of independent agents and powers, and should exercise only limited powers of its own, steering and regulating rather than rowing and providing. There has been a fragmentation of 'the social' as a field of action and thought, a unitary domain more or less coterminous with a national territory and coincident upon a single national economy. In its place we see economic circuits territorialized in other ways, for example in the themes of globalization and localization. The idea of a unified solidary social domain and a single national culture is displaced by images of multiple communities, plural identities, and cultural diversity. A whole range of new technologies—'technologies of freedom'—have been invented that seek to govern 'at a distance' through, not in spite of, the autonomous choices of relatively independent entities. Hence, as far as organizations are concerned, privatization, marketization, consumerization have been accompanied by the increased use of techniques of accountability such as centrally set but locally managed budgets, and the practices of evaluation and auditing. As far as individuals are concerned, one sees a revitalization of the demand that each person should be obliged to be prudent, responsible for their own destinies, actively calculating about their futures and providing for their own security and that of their families with the assistance of a plurality of independent experts and profit-making businesses from private health insurance to private security firms. This alloy of autonomization and responsibilization underpins shifts in strategies of welfare, in which substantive issues of income distribution and poverty have been displaced by a focus upon processual issues that affiliate or expel individuals from the universe of civility, choice and responsibility, best captured by the dichotomy of inclusion and exclusion. And, in the recent interest in the politics of communitarianism, associationalism and the 'Third Way', ones sees an accentuation of the strategies that I term 'ethopolitics' (Rose 1999b). These seek to regenerate and reactivate the ethical values that are now believed to regulate individual conduct and that help maintain order and obedience to law by binding individuals into shared moral norms and values: governing through the self-steering forces of honour and shame, of propriety, obligation, trust, fidelity, and commitment to others.

Taking these themes as my guides, and drawing upon the work of other researchers, I would like to suggest that we are, indeed, witnessing some intelligible shifts in ways of thinking about and seeking to ensure control. However, to understand such shifts, it is necessary to de-centre analysis from 'the criminal justice system'—codes, courts and constables—and to relocate the problem of crime and its control within a broader field of rationalities and technologies for the conduct of conduct. At least since the mid-nineteenth century, schooling, family life, the labour market and factory organization, public architecture and urban planning, leisure facilities, the mass media and much more have been mobilized and instrumentalized governmentally in the name of good citizenship, public order and the control or elimination of criminality, delinquency and anti-social conduct. In many ways, the criminal justice system itself plays a minor role in control practices—a role that is historically variable and should itself be the subject of analysis. From this perspective, I shall suggest that, despite their apparent complexity and heterogeneity, contemporary control strategies do show a certain strategic coherence. They can be broadly divided into two families: those that seek to regulate conduct by enmeshing individuals within circuits of inclusion and those that seek to act upon pathologies through managing a different set of circuits, circuits of exclusion.

Inclusion: Circuits of Security

In advanced liberal societies, one family of control practices operates by affiliating subjects into a whole variety of practices in which the modulation of conduct according to certain norms is, as it were, designed in. These are the practices that Deleuze referred to in his thesis that we now lived in 'societies of control' (1995). In disciplinary societies it was a matter of procession from one disciplinary institution to another—school, barracks, factory . . . —each seeking to *mould* conduct by inscribing enduring corporeal and behavioural competences, and persisting practices of self-scrutiny and self-constraint into the soul. Control society is one of constant and never ending *modulation* where the modulation occurs within the flows and transactions between the forces and capacities of the human subject and the practices in which he or she participates. One is always in continuous training, life-long learning, perpetual assessment, continual incitement to buy, to improve oneself, constant monitoring of health and never-ending risk management. Control is not centralized but dispersed, it flows though a network of open circuits that are rhizomatic and not hierarchical. In such a regime of control, we are not dealing with subjects with a unique personality that is the expression of some inner fixed quality, but with elements, capacities, potentialities. These are plugged into multiple orbits, identified by unique codes, identification numbers, profiles of preferences, security ratings and so forth: a 'record' containing a whole variety of bits of information on our credentials, activities, qualifications for entry into this or that network.

In our societies of control, it is not a question of socializing and disciplining the subject *ab initio*. It is not a question of instituting a regime in which each person is permanently under the alien gaze of the eye of power exercising individualizing surveillance. It is not a matter of apprehending and normalizing the offender *ex post facto*. Conduct is continually monitored and reshaped by logics immanent within all networks of practice. Surveillance is 'designed in' to the flows of everyday existence. In these circuits of inclusion, the calculated modulation of conduct according to principles of optimization of benign impulses and minimization of malign impulses is dispersed across the time and space of ordinary life. This is not a rehearsal of the sociological thesis perhaps first proposed by E. A. Ross, who, in 1894, 'jotted down 33 ways in which society exercised social control . . . [and then] proceeded to develop these preliminary thoughts into the organizing principles of sociology': the assertion that informal controls upon conduct are exercised in all areas of social life (Kay 1993: 22–3; cf. Ross 1901; Hamilton and Sutton 1989: 14–15, Lumley 1925; Rose 1999: 120–4). For what is entailed here is the calculated instrumentalization and enhancement of control features that are potential within a whole variety of practices in the service or specific projects for the management of conduct.

Inclusive identities

Perhaps the clearest example of such control strategies concerns identity itself. The exercise of freedom in the regulated societies of consumption that took shape in the second half of the twentieth century required incessant proof of legitimate identity. These link identification, individuation and control: computer-readable passports, driving licences with unique identification codes, social insurance numbers, bank cards, credit cards, debit cards electronically checking available resources at the point of sale, store cards . . . —the list could be prolonged (cf. Gandy 1993; Gordon 1987; Marx 1988; Poster 1990; Webster and Robins 1986). Each identifies the bearer with a virtual identity—a database record storing personal details—whilst at the same time allowing access to various privileges. Each access to such a privilege, for example the purchase of an item using a credit card, entails a further entry upon the database, a further accretion to the virtual identity. Access to other privileges, to mortgages, to credit purchase facilities, to accounts allowing use of telephone, electricity or gas, is dependent upon the provider accessing and checking these databases, through specialist intermediaries. Other databases, such as those of criminal records, may be linked into these circuits of information flow; government agencies use computer matching facilities to compare data from different sources in order to identify miscreants, for example those making false claims for social security benefits. Information on driving licences can be linked with police and court records in criminal investigations. Insurance companies check databases held by banks and credit card companies in order to identify bad risks. Proposals are made for national databanks of 'DNA fingerprints' in which the identity of each individual, written indelibly in their body, will act as a unique identifier that will not only qualify or disqualify them for entry into these circuits of consumption but will also identify them in a host of other potential encounters.

Critics have tended to stress the totalitarian potentials in the dissemination of networks of surveillance across the territory of everyday life (see Marx 1988 for this list). They overcome the barriers of space and time involved in physical surveillance; they are not labour intensive; they are of low visibility; they are of high durability; they have high transferability across domains; they are largely involuntary or participated in as an uncalculated side-effect of some other action; they are pre-emptive and preventive, denying access to benefits on the basis of what one might do rather than apprehending one after the act; they are amenable to rapid augmentation as new modes of identification come on stream. But the image of a 'maximum security society' or an 'electronic Panopticon' is misleading (cf. Lyon 1994). Totalitarian control is neither the intended or unintended consequence of the new technologies of securitization of identity. Of course, there is no doubt that law enforcement agencies and other similar control agencies will utilize these new sources of information in any ways that they can. They will use them to identify and monitor offenders. They may also utilize them to profile and identify potentially pathological individuals and groups. But the control practices of identification that do not principally involve the tentacles of the state are spreading across everyday life. The securitization of identity is dispersed and disorganized. Problems of the individualization of the citizen have formed in a whole variety of sites and practices—of consumption, of finance, of police, of health, of insurance—to which securitization of identity can appear as a solution. Does this person have sufficient funds to make this purchase; is this citizen entitled to enter this national territory; is this person creditworthy; is this individual a potential suspect in this criminal case; is this person a good insurance risk? The image of control by totalizing surveillance is misleading. Control is better understood as operating through conditional access to circuits of consumption and civility: constant scrutiny of the right of individuals to access certain kinds of flows of consumption goods; recurrent switch points to be passed in order to access the benefits of liberty.

Control, here, is related to the very form that citizenship had been given by the close of the twentieth century. Citizenship is not primarily realized in a relation with the state, nor does it involve participation in a uniform public sphere; citizenship, rather, entails active engagement in a diversified and dispersed variety of private, corporate and quasi-corporate practices, of which working and shopping are paradigmatic. In this context, the securitization of identity is a control strategy that operates by securing the obligatory access points for the exercise of such active citizenship. This strategy produces the obligation to continuously and repeatedly evidence one's citizenship credentials as one recurrently links oneself into the circuits of civility. In a society of control, a politics of conduct is designed into the fabric of existence itself, into the organization of space, time, visibility, circuits of communication. And these enwrap each individual life decision and action—about labour, purchases, debts, credits, lifestyle, sexual contacts and the like—in a web of incitements, rewards, current sanctions and forebodings of future sanctions which serve to enjoin each citizen to maintain particular types of control over their conduct. These assemblages which entail the securitization of identity are not unified, but dispersed, not hierarchical but rhizomatic, not totalized but connected in a web or relays and relations. But in policing the obligatory access points to the practices of inclusion, they inescapably generate novel forms of exclusion.

Partners in prudence

Political discourse stresses not merely the economic and technical limits of what can be provided by the state for its citizens but also the paradoxical and undesirable effects of the promise of total social protection. The dream of the social state gives way to the metaphor of the facilitating state, the state as partner and animator rather than provider and manager. Individuals, families, firms, organizations, communities are urged to *take upon themselves* the responsibility for the security of their property and their persons, and for that of their own families. Protection against risk of crime through a investment in measures of security becomes part of the responsibilities of each active individual, each responsible employer, if they are not to feel guilt at failing to protect themselves, their loved ones, their employees against future misfortunes. And, in exercising prudence, individuals cannot look solely to the public police and the formal mechanisms of the legal system: they must educate themselves with the assistance of experts and must actively engage in partnerships with expertise to maintain order and combat threats to individual and collective security.

These reactivated technologies of prudentialism have been best analysed by Pat O'Malley (1991, 1992, 1996). Prudentialism is most usually associated with the last half of the nineteenth century (O'Malley 1995; Ewald 1986, 1991). Twentieth century programmes for social insurance always sought to maintain this prudence and not destroy it, but the new technologies of social citizenship nonetheless mitigated and socialized these obligations: welfare states assumed the responsibility of being both the ultimate and the proximate guarantor of security. But within the economic rationalities of advanced liberalism, the implicit contract between state and citizen was no longer valued for its socializing consequences and the creation of solidarity. It appeared that, in any case, the promise of universal security had never been delivered; but further, the drain on individual incomes and on national finances was unwarranted and unbearable, responsibility was being stifled, risk-taking inhibited; entrepreneurship penalized, dependency induced. Hence a society of security now appeared to exacerbate, rather than reduce, the division between the included and the excluded. In the strategies that took shape in the shadow of these criticisms, individuals were not only to be encouraged to provide for their own future security through such measures as private health insurance, private pensions. They were also to secure themselves against crime risks and to take care not to make themselves the victims of crime. As O'Malley puts it, 'not only does responsibility for crime-risk-management shift, but co-relatively, the rational subject of risk takes on the capacity to become skilled and knowledgeable about crime prevention and crime risks' (O'Malley 1996: 201).

Hence security is no longer a matter of a national monopoly of actuarial wisdom, but nor is it to be assured through the encouragement of thrift by means of the personal relation with the contributions collector, or through the link to a commercial organization whose 'rock-like' reputation for stability and probity will assure peace of mind. Each of us is to be our own rock: insurance is now part of a politics of choice and lifestyle, sold through market mechanisms, and promoted though consumerized dreams of desired futures, which thrive on the reciprocal—if often implicit—exacerbation of anxiety. Further, insurance agents now offer themselves as versatile advisers in the techniques of risk reduction and risk management, providing information 'about local crime rates, about how to recognize suspicious persons, how to make the home and its contents secure, how to recognize and avoid high-crime-risk-situations, about the value of insuring and marking property and so on' (O'Malley 1996: 201, cf. O'Malley 1991). This responsibilization of the subjects of government is not restricted to individuals in their 'private lives'—it extends to firms, neighbourhoods, communities, none of whom can now allocate responsibility for crime control to an all powerful state. As David Garland has pointed out, the message now is that 'Property owners, residents, retailers, manufacturers, town planners, school authorities, transport managers, employers, parents and individual citizens' must recognize their responsibilities in the reduction of criminal opportunities and the increase of controls, working in partnership with the public police, with the burgeoning empire of private security, with other traders, with neighbours in their locality (Garland 1996: 453). In these partnerships in prudence, the social space of welfare is fragmented into a multitude of diverse pockets, zones, folds, each comprised of a linking of specific persons, organizations, spaces and types of conduct, each with their own dangers and risks.

Territories of security

The security practices of the social state were, in principle at least, territorialized across a single uniform plane, that of 'society'. A domain of collective security was to be maintained by the state on behalf of all citizens, through universal measures ranging from old age pensions to a unified and socially funded police force. In the new, fragmented political space, each community is to take responsibility for preserving the security of its own members, whether they be the residents of a neighbourhood, the employees of an organization, the consumers and staff of a shopping complex. Security, here, is to be managed within a variety of discrete spatio-ethical zones, each of which circumscribes what Clifford Shearing has termed a 'contractual' community. And this community assumes—or is forced to assume—responsibility for 'its own' risk management (Shearing 1995; O'Malley 1992; O'Malley and Palmer 1996; Stenson 1993, 1999).

As space is reconfigured in the name of security, new conceptions of 'criminogenic spaces' and new strategies of 'situational crime control' have taken shape. These strategies have given us two striking images: the 'gated community', internally monitored and pacified, surrounded by walls, with entry and exit controlled by security guards; the 'fortress city' so vividly portrayed by Mike Davis in his account of downtown Los Angeles (Davis 1990). These strategies involve a reconfiguration of the work of the security agencies. Not merely the private security firms who undertake the labour-intensive work of guarding, patrolling, surveilling and all the rest. But also the public police (Ericson and Haggerty 1997, chs 7,8 9). They are involved in tracing out the territories for surveillance using high-tech electronic surveillance and data-analysis systems. They use their information technology and database resources to provide information on types of crime and suspects prevalent in particular zones. They alert inhabitants to the dangers of crime through leaflets warning of risks and exhorting alertness and responsibility. They mobilize territories through residential watch programmes. They advise on design and security features of new homes and conversions. They visit schools and colleges. They help make up communities of active citizens committed to the securitization of their habitat. They become advisers on risk management in public and private spaces intersecting with a whole range of other professions involved in this task: licensing and certifying security technology, advising on the information technology necessary for securitization, advising on the location of such things as automatic banking machines, underwriting particular alarm systems and much more. And a host of new professions becomes expert in security—architects, store designers, manufacturers of street furniture, management consultants, those running training courses for staff, insurance companies, high-tech designers of video and audio systems and many more.

Through this multiplication of expertise in alliance with responsibilization, the collective logics of community come into alliance with the ethos of individual autonomy characteristic of advanced forms of liberalism: choice, personal responsibility, control over one's own fate, self-promotion and self-government. They are also brought into line with prevailing anti-political themes in political discourse, in that self-activating communities are promoted as an antidote to the combined depredations of market forces, remote central government, insensitive local authorities and ineffective crime control agencies, which have combined responsibility for the breakdown of law and order at the heart of urban—and rural—existence. New modes of neighbourhood participation, local empowerment and engagement of residents in decisions over their own lives will, it is thought, reactivate self-motivation, self-responsibility and self-reliance in the form of active citizenship within a self-governing community (Rose 1999b; cf. Stenson 1993). Government of security here operates through the activation of individual commitments, energies and choices, through personal morality within a community setting. Community is not simply the territory within which crime is to be controlled, it is itself a *means* of government: its detailed knowledge about itself and the activities of its inhabitants are to be utilized, its ties, bonds, forces and affiliations are to be celebrated, its centres of authority and methods of dispute resolution are to be encouraged, nurtured, shaped and instrumentalized to enhance the security of each and of all.

These patterns of reconfiguring urban space inaugurate a spiral of amplification of risk—as risk is managed in certain secure zones, the perceived riskiness of other unprotected zones is exacerbated. Nowhere is this clearer than in the fortress city, where a corporate citadel of offices and shopping malls, and their attendant facilities such as car parks and walkways, is enclosed and gated off from the poor neighbourhoods that surround it (Davis 1991). In these regenerated downtowns, space is reconfigured in a project of control and urban design, architecture and the police apparatus have merged into an integrated programme in the name of security. The civilizing public spaces of nineteenth century liberalism and twentieth century social architecture—public parks, libraries, playgrounds, the streets themselves—are increasingly abandoned, desolate and dangerous. They are replaced by an archipelago of secured spaces—shopping malls, arts centres and gourmet restaurant strips. Access to each is guarded, the internal space is under electronic surveillance and private security policing, its architecture and design so organized as to eliminate or expel those who have no legitimate—that is to say, consumerized—reason to be there. In fact, a double exclusion occurs. The third world proletariat who service these spaces of consumption are herded into public housing zones that are expelled to the outer rings of the city. And the poor, 'street people', the homeless and workless are expelled to spaces outside the circuits of security and inclusion, spaces which are increasingly avoided and feared by those who used to walk, shop and visit there. Hence, whilst this securitization of consumption may succeed in producing enclaves of contentment and encouraging the pursuit of pleasure, it is grounded in an exclusionary logic: those who are excluded—the new 'dangerous classes'—are forced to consume elsewhere.

Exclusion: Circuits of Insecurity

Opposed to inclusion, and the circuits that maintain it, stands exclusion. Not that the excluded are to be merely cast out—they are also to be subject to strategies of control. On the one hand, there are those strategies that seek to reaffiliate the excluded, through a principle of activity, and to reattach them to the circuits of civility: active labour market policies emphasizing the retraining of the unemployed, interventions to regenerate and empower disadvantaged communities and individuals, programmes to 're-familialize' life in the inner cities. On the other hand, there are the strategies which deem affiliation impossible for certain individuals and sectors, and seek to manage these anti-citizens and marginal spaces through measures which seek to neutralize the dangers they pose. Here one can locate 'three strikes' policies, the upsizing of the penal complex, the increase in the prison population and strategies for the preventive detention of incorrigible individuals such as paedophiles.

Subjectification

Since at least the eighteenth century, the political imaginations of most
European countries have been haunted by a succession of figures that
seem to condense in their person, their name, their image, all that is disorder, danger, threat to civility: the vagrant, the pauper, the degener-
ate, the unemployable, the residuum, the social problem group. Even
over the last decades of the nineteenth century and the first half of the
twentieth, when projects to forge universal social citizenship were
being formulated and set in place, not all were thought to be includ-
able, notably the mad, the criminal, those who refused the bonds of
regular labour, but also, in different ways at different times, the child,
the African, the woman and the Jew. But to think of the excluded as a
kind of eternal presence, an inescapable other to the aspirations of
civilization is to oversimplify. Who, or what are today's excluded?

The contemporary specification of exclusion arises out of a problematization of the social states that formed in the second half of the
twentieth century. 'We tried to provide for the poor and produced
more poor instead. We tried to remove the barriers to escape from
poverty and inadvertently built a trap' (Murray 1984: 9). Charles
Murray's welfare dependants were rational individuals, calculating
that they could earn more or live better by not working, and using the
welfare system to their own advantage. Lawrence Mead's dependents
lacked competence: 'Victims of a culture of dependence spawned by
well-meaning but misguided liberal policy, they had lost the capacity to
work and to carry out the ordinary duties of citizens' (Katz 1993: 15; cf.
Mead 1986). In either case, the problem created by welfare was essentially a moral and ethical one (Himmelfarb 1995): some were lured into
welfare dependency by the regimes of social security themselves, some
were unable to accept their moral responsibilities as citizens for reasons
of psychological or other personal incapacity, some were enterprising,
rational and calculating but enterprised themselves in the culture of
anti-civility, of crime and drugs, rather than within the values of civility and responsible self-management.

New political rationalities, including those of crime control, came to
be articulated in terms of this distinction between a majority who can
and do ensure their own well-being and security through their own
active self-promotion and responsibility for themselves and their families, and those who are outside this nexus of activity: the underclass,
the marginalized, the truly disadvantaged, the criminals. These

excluded sub-populations have either refused the bonds of civility and self responsibility, or they are unable to assume them for constitutional reasons, or they aspire to them but have not been given the skills, capacities and means. It appears as if, outside the circuits of inclusion—in 'marginalized' spaces, in the decaying council estate, in the chaotic lone parent family, in the shop doorways of inner city streets—exists an array of micro-circuits, micro-cultures of non-citizens, failed citizens, anti-citizens, comprised of those who are unable or unwilling to enterprise their lives or manage their own risk, incapable of exercising responsible self-government, either attached to no moral community or to a community of anti-morality. It is in relation to these zones of exclusion that the new strategies of risk management are directed.

Managing risk

Malcolm Feeley and Jonathon Simon have suggested that a 'new penology' is taking shape which is 'markedly less concerned with responsibility, fault, moral sensibility, diagnosis, or intervention and treatment of the individual offender. Rather, it is concerned with techniques to identify, classify, and manage groupings sorted by dangerousness. The task is managerial not transformative . . . It seeks to *regulate* levels of deviance, not intervene or respond to individual deviants or social malformations' (1992: 452). They suggest that this new penology is actuarial in character, not seeking to discipline and normalize individual offenders but to map out distributions of conduct across populations and to reshape the physical and social habitat in which individuals conduct their lives so as to minimize criminal conduct and maximize efficiency of the population as a whole. For those whose risk cannot be managed in these ways, imprisonment is utilized as a means of enduring incapacitation, whilst for those who appear to present lower risk, conduct can be managed through measures like probation, valued now only to the extent that they can demonstrate themselves as efficient techniques for the more or less permanent management of dangerous sectors of the population.

This thesis is suggestive, and finds confirmation from shifts in other areas such as psychiatry (Castel 1981, 1991; Rose 1996, 1998). We should not, however, misunderstand the argument, and assume that the increasing focus upon factors influencing the distribution of behaviours in the population and on strategies for prevention and risk minimization amounts to a totalized shift towards actuarial control (cf. Feeley and Simon 1994). The languages of description and techniques of calculation that are pervading the work of control professions may be probabilistic, but they are seldom actuarial, and are often only weakly numericized. For the control professionals, it is probably better to understand what is happening in terms of the emergence and routinization of a particular style of thought: risk thinking. This is concerned with bringing possible future undesired events into calculations in the present, making their avoidance the central object of decision-making processes, and administering individuals, institutions, expertise and resources in the service of that ambition. Understood in this way, risk thinking has become central to the management of exclusion in post-welfare strategies of control.

Take, for example, the public police. Ericson and Haggerty suggest that in the contemporary work of the police 'categories and classifications of risk communication and . . . the technologies for communicating knowledge [about risk] internally and externally' prospectively structure the actions and deliberations not just of police officers and police tactics, but also of other professionals who are now enrolled in the business of control by risk management—welfare workers, psychiatrists, doctors, teachers . . . (Ericson and Haggerty 1997: 33). Once stabilized in 'communication formats'—more or less systematic rules for the organization and presentation of information and experience—risk classifications tend to become the means by which such professionals think, act and justify their actions. In that sense, the very gaze of the control professional and the nature of their encounter with their client, patient or suspect, is liable to be formatted by the demands and objectives of risk management. Ericson and Haggerty suggest that this constitutes a dispersed 'expert system' of risk management, to which the professionals are subject: 'He or she is one of many contributors to the expert system of risk management that creates the patient's dossier, and therefore lose control over particular outcomes as well as over the progress of cases' (Ericson and Haggerty 1997: 37–8). The central work of such agents is thus structured around information.

This is not just information on the internal characteristics of particular persons—the extent to which they are 'dangerous individuals'—but concerns an array of factors that—formally via research or informally via professional beliefs—are associated with an increased likelihood of undesirable conduct (housing conditions, employment history, abuse of alcohol or drugs, family circumstances . . .). It is these factors that become the focus of the risk gaze, and that are increasingly organized and packaged by structured risk assessments, risk schedules,

forms and proformas, database fields, into indicators of risk, risk classifications and the like that are communicated to other professionals,
to law enforcement agencies, to the courts, to other decision makers,
with consequences far removed from those surrounding the initial consultation, encounter, or occasion which led to the collection of the
information in the first place (cf. Castel 1991: 281).

Control workers, whether they be police or psychiatrists, thus have
a new administrative function—the administration of the marginalia,
ensuring community protection through the identification of the riskiness of individuals, actions, forms of life and territories. Hence the
increasing emphasis on case conferences, multidisciplinary teams,
sharing information, keeping records, making plans, setting targets,
establishing networks for the surveillance and documentation of the
potentially risky individual on the territory of the community. In the
circuits of exclusion, control is not merely a matter of constraining
those who are individually pathological; it is about the generation of
'knowledge that allows selection of thresholds that define acceptable
risks' and generates practices of inclusion and exclusion that are based
on that knowledge (Ericson and Haggerty 1997: 41). A plethora of
quasi-autonomous agencies work upon the territories of control that
have taken shape after the welfare state, within the 'savage spaces' of
exclusion, in the 'anti-communities' on the margins, or with those
abjected from civility by virtue of their lack of competence or capacity
for responsible ethical self-management. Within this new territory of
exclusion, a whole array of control agencies—police, social workers,
doctors, psychiatrists, mental health professionals—seek to link up in
circuits of surveillance and communication in a perpetually failing
endeavour to minimize the riskiness of the most risky. They form a
multiplicity of points for the collection, inscription, accumulation and
distribution of information relevant to the management of risk.

Whereas social notions of risk were universalizing, these risk agencies focus upon 'the usual suspects'—the poor, the welfare recipients,
the petty criminals, discharged psychiatric patients, street people. The
logics of risk inescapably locate the careers and identities of such
tainted citizens within a regime of surveillance which actually constitutes them all as actually or potentially 'risky' individuals. The incom-
pleteness, fragmentation and failure of risk assessment and risk
management is no threat to such logics, merely a perpetual incitement
for the incessant improvement of systems, generation of more knowledge, invention of more techniques, all driven by the technological

imperative to tame uncertainty and master hazard. Risk management—the identification, assessment, elimination or reduction of the possibility of incurring misfortune or loss—has thus become an integral part of the professional responsibility of a host of professionals. The respecification of one dimension of the problem of control in terms of risk is bound to a revised governmental role for such professionals, to manage dangerous sites and dangerous persons on the territory of the community, under the threat of being held accountable for any harm to 'the general public'—'normal people'—which might result. However the emphasis on factors, probabilities and categories of sub-populations does not efface the pathological individual as a key object of attention and intervention. Indeed, the problem is precisely to deploy actuarial classifications of risk to identify and control risky individuals in order to ascertain who can, and who cannot, be managed within the open circuits of community control.

In these exclusionary circuits, the role of custodial institutions is redefined. They are understood and classified not in terms of their reformatory potential, but in terms of the secure containment of risk. On the one hand, confinement becomes a way of securing the most risky until their riskiness can be fully assessed and controlled. On the other, a group of individuals emerge who appear intractably risky—'monstrous individuals', who either cannot or do not wish to exercise the self-control upon conduct necessary in a culture of freedom. Sexual predators, paedophiles, the incorrigibly anti-social are representatives of a new 'human kind'—individuals whose very make up as human beings appears somehow faulty or incomplete, and whose very nature thus seems to place them permanently beyond the limits of civility and its demands on subjectivity. For such monstrous individuals a whole variety of paralegal forms of confinement are being devised, including pre-emptive or preventive detention prior to a crime being committed or after a determinate sentence has been served, not so much in the name of law and order, but in the name of the community that they threaten, the name of the actual or potential victims they violate. It appears that the conventions of 'rule of law' must be waived for the protection of the community against a growing number of 'predators', who do not conform to either legalistic or psychiatric models of subjectivity (see Pratt 1999; Simon 1998; Scheingold *et al.* 1994).

From dependency to activity

Whilst confinement without the aspiration of reformation is certainly on the increase in these new control practices, it would be a mistake to think that the logics of control pay no attention to the transformation of the excluded individual. Whilst analysts of the prisons have focused on the shift from reformation to incapacitation and punishment, at a more general level, the ethical reconstruction of the excluded individual is a central problem for one set of control strategies. Thus workfare programmes in the United States and welfare reform in the United Kingdom seek to micro-manage the behaviour of welfare recipients in order to remoralize them. They stress the need to reform habits as a condition of receipt of benefits, and ultimately, to seek to get all those physically able to work off benefits entirely. The aim, once more, is responsibilization: to reconstruct self-reliance in those who are excluded. But responsibilization here takes a characteristic form. Within this new politics of conduct, the problems of problematic persons are reformulated as moral or ethical problems, that is to say, problems in the ways in which such persons understand and conduct themselves and their existence. This ethical reformulation opens the possibility for a whole range of psychological techniques to be recycled in programmes for governing 'the excluded'. The imperative of activity, and the presupposition of an ethic of choice, is central not only to the rationale of policy but also to the reformatory technology to which it is linked.

Barbara Cruikshank in the United States and Karen Baistow in the UK have drawn attention to the significance of the language of empowerment for professionals operating within such technologies (Cruikshank 1994; Baistow 1995). For empowerment—or the lack of empowerment—codes the subjective substrate of exclusion as lack of self-esteem, self-worth and the skills of self-management necessary to steer oneself as an active individual in the empire of choice. The relations that humans have with themselves are to be the target of professional reconstruction, often backed with the power of law. The beauty of empowerment is that it appears to reject the logics of patronizing dependency that infused earlier welfare modes of expertise. Subjects are to do the work on themselves, not in the name of conformity, but to make them free. The binary of dependency and control becomes a powerful formula for judging the conduct by others, and for judging oneself. Autonomy is now represented in terms of personal power and the capacity to accept responsibility—not to blame others but to recognize your own collusion in that which prevents you from being yourself, and in doing so, overcome it and achieve responsible autonomy and personal power. High self-esteem is linked to the power to plan one's life as an orderly enterprise and take responsibility for its course and outcome. The vocabulary of dependence as a problem of the will provides the common language of description for conditions ranging from lack of work to dependence on alcohol (cf. Sedgwick 1992; Fraser and Gordon 1994; Valverde 1998).

The tactics of empowerment exemplify a much wider phenomenon—exclusion has become a fundamentally subjective condition. It is not a psychological subjectivity with social determinants, as in welfare regimes. It is an ethical subjectivity, and a cultural subjectivity. Hence welfare to work, zero tolerance, 'naming, blaming and shaming', parental responsibility for the crimes of their children. This is 'tough love', 'compassion with a hard edge'. The problems of the excluded, of the underclass are to be resolved by a kind of moral rearmament: 'a politics of conduct is today more salient than a politics of class' (Mead 1991: 4, quoted in Procacci 1998: 30). It is through moral reformation, through ethical reconstruction, that the excluded citizen is to be reattached to a virtuous community. Within such programmes for the ethical reconstruction of the excluded, everyone within the ghetto, every member of the underclass, each excluded person, even the convicted prisoner, should be 'given the opportunity' to achieve full membership in a moral community, and to adhere to the core values of honesty, self-reliance and concern for others. Their willingness to do so is to form the object of scrutiny of new moral authorities. For those who can be included, control is now to operate through the rational reconstruction of the will and self-control, of the habits of independence, life planning, self-improvement, autonomous life-conduct, so that the individual can be reinserted into family, work and consumption, and hence into the continuous circuits and flows of control society. But as I have already suggested, for those who cannot or will not be included, and who are too risky to be managed in open circuits—the repeat offender, the predator, the irredeemably anti-social, the irretrievably monstrous, the paedophile, the psychopath—control will take the form of more or less permanent sequestration. Those who refuse to become responsible, to govern themselves ethically, have also refused the offer to become members of our moral community. Hence, for them, harsh measures are entirely appropriate. Three strikes and you are out: citizenship becomes conditional upon conduct.

The penal-welfare complex

The theorists of decarceration in the 1970s suggested that advanced industrial societies were witnessing a sharp decline in the size of the populations who were confined. There has, indeed, been a marked reduction in the numbers of inmates of many publicly run institutions, notably mental hospitals and old people's homes. In the United States, for example, by 1990 the rate of incarceration in state mental hospitals had dropped to less than 50 per 100,000 residents aged 15 and over, from a peak in 1955 of over 450 per 100,000. Yet this 'decarceration' has led to a new incarceration, in the growth of a highly lucrative market sector in private residential facilities run for profit. And at the same time, many jurisdictions are introducing new measures for the preventive detention of those thought to present a threat to the public: a new archipelago of confinement without reformation is taking shape. In the criminal justice system, despite the proliferation of non-custodial punishments, there has been no reduction in the prison population in Britain and the United States. By the end of the 1980s, Britain's rate of imprisonment was around 100 persons for every 100,000 population: more than almost any other European state. But the American example is even more striking. In 1996, the incarceration rate for sentenced adult prisoners in the United States had risen to over 400 for every 100,000 of the population; where all jail inmates are included, the figure reaches over 600 per 100,000. Almost 1.2 million inmates were serving sentences of a year or more in state and federal prisons, and almost 4 million were on parole or probation: almost 3 per cent of the adult population and 7 per cent of the male adult population was subject to the control practices of the criminal justice system.

There are undoubtedly many reasons for the use of imprisonment in the United States, as elsewhere, and many plausible explanations of the rise in the penalized population can be provided. But I think it is possible to argue that the new regimes of welfare and control that I have described in this essay entail a new relation between the penal and welfare complexes. The prison, and penality more generally, have become crucial elements in the government of insecurity. If the United States can be regarded as a test case in this developing diagram of control, the poor, the dispossessed, the unemployed and the recipients of benefits are, in Jonathan Simon's telling phrase, 'governed through crime'. It is not merely that prisoners are overwhelmingly recruited from the ranks of the poor, the uneducated and unaffiliated, as everywhere, and from

African-Americans. Nor is it merely that that tough crime control and the virtues of penality have become vital elements in political rhetoric. Nor is it merely that the criminal justice system is used to fight a war that is undoubtedly the longest, costliest and least effective in human history—the 'war on drugs'—although drug convictions have been a powerful contributor to the growth of the penalized population. Rather, it is that the obverse of the responsibilizing moral imperatives of welfare reform is the construction and exclusion of a semi-permanent quasi-criminal population, seen as impervious to the demands of the new morality. Of course, within the prisons there are many projects that seek to reconstruct the will of the confined individual in the name of self-control or even enhanced entrepreneurship (Garland 1997; Fox 1999). And, in the community there are innumerable 'inter-agency' programmes—involving police, welfare agencies, health agencies, school staff, family members and the like—that seek to do the same prior to incarceration, targeting the select few from high risk youth, habitual offenders and so forth: these redeploy all the moralizing techniques of ethical reconstruction in the attempt to instil the capacity for self-management—'naming, shaming and blaming'—or 'reintegrative shaming' as it is more properly known—has become a great favourite in these techniques of ethical reconstruction (Braithwaite 1989). But the procedures for the selection of these experimental subjects themselves arise out of the detailed profiles that identify risky individuals on the basis of the compilation of all manner of data on crime, criminal records, offender profiles and the like. In the same movement as the circuits of insecurity exclude the homeless, the workless and all those other non-consumers from the inclusory logics of control, they are consigned to unending management by the agents, agencies and technologies of the new penal complex. Exclusion itself is effectively criminalized, as crime control agencies home in on those very violations that enable survival in the circuits of exclusion: petty theft, drinking alcohol in public, loitering, drugs and so forth. These new circuits cycle individuals from probation to prison because of probation violations, from prison to parole, and back to prison because of parole violations (cf. Simon 1993). Whilst the welfare budgets are cut, the penal budgets expand, and police, magistrates, parole officers and a host of others have become integral to the management of exclusion, playing a key role in the government of insecurity. A penal grid comes to overlay and define zones of exclusion.

Conclusion

I have suggested that a number of current features of crime control become intelligible when located within with some rather general mutations and reconfigurations in the rationalities and technologies of government that I have termed 'advanced' forms of liberalism. Central to these are the revised ambitions of political government, the aspiration to govern 'at a distance', the fragmentation of sociality and subjectivity into communities and identities, the emphasis upon creating active individuals who will who take responsibility for their own fates through the exercise of choice, and the organization of socio-political concerns around the management and minimization of risks to lifestyles of contentment and consumption.

Approached in this way, contemporary control strategies do have a strategic coherence. Although the problems addressed by these new strategies of control are varied, at their heart lies the problem of control in a 'free society' and hence the kinds of subjects that are imagined to inhabit and deserve such a society. The pervasive image of the perpetrator of crime is not one of the juridical subject of the rule of law, nor that of the social and psychological subject of criminology, but of the individual who has failed to accept his or her responsibilities as a subject of moral community. Punishment by shaming and reform by ethical reconstruction seek to reconstruct these ethical self-steering mechanisms. And the increased punitiveness of the welfare and penal systems, which many have remarked upon, is also linked to the conception of the criminal as a violator of his or her moral responsibilities to others: violating the bonds of obligation and trust of community life; violating individual rights to contentment and the pursuit of happiness; violating legitimate pride in the personal possessions that define our existence as certain kinds of self; violating the personhood of the victim; violating the love of their families. Conduct is problematized as an infraction of freedom. The problem of control today is increasingly understood in terms of the violation of the assumptions of subjectivity—of responsible morality, self-control and self-advancement through legitimate consumption—upon which contemporary strategies for the government of freedom have come to depend. But, just because of that, a whole variety of spaces and practices of control are open for contestation, not in the name of universal principles of justice and the rule of law, but in the name of the capacities and obligations that have been conferred upon us by those who claim to govern us as ethical subjects of freedom.

References

BAISTOW, K. (1995), 'Liberation or Regulation?: Some Paradoxes of Empowerment', *Critical Social Policy*, 42: 34–46.

BARRY, A., OSBORNE, T. and ROSE, N., eds. (1996), *Foucault and Political Reason*. London: UCL Press.

BRAITHWAITE, J. (1989), *Crime, Shame and Reintegration*. Cambridge: Cambridge University Press.

BURCHELL, G., GORDON, C. and MILLER, P., eds. (1991), *The Foucault Effect: Studies in Governmentality*. Hemel Hempstead: Harvester Wheatsheaf.

CASTEL, R. (1981), *La gestion des risques: de l'anti-psychiatrie a l'après-psychanalyse*. Paris: Edition de Minuit.

—— (1991), 'From Dangerousness to Risk', in Burchell, Gordon and Miller, 281–98.

CRUIKSHANK, B. (1994), 'The Will to Empower: Technologies of Citizenship and the War on Poverty', *Socialist Review*, 23/4: 29–55.

DAVIS, M. (1990), *City of Quartz: Excavating the Future in Los Angeles*. London: Verso.

DEAN, M. (1999), *Governmentality*. London: Sage.

DEAN, M. and HINDESS, B. (1998), *Governing Australia: Studies in Contemporary Rationalities of Government*. Cambridge: Cambridge University Press.

DELEUZE, G. (1995), 'Postscript on Control Societies', in *Negotiations*, translated by M. Joughin, 177–82. New York: Columbia University Press.

ERICSON, R. and HAGGERTY, K. (1997), *Policing the Risk Society*. Toronto: University of Toronto Press.

EWALD, F. (1986), *L'Etat providence*. Paris: Grasset.

—— (1991), 'Insurance and Risk', in Burchell, Gordon and Miller, 197–210.

FEELEY, M. and SIMON, J. (1992), 'The New Penology: Notes on the Emerging Strategy of Corrections and its Implications', *Criminology*, 30/4: 449–74.

—— (1994), 'Actuarial Justice: Power/Knowledge in Contemporary Criminal Justice', in D. Nelken, ed., *The Futures of Criminology*, 173–201. London: Sage.

FOUCAULT, M. (1991), 'Governmentality', in Burchell, Gordon and Miller, 87–104.

FOX, K. (1999), 'Changing Violent Minds: Discursive Correction and Resistance in the Cognitive Treatment of Violent Offenders in Prison', *Social Problems*, 46/1: 88–103.

FRASER, N. and GORDON, L. (1994), 'A Genealogy of Dependency: Tracing a Keyword of the US Welfare State', *Signs*, 19/2: 311–36.

GANDY, O. (1993), *The Panoptic Sort: Towards a Political Economy of Information*. Boulder, CO: Westview.

GARLAND, D. (1996), 'The Limits of the Sovereign State: Strategies of Crime Control in Contemporary Society', *British Journal of Criminology*, 36/1: 445–71.

—— (1997), ' "Governmentality" and the Problem of Crime', *Theoretical Criminology*, 1/2: 173–215.

GORDON, D. (1987), 'The Electronic Panopticon: a Case-study of the Development of the National Criminal Records System', *Politics and Society*, 15: 483–511.

GREIG, D. (1997), 'The Politics of Dangerousness', in S. A. Gerull and W. Lucas, eds., *Serious Violent Offenders: Sentencing, Psychiatry and Law Reform*, 47–66. Canberra: Australian Institute of Criminology.

HAMILTON, G. and SUTTON, J. (1989), 'The Problem of Control in the Weak State: Domination in the United States, 1880–1920', *Theory and Society*, 18: 1–46.

HIMMELFARB, G. (1995), *The Demoralization of Society: From Victorian Virtues to Modern Values*, revised edn. London: Institute of Economic Affairs.

KATZ, M. (1993), ' "Underclass" as Metaphor', in *The 'Underclass' Debate*, 3–26. Princeton, NJ: Princeton University Press.

KAY, L. (1993), *The Molecular Vision of Life: Caltech, The Rockefeller Foundation and the Rise of the New Biology*. New York: Oxford University Press.

LUMLEY, F. (1925), *Means of Social Control*. New York: Century.

LYON, D. (1994), *The Electronic Eye: The Rise of Surveillance Society*. Cambridge: Polity.

MARX, G. (1988), *Undercover: Police Surveillance in America*. Berkeley: University of California Press.

MEAD, L. (1986), *Beyond Entitlement: The Social Obligations of Citizenship*. New York: Free Press.

—— (1991), 'The New Politics of the New Poverty', *Public Interest*, 105: 3–20.

MURRAY, C. (1984), *Losing Ground: American Social Policy 1950–1980*. New York: Basic Books.

O'MALLEY, P. (1991), 'Legal Networks and Domestic Security', *Studies in Law, Politics and Society*, 11: 181–91.

—— (1992), 'Risk, Power and Crime Prevention', *Economy and Society*, 21/3: 252–75.

—— (1995), 'The Prudential Man Cometh: Life Insurance, Liberalism and the Government of Thrift', paper presented to the Annual Meeting of the Law and Society Association, Toronto, June 1995.

—— (1996), 'Risk and Responsibility', in Barry, Osborne and Rose, 189–208.

—— (1999), 'Volatile Punishments: Contemporary Penality and the Neo-liberal Government', *Theoretical Criminology*, 3/2: 175–96.

O'MALLEY, P. and PALMER, D. 'Post-Keynesian Policing', *Economy and Society*, 25/2: 137–155.

POSTER, M. (1990), *Mode of Information*. Cambridge: Polity.

PRATT, J. (1999), 'Sex Crime and the New Punitiveness', *International Journal of Law and Psychiatry*.

PROCACCI, G. (1998), 'Poor Citizens: Social Citizenship and the Crisis of Welfare States', in S. Hänninen, ed., *Displacement of Social Policies*. Jyväskylä SoPhi, University of Jyväskylä, 7–30.

ROBINS, K. and WEBSTER, F. (1989), 'Plan and Control: Towards a Cultural History of the Information Society', *Theory and Society*, 18: 323–51.

ROSE, N. (1996), 'Psychology as a Political Science: Advanced Liberalism and the Administration of Risk', *History of the Human Sciences* 9, /2: 1–23.

ROSE, N. (1998), 'Governing Risky Individuals: The Role of Psychiatry in New Regimes of Control', *Psychiatry, Psychology and Law*, 5/2: 177–95.

—— (1999a), *Powers of Freedom: Reframing Political Thought*. Cambridge: Cambridge University Press.

—— (1999b), 'Inventiveness in Politics: Review of A. Giddens, The Third Way', *Economy and Society*, 28/3.

ROSS, E. A. (1901), *Social Control: A Survey of the Foundations of Order*. New York: Macmillan.

SCHEINGOLD, S., PERSHING, J. and OLSON, T. (1994), 'Sexual Violence, Victim Advocacy and Republican Criminology', *Law and Society Review*, 28/4: 729–63.

SEDGWICK, E. (1992), 'Epidemics of the Will', in J. Crary and S. Kwinter, eds. *Incorporations*, 582–95. New York: Zone Books.

SHEARING, C. (1995), 'Reinventing Policing: Police as Governance', in O. Marenin (ed.), *Policing Change: Changing Police*. New York: Garland Press.

SHEARING, C. and STENNING, P. (1985), 'From the Panopticon to Disneyworld: The Development of Discipline', in E. Doob and E. L. Greenspan, eds., *Perspectives in Criminal Law*, 335–49. Aurora: Canada Law Books.

SIMON, J. (1993), *Poor Discipline: Parole and the Social Control of the Underclass, 1890–1990*. Chicago: University of Chicago Press.

—— (1998), 'Managing the Monstrous: Sex Offenders and the New Penology', *Psychology, Public Policy and Law*, 4: 452–67.

STENSON, K. (1993), 'Community Policing as a Governmental Technology', *Economy and Society* 22/3: 373–89.

—— (1999), 'Crime Control, Governmentality and Sovereignty', in R. Smandych, ed., *Governable Places: Readings on Governmentality and Crime Control*, 45–73. Aldershot: Dartmouth/Ashgate.

VALVERDE, M. (1998), *Diseases of the Will: Alcohol and the Dilemmas of Freedom*. Cambridge: Cambridge University Press.

WEBSTER, F. and ROBINS, K. (1986), *Information Technology: A Luddite Analysis*. Norwood, NJ: Ablex.

Index

Mawby, R. 96
Mead, G. H. 13, 151 n., 152, 160
Mead, Lawrence 196
media 16, 151, 158
  mass 15, 36
mediation 72–3, 119
  technological 105
Meidinger, E. 50
Melossi, D. 104 n., 150–4 *passim*, 159, 165, 166, 170, 172 n., 173 n., 175
Melucci, A. 32
mental hospitals 203
mental patients 53, 128
Merry, S. 73, 74
Merton, R. 117
micro-management 136–7
middle class 75, 84, 130, 137, 140, 168
  boundaries between the poor and 131
  choice largely confined to upper echelons 145
  lifestyle choice of men and women 171
migration 51, 159–61, 172
Miller, Emmanuel 8
Miller, Errol 88
Miller, J. 166
millet system 143
millionaires 130
minor offenders 8, 9
minority groups 15, 123
  moral 143
misanthropy 23, 24
models 184, 200
modernism/modernity 8, 10–14, 34, 105, 156
  late 1, 14–18, 112, 122
Mods and Rockers 163
Mohammed, P. 88, 92, 96
Molfese, F. 155
monitoring 190
monstrosities 155, 158, 169, 200, 202
Moody's 51
moral decline/breakdown 10, 17
moral individualism 15
moral philosophy 64
morality 151, 154, 171, 197
  'bad' 169
  common 140
  new 204
mores 130
Morgan (J. P.) 55, 63
Morris, R. 171 n.
Mortenson, T. 53
Mosco, V. 116

motivation 9, 60
  self 194
'motorized legislation' 132
Mugford, S. 72, 74
Mulgan, G. 60
murder 90, 140
Murray, C. 167, 169, 171 n., 196
Muslims 143, 144, 146

Namenwirth, J. Zvi 173 n.
naming/shaming/blaming 183, 202, 204
Naples 159
'natural' crimes 158
neglect 130
negotiation 106
Negroes 171, 172
neighbourhood disputes 72, 73
neighbourhood watch 39, 80–7, 183
Nelken, D. 150 n.
neo-Chicagoans 163–5
neo-classical economics 63
Netherlands, *see* Holland
New Left 163
New Mexico State prison 171 n.
New Times 14
New York 56, 129, 137, 160
New Zealand 53–4, 62, 136
  Maori communities 74
NGOs (non-governmental organizations) 50, 60, 61
  women's movement 89, 90–1, 92, 95, 97
Nicholas, E. 89, 91
nightwatchman state 48, 63
Nixon, Richard M. 166
no-go areas 42
normalcy 79
'normality' 106, 110, 156
norms 23, 24–5, 104, 108, 129, 187
  breach of 26
  community, conflicting 140
  evaluative 105
  legal 128
  overlapping 132
  performance 128, 133, 136
  social 29
  work 134
Northern Ireland 60, 172 n.
Norway 34
Nozick, R. 48
nuclear industry 55

obedience 137, 187

Index compiled by Frank Pert